THE USES OF REASON

THE MACMILLAN COMPANY
NEW YORK · BOSTON · CHICAGO
DALLAS · ATLANTA · SAN FRANCISCO

MACMILLAN AND CO., LIMITED
LONDON · BOMBAY · CALCUTTA
MADRAS · MELBOURNE

THE MACMILLAN COMPANY
OF CANADA, LIMITED
TORONTO

The Uses of Reason

BY

ARTHUR E. MURPHY

University of Illinois

*Truth, freedom, humanity, law: intellect ventures to take
these words in its mouth once more—a nobler venture than to
pour scorn and confusion on them. It is no longer ashamed of
them, as it thought it had to be as long as they were taken for
granted. Now, when they are in extremity, the mind becomes
aware that they are its daily bread, the air it breathes, dear life
itself; that they must be fought for lest they perish.*

—THOMAS MANN

BD161.M88
ST. JOSEPH'S UNIVERSITY
The uses of reason.

3 9353 00135 3869

ACADEMY
REF
MARKETING,
COLLEGE
A., P.A. 19131

BD
161
M88

New York · 1943

THE MACMILLAN COMPANY

237206
000007
BD 161
.M88

Copyright, 1943, by
THE MACMILLAN COMPANY.

All rights reserved—no part of this book
may be reproduced in any form without
permission in writing from the publisher,
except by a reviewer who wishes to quote brief
passages in connection with a review written
for inclusion in magazine or newspaper.

FIRST PRINTING.

PRINTED IN THE UNITED STATES OF AMERICA
AMERICAN BOOK—STRATFORD PRESS, INC., NEW YORK

PREFACE

To write philosophy in the present tense and with explicit reference to contemporary issues and doctrines is a hazardous enterprise. For the present of the writer will inevitably, even under the most fortunate conditions of publication, have become the past of the reader and will have lost something of its urgency and altered somewhat in emphasis and perspective with this change in temporal status. This book was written in the summer and autumn of 1942, in the first year of America's participation in the Second World War. Some of the things it says would be said in a different tone today, with El Alamein and Stalingrad safely between us and the more immediate dangers of those times. One or two of the theories it criticizes have already begun to fade in popular esteem and it seems more necessary now than it did some months ago to remind the reader that they are here considered not chiefly for their individual importance but as symptoms of a state of mind which has a variety of spokesmen but does not alter in its animus or in its potency to confuse the issues of social policy. It would have been safer, surely, to discourse more largely on the eternal verities and maintain a cautious distance from the shifting particularities of the sequence of events.

It is, however, of the essence of the philosophy presented in this book that it can practice no such aloofness and claim no such immunity from the hazards and the lessons of history. The philosophic reason it is concerned to exemplify is inescapably involved in the process in which events, losing their immediate urgency as occasions for action, become the

v

subject-matter for reflection and critical evaluation—the process through which we learn from and by experience and apply what is learned to the intellectual mastery of a new present, thus gathering the fruits of temporal experience in a practical wisdom that will stand the test of time. To that test the conclusions of this volume are herewith submitted.

For permission to quote from the volumes here listed grateful acknowledgment is made to the following publishers:

To the D. Appleton-Century Company for quotations from *Old Errors and New Labels* by Fulton J. Sheen.

To the Conference on Science, Philosophy and Religion for quotations from "In Search of Man" by Anton J. Pegis in *Science, Philosophy and Religion*, Vol. I, and from "The Spiritual Basis of Democracy" by seven Princeton professors in Vol. II.

To the John Day Company for quotations from *The Managerial Revolution* by James Burnham and *The Future of Industrial Man* by Peter F. Drucker.

To E. P. Dutton & Company for quotations from *The Present Crisis of Our Age* by P. Sorokin.

To Harcourt, Brace and Company for quotations from *The Tyranny of Words* by Stuart Chase, from *Language in Action* by S. I. Hayakawa, from *The Mind and Society* by V. Pareto, from *America's Strategy in World Politics* by N. Spykman, from *Equality* by R. H. Tawney and from *Ethical Relativity* by E. Westermarck.

To the Institute for Propaganda Analysis for quotations from Vols. I, III and IV of its *Bulletins*.

To Alfred A. Knopf, Inc., for the quotation from Thomas Mann's *Orders of the Day* which appears on the title page, for lines from Wallace Stevens' "Hymn from a Watermelon Pavilion" in *Harmonium*, and for quotations from *The Declaration of Independence* by Carl Becker and *The Hour of Decision* by Oswald Spengler.

To The Macmillan Company for quotations from *The*

Intelligent Individual and Society by P. W. Bridgman, from *Conditions of Peace* by E. H. Carr, from *Intellectual America* by O. Cargill, from *Adventures of Ideas* by A. N. Whitehead and from articles by B. Ginzburg and H. M. Kallen in *The Encyclopaedia of the Social Sciences*, Vols. XIII and X respectively.

To the W. W. Norton Company for quotations from *The Anatomy of Revolution* by Crane Brinton and *The Scientific Outlook* by Bertrand Russell.

To the Princeton University Press for quotations from *Knowledge for What?* by Robert Lynd.

To Random House for quotations from *The Retreat from Reason* by L. Hogben.

To Charles Scribner's Sons for quotations from *Christianity and Power Politics* and *The Nature and Destiny of Man*, Vol. I, by Reinhold Niebuhr.

To the Viking Press for quotations from *The Place of Science in Modern Civilization* by Thorstein Veblen.

To the Yale University Press for quotations from *The Folklore of Capitalism* by Thurman Arnold and *The Heavenly City of the Eighteenth Century Philosophers* by Carl Becker.

The manuscript has been read by my friends Max Black, Ralph Blake, Sterling Lamprecht and Fred Will and has profited much from their discerning criticism. My warmest thanks to them, to Louise Will for the preparation of the index, and to my sister, Gladys Murphy Graham, whose use of practical reason instances and verifies the theories of this volume and whose encouragement and sound judgment have aided mightily in its preparation.

Sept. 1, 1943.

CONTENTS

THE USES OF REASON

INTRODUCTION

THE FOUNDATIONS OF RATIONAL BELIEF

Our Contemporary Situation. In Saroyan's play *The Time of Your Life*, a somewhat somber character, identified by the author as "The Arab, an Eastern philosopher and harmonica player," wanders in and out, observing the proceedings and remarking, at approximate intervals, "No foundation. All the way down the line." The remark is directed, I take it, not merely at the behavior of the other characters of the play, to which it has an undeniable pertinence, but at "life" as the Arab and Saroyan observed it in prewar America. The sentiment it voices with commendable brevity is widespread and significant. It is a sense of mental and moral instability arising from the fact that we have largely lost our confidence in the ideas and principles to which we should once have appealed to interpret and justify our conduct, and have so far found no others fit to take their place. In such a situation we no longer know, from any long-run point of view, what we are doing, and those sensitive enough to be disturbed by this are likely to take refuge in a calculated superficiality—a refusal to look beyond quite tangible interests and short-run satisfaction for a securer basis for their lives, not because they do not want one, but because they think they know in advance that none is to be found. One need be neither an Eastern philosopher nor a harmonica player to diagnose the insecurity of such a way of life and to pass an appropriate judgment upon it.

Yet men will not long be content with mere absence of

belief on fundamental issues. And in a period, like the present, of rapid social change, when they feel themselves threatened from all sides by forces they do not understand, and whose bearing on their fortunes is incalculable, they are naturally prone to turn to soothsaying, divination and the propitiation of the unknown for relief from their anxieties. Any new thing confidently presented as the inevitable next step in history—whether it be the dictatorship of the proletariat, the managerial revolution, or the latest and shallowest splash in an advertised "wave of the future"—will find excited devotees prepared to prostrate themselves before its conquering advance. And some very old things that vividly recall an era of order and stability, to which the present seems to stand in unhappy contrast, will once more take on the sanctity of eternal truth in the minds of hopeful believers. The need for faith is felt on all sides; but the varieties of faith are many and conflicting. Where are we to turn for foundations of belief that will stand inspection?

There are times, to be sure, when we seem to know the answer without having to think about it—times of crisis when the imminence of some great and obvious danger presents us with an immediate objective so undoubtedly imperative as to organize our purposes and lend sense to activities which, however arduous and violent, seem meaningful and excellent in contrast to our previous aimlessness. The present war is such a crisis, and the way in which many men have responded to it is renewed evidence of the heights to which human nature can rise when it finds a stimulus adequate to elicit its whole-hearted effort. But war, while it can make sense of and organize other activities, does not make sense by itself. If we are sane men we make war, as Aristotle long ago insisted, for the sake of peace, and if we cannot organize a peace worth having and a world worth living in on a level of purposeful and hence meaningful action, a world in which we know the worth of what we are doing and can justify to our minds and wills the ends for the sake of which we act, we shall have been defeated indeed, and on the issues that matter most.

Our question therefore recurs, and with renewed urgency. The answer to it that would once have been given by many reflective men is that we can appeal to reason as a principle of discrimination and hence as a guide to the right appraisal of beliefs on basic issues of thought and conduct. But one of the most striking factors in our present mental insecurity is the pervasive doubt that prevails about the capacity of human reason to perform this essential function. To make judgments as to what is "really" true and good has seemed to many of our contemporaries either an illegitimate and dogmatic pretension or a responsibility too heavy to be borne. As Monsignor Fulton J. Sheen observes: "The mass of people have kept up hard and fast distinctions between dollars and cents, battleships and cruisers, 'You owe me' and 'I owe you,' but they seem to have lost entirely the faculty of distinguishing between the good and the bad, the right and the wrong." [1] It is not only among the masses that this incapacity, or refusal, to make basic intellectual and moral discriminations prevails. It is the advanced thinkers of the time who have taught us to enclose "true" and "false," "good" and "bad," in noncommittal quotation marks and to speak with critical caution of what is *called* "good" or *accepted as* "true" in one social group or another, making no claim in the process to pronounce judgment on what is "really" good or true or just. Nor is this by any means a mere academic affectation. It is the expression of a state of mind, to be more fully examined later, which refuses on principle to make distinctions of principle because it can find nothing in "the facts" which a critical mind acknowledges to justify them. The "rational man" has come, in fact, to have a thoroughly bad reputation in sophisticated circles, and those who try to give good reasons for what they think and do are more likely to be viewed with suspicion as hypocrites or wishful thinkers than with friendli-

[1] Fulton J. Sheen, *Old Errors and New Labels*, p. 104.

ness as responsible moral agents. This anti-intellectualism—the turning of the intellectuals against the rational authority of intelligence—had its philosophical flowering in the last decades of the nineteenth century and has now penetrated through the several layers of educated opinion to become the accepted standpoint and uncriticized preconception of most of those who interpret the methods and findings of modern science and the goods of modern culture to the general public. Combining in ways not always anticipated by its philosophical parents with more robust and less measured versions of the revolt against reason, it has had its considerable part in enhancing our current mental and moral instability and confusion.

The situation in which we find ourselves is of practical as well as theoretical importance. We should hardly, in any case, have been naïve enough, in these difficult and uncertain times, to claim that reason rules the world, or human behavior, in any very obvious or easily verifiable sense. Those who put their faith in the inscrutable ways of Providence can rarely have found them more inscrutable than today, and those who like to think that man is in his essence a rational animal have more need than ever to distinguish this essential human nature from the observable behavior in which it finds, at best, an oblique and equivocal expression. But so long as we believed that we knew at least how to proceed to find out the truth and how to distinguish it from its opposite when we found it, the work of reason could be carried on. When, however, we lose our confidence in the capacity of tested inquiry to arrive at truth, and of moral judgment to distinguish right from wrong, in any sense in which a contradictory judgment would not be equally legitimate if one cared to adopt it, we not only admit that we do not possess the truth we seek, but that we should have no reasonable means of knowing it if we saw it. This does not mean, of course, that we stop having beliefs, or preferring one course of action to another. It means rather that we accept arbitrarily and without rational warrant ideas that would antecedently have seemed to require such warrant, because we are assured on the best academic authority that no such validation could in the nature of things have been expected. Skepticism about the cognitive claims and efficacy of reason is no enemy to many varieties of belief, as Santayana has pointed out in his *Scepticism and Animal Faith*. On the contrary it may encourage the acceptance of many congenial dogmas, where critical reason would have had a cold and inhibiting influence. But beliefs and practical commitments accepted *as arbitrary*, with the knowledge that they possess, "in the end," no further justification than the willfulness with which they are affirmed or the convenience with which they can be employed for ulterior ends, themselves quite groundlessly desired or demanded, are maintained with a different temper than those which looked to reason for their validation. The whole direction of men's thought and purpose is altered when such an attitude is seriously accepted, and we have seen something of the consequences of this alteration in our contemporary social environment. The specialist may, of course, go on using his reason with amazing skill and precision in the restricted activities, e.g., chemistry and medicine, where such use is socially accepted as both safe and convenient. And the reserve supply of public regard for "culture" and "education" built up in a period when men really did believe in the cogency of principles of rational discrimination may still be sufficient to support for a while the humanistic disciplines, with the values they represent, in something like the manner to which they have become accustomed. But we cannot expect such a cultural lag to continue indefinitely, and there are signs enough already that the public credit of a "reason" which has lost its intellectual and moral authority is fast running out. It is hard to see what other outcome could reasonably have been expected.

It was equally to be expected that those who value the

cultural, or spiritual, goods once associated with the name of reason, and who see clearly the insecure position in which these are placed when the authority of rational standards and principles is undermined, would come to the defense of these values with all the resources at their command. Such a thinker is Monsignor Fulton J. Sheen, whose comment on our contemporary inability to distinguish right from wrong and true from false we have already recorded. His further examination of our intellectual ills is penetrating and explicit, and the remedy he proposes is forthright. Both diagnosis and proposed cure will repay our further consideration.

He puts his finger at once on the central difficulty—the "disrespect for rational foundations" [2] now widely manifest in secular intellectual circles. It is this which accounts, in turn, for that undiscriminating tolerance or false broadmindedness, that "lack of intellectual backbone" which, whatever may have been the intentions of its sponsors, has become in effect an evasion of the responsibility for making moral distinctions which are rationally grounded and rationally defensible. Mr. Sheen holds, quite correctly, I think, that this is a bad state of affairs and one that requires correction. In contrast to this unhappy "liberal" position, he places that of the Roman Catholic Church, which, he tells us, is "madly in love with rationalism." [3] "The Church is accused of being the enemy of reason; as a matter of fact, she is the only one who believes in it. Using her reason in the Council of the Vatican, she officially went on record in favor of Rationalism, and declared, against the mock humility of the Agnostics and the sentimental faith of the Fideists, that human reason by its own power can know something besides the contents of test-tubes and retorts, and that working on mere sensible phenomena it can soar even to the 'hid battlements of Eternity,' there to discover the Timeless beyond time and the Spaceless beyond

[2] *Ibid.*, p. 6.
[3] *Ibid.*, p. 7.

space which is God, the Alpha and Omega of all things." [4]

This confidence in reason is not to be maintained, it seems, in the easy atmosphere of tolerance which liberalism generates. There are bad thoughts as well as good, and they are to be rigorously dealt with, for "a bad thought set loose is more dangerous than a wild man. . . . There was once a time when Christian society burned the thought in order to save society, and after all, something can be said in favor of this practice. To kill one bad thought may mean the salvation of ten thousand thinkers." [5] Such a disposal of dangerous thoughts requires a kind of intolerance—not toward persons, who may be dealt with in reasoned patience, but toward false principles whose corrupting influence has now been amply exhibited. "Tolerance does not apply to truth or principles. About these things we must be intolerant, and for this kind of intolerance, so much needed to rouse us from sentimental gush, I make a plea. Intolerance of this kind is the foundation of all stability." [6]

There is little doubt that this outspoken appeal will strike a responsive chord in the heart of many a troubled and conscientious rationalist. Authority was wanted for the deliverances of reason, and here is an authority of the highest eminence making a most heartening pronouncement in its favor. Nor is the use of the term "intolerance" likely to be as disturbing as it would once have been. If it was a non-discriminating tolerance which culminated by confessing its own incapacity to distinguish on rational grounds between right and wrong, it seems natural to expect as its needed corrective a new intolerance that will once more condemn what it knows to be false and evil, and set up an unequivocal standard of truth and righteousness to which the judicious and well-intentioned can repair. It is not surprising that the influence of

[4] *Ibid.*, pp. 9-10.
[5] *Ibid.*, p. 11.
[6] *Ibid.*, p. 107.

the philosophy Mr. Sheen represents and of the authority to which he appeals have grown substantially in recent years.

Yet it must be clear, I think, on further reflection, that the sort of support for human reason he offers is not adequate to the demands of the existing situation. It is not enough to be madly in love with Rationalism. If the "reason" defended is worth defending, it is necessary, also, for those who profess it to be rigorously and consistently addicted to the use of the methods of rational inquiry, for it is by these, rather than by the decisions of Church Councils, that the guarantee of the validity of reason can authoritatively be made out. Nor is the plea for a new intolerance, however well-intentioned, a reliable contribution to the rehabilitation of the sway of reason in the affairs of men. If intolerance meant merely the reasoned rejection as false of beliefs which can be proved to be so, or the condemnation of injustice where it can be shown to exist, it would indeed be fully justified. But Mr. Sheen's reference to burning thoughts to save society is disquieting. I do not know how, precisely, one burns a thought save by burning the book in which it is set down or the thinker who proclaims it, but I do know that it is not by such methods that the rational authority of human reason is made good in the minds of free men. Reason as a fetish, enshrined in ideas and assumptions which, through habitual use, have acquired a specious self-evidence or sanctity, may profit by such authoritarian sanction, but reason as a function of inquiry and responsible judgment has rarely prospered in such an atmosphere. It must justify itself, not by recourse to such extrinsic supports and sanctions, but by evidence, provided in the course of its application in the contexts in which it has a reliable use, to show that it can perform what it promises and maintain itself in the light of the best we know of the nature of the world and the conditions of effective action in it.

There are other plausible proposals for the recovery of the higher values which skepticism about and indifference to the rational foundations of belief are held to have undermined. In most cases it is some form of faith that is brought to the aid of reason—a reason which is held to be unduly limited and even distorted by its modern practitioners and in need of supplementation from higher sources if its proper status is to be understood. Mr. Lewis Mumford, in violent reaction against what he calls the "pragmatic liberalism" of our time, offers a "faith for living" of impressive dimensions. This faith, which is judicious and specific in some of its recommendations for a recovery of purpose in our lives, goes on to link human purpose hopefully, though a little vaguely, to the "promise" of a cosmic purpose which "bottoms all purposes." [7] The significance of this is appreciated when we learn further that "Men are individually nothing except in relation to that greater reality, Man. And man himself is nought except in relation to that greater reality which he calls divine." [8] Believing this, men will perhaps think better of their fellows, and more seriously of their own obligations, and that lack of moral stamina for which pragmatic liberalism is held responsible may be made good.

Professor Hocking, in *Fortune Magazine*, combines an attack on a "modernism" which has much in common with the pragmatic liberalism to which Mr. Mumford objects, with a somewhat similar faith to confirm his valuations. He notes with approval the benefits that men in past ages derived from belief in a cosmic purpose supporting their own, and holds that the recovery of the assurance of such a "healing fact" would be a great boon for those who now turn to psychiatrists for a more dubious consolation. "The great religious ones seem to have had a certainty that they were going along with the trend of the world. They have had a passion for right living which they conceived of as a cosmic demand." [9] It is this

[7] Lewis Mumford, *Faith for Living*, p. 205.
[8] *Ibid.*, p. 210.
[9] W. E. Hocking, "What Man Can Make of Man," *Fortune Magazine*, February, 1942.

certainty, he believes, which must be rewon, and we can no longer put up with the negations of modernism which stand in the way of its acceptance.

I have cited these instances as characteristic of a widespread tendency in current thought. A renewed attachment, enhanced by anxiety, to the spiritual good in which the ideal values of our culture are enshrined, here unites with a sharp distrust of the results to which modern thought, especially in its scientific and pragmatic aspects, seems to have led us. Hence the need of faith to supplement the inadequacies and correct the mistakes of a too narrowly conceived reason. The distinctive function of reason in this recovery appears to be not to substantiate the faith, nor to judge it, but to get out of its way and let it do its healing work with the assurance that the benefits that will thus ensue will justify the method used in attaining them. What are we to think of such proposals, and how are we to judge their contribution to the solution of our current problems?

It would be folly to claim that we can dispense with faith or that "reason alone" can remedy our spiritual ills. Indeed, as we shall see, it is a distinguishing characteristic of reason when it is about its appropriate business that it never works alone, but has its function in the criticism, coordination and redirection of impulses, emotions and beliefs which, apart from their contribution to or conflict with the order it proposes, are neither rational nor irrational in character. We shall have need in the future of all the inspiration and renewal of purpose which any faith that can work with and build upon the best we know can supply. But, important as this renewal of faith may be, there is a prior issue which must first concern us, and—for the reasonable ordering of our beliefs—a more fundamental one. The defense of ideal values against their enemies, foreign and domestic, will be a worth-while undertaking only if there is good ground for believing that these values are worth defending, and that the "reason" which supports them can in fact perform its guiding function in thought and conduct better and more reliably than any rival or substitute so far proposed. The difficulties that have led men to doubt that this is true are by no means wholly gratuitous; they arise in considerable part not from mere ill-will or moral depravity, but from genuine critical scruples, and if they are to be honestly met and overcome we shall need to know how to use our reason more accurately and adequately, not merely to be reassured in general that the higher powers in the Universe are on its side, and ours. If we can see how good judgment and good will, enlightened by reliable information and guided toward a sharable good, can carry through the organization of human interests to a reasonable satisfaction, we shall have good ground for confidence in the work of practical reason and a worth-while assurance of the validity of its claims. So long as we cannot see this, the confidence in a more general purpose that "bottoms all purposes" will hardly serve as a reliable guide. The reality that "men call divine" may indeed be on the side of righteousness and, like Mumford, against pragmatic liberals and political isolationists; but unless we can tell what righteousness is, and by what methods it is rightly to be pursued, how shall we know it when we see it?

This question is of primary importance. For while it is true, as Professor Hocking told us, that "the great religious ones" have conceived their passion for right living as a cosmic demand, it is equally true that some of the most violent and fanatical of men have similarly conceived their own less admirable passions. We shall need some surer guide than the urgency of such convictions and the inspiration they provide for their devotees, if we are to discriminate the true prophets from the false among those who identify their own demands, made in the name of righteousness, with the trend and purpose of the cosmos. There is no lack of faiths of one sort or another at the present time; faith in the higher destiny of the Aryan, faith in the spiritual efficacy of breathing exercises and a vegetarian diet, faith in the verbal inspiration of the scriptures or the dialectical triumph of the proletariat, have lent meaning to the lives of those who accepted them and renewed and hardened their purposes to arduous and sustained endeavor. What we now need, with peculiar urgency, is the wisdom to find a faith that can maintain itself in practice and in the open, as the spokesman for a good that is in fact what it purports to be and can perform what it promises, and what its disciples profess. For the attainment of such a faith we shall need the best use of all our powers, those of rational discrimination and comprehensive understanding not least among them. While, therefore, we shall welcome any aid that faith can bring to reason, we shall have to ask that faith to identify itself and present its credentials. It is the reason that judges of the authenticity of that identification with which we are, in this volume, to be proximately concerned.

The Claims of "Reason" and the Uses of Reason. It will be well, if we are to pursue this considerable undertaking with any prospect of success, to know clearly from the outset what we are doing. The quarrel between the defenders of "Reason" and its critics is, of course, a very old one. Nor have all the merits, in this prolonged dispute, been on the side of its professed defenders. The champions of the "heart" against the "head," of "will" and "action" against a "vicious intellectualism," and of "life" against "logic" have frequently had something sound and important to say, though they have not infrequently chosen a confused and misleading way of saying it. The good to which men reasonably aspire is a full and harmonious development of all their human powers. A one-sided or exclusive emphasis on any special interest or faculty, whether it be labeled "feeling," "will," or "intellect," is an offense against that good and, as such, is properly to be condemned. The friends of "Reason" have sometimes been guilty of such overemphasis, and their critics were right in defending against them the claims of aspects of experience which an unreasonable rationalism had distorted or denied. "Reason" as one competitor among others for an unqualified primacy in human concerns has no special sanctity about it, and is quite as much in need of criticism as the rest. It is not our purpose to defend it, or to prolong the unprofitable dispute to which the excessive claims of its protagonists have led. What we shall find important is rather this: that the criticism of all such questionable pretenders be wisely and reasonably made, in the light of the most reliable knowledge available and the soundest ideals by which men of good will would wish to be guided, and that its conclusions be tested by reference to the widest possible area of humanly relevant experience. It is the work of rational inquiry in the acquisition of that sort of knowledge, the development of such ideals, and the attainment of the philosophic standpoint from which experience in its most inclusive aspects can be justly understood that makes such criticism possible and entitles it, when valid, to our credence and respect. If those who protest against "rationalism" have good reasons for so doing, if there are facts, authentically established, to which they appeal, valid ideals of human excellence in whose name they speak, and a philosophically just and comprehensive standpoint from which their claims can be made good, then we shall have good reason to believe what they say, and to follow their advice. But we shall need first of all to know that the "facts" are what they purport to be, the ideals invoked valid as alleged, and the interests for which they speak comprehensive enough to justify themselves to an understanding of philosophic adequacy and scope. Given these prior assurances we shall have the means of judging justly and responsibly on the further issues with which the friends and the critics of "Reason" confront us. Without them the dispute must remain on that level of controversy in which the large and loose generalizations of one side invite a compensatory overstatement from the other and each seems securely right only in its claim that its antagonist is to a considerable extent mistaken.

An instance may help to clarify this point, which will be of increasing importance as we proceed. William James, that most genial and generous of philosophers, once startled his colleagues and contemporaries by his announced determination, in the face of a conflict between logic and experience, to which his theories seemed to have led him, *"to give up the logic,* fairly, squarely, and irrevocably." [10] Experience, he believed, indicated plainly that states of consciousness could be compounded. Logic—the "logic of self-identity"—denied this. And he chose, in this "tragic predicament," to trust experience and part company with logic. The shock in academic circles was considerable. McTaggart of Cambridge warned that "no one ever broke with logic but logic broke him," and there were other and equally portentous pronouncements. Nor were such admonitions by any means without their measure of justification. The equivocal blessing which James seemed at times to give to the forces of unreason in human life has since been used by violent and willful men to excuse their willful and violent acts, and so has played its part in the current breakdown of rational standards. Yet it evidently was not so intended. James thought he had the best of reasons for his quarrel with "logic," and was prepared to reason long and earnestly with those who disagreed with him. It was because the logic employed did not fit the facts of experience that he felt justified in rejecting it. He wrote of his great *Principles of Psychology* that every sentence in it was "forged in the teeth of irreducible and stubborn facts," and few men have tried to understand the facts as they saw them more honestly than did James. And it was in the name of philosophical adequacy that he asked his readers to turn from the abstractions of a "vicious intellectualism" to the realities of their own experience, and to make the most of them. Thus, though to

[10] William James, *A Pluralistic Universe,* p. 212. Italics in text.

some degree he was wrong in his theory of the relation of logic to experience, his mistake occurred within the area in which beliefs and theories are rationally examinable, and his philosophy is properly understood as an episode in, and an intended contribution to, the work of philosophical reason, not as an attack upon it. The misfortune was that both James and his readers often failed to distinguish the criticism of the too sweeping claims of "intellectualism" and its "logic" as spokesmen for "reality" from an attack on the authority of conclusions reasonably arrived at and tested as guides for belief and action. The former may well be a contribution to the work of rational understanding. The latter is a rebellion against it which, in the measure that it is successful, destroys all standards of intellectual integrity and responsible inquiry.

In the easy-going days when "irrationalism" was a gospel preached by eloquent professors to pleasantly shocked ladies' study groups, this confusion was of no great practical importance. Today, however, we are in a different and a grimmer situation. The standards of rational belief and conduct are under attack from men who know quite clearly what they are doing, and we must meet them if we can, not on the level of literary or speculative pronouncements about the respective charms of "Life" and "Logic," but by looking to the cogency and security of those basic processes which provide us with the only means we have of distinguishing justice from injustice, right from wrong, and the well-grounded results of tested inquiry from the obscurantism and superstition by which they are now so gravely threatened. If we can be clear about the validity of reason in these primary uses, we may later be in a position to say something useful about the various "isms" that contend for the primary or exclusive right to speak for the "reality" to which their speculations are addressed. If we cannot, nothing that we should be inclined to say now or later on such high matters will have any testable claim to rational cogency.

The Plan of This Inquiry. The procedure to be followed is quite plainly dictated by the aim of our inquiry and by the conditions to be met if that aim is to be accomplished. The first requirement for truthful and accurate thinking is that it be securely based on reliable information concerning such matters of fact as are pertinent to its conclusions. Where and under what conditions is such reliable information available and what part does it properly play in our further reasonings about the world and ourselves? Part I attempts to answer this question, not in detail, to be sure, for it does not pretend to be an encyclopedia of human knowledge, but so far as is necessary to show that trustworthy criteria for the distinction between truth and error can in some fields be established, and that conclusions certified as true by such criteria can stand the test of criticism that has been or can pertinently be brought against them. The rational use of ideas in the pursuit of truth thus tested or testable is essential to the acquisition of this reliable information, and we shall find, I believe, that reason in this use is sometimes clearly justified in its fruit, which is knowledge of matters of fact. If those who profess to deny the authority of reason have meant to say that *in this usage* it cannot perform what it promises, or that there are higher grounds on which the properly tested findings of rational inquiry can be set aside, we can show that they are mistaken. They may not choose to acknowledge truth thus established, having loftier and more congenial objects with which to concern themselves; but if they deny it, or its primary place in the rational organization of beliefs, they will be wrong, whether they choose to be or not. For what discredits their claim is not a matter of choice or of preference or point of view, but of ascertainable fact which does not wait upon our choice or preference to be what it is but, being what it is, is the standard for beliefs that purport to be the truth about it. That some such matters of fact are accessible to rationally directed inquiry and that, on the terms they offer, we can sometimes see things as they are and correct our beliefs and enlighten our conduct accordingly, is the most fundamental of all the conclusions which, in this inquiry, we shall be able to establish. To the reader unacquainted with the sources of current skepticism and irrationalism this may seem an obvious and almost trivial truism. He will find, however, that it is widely questioned and more often set in the context of theories which, if true, would render it highly questionable. Our reaffirmation of it has indeed, from the standpoint of the current intellectual fashions, the appearance of temerarious and dogmatic self-assurance. We shall not be much alarmed about the appearances, however, if we can establish the fact. For the right use of reason here provides us with a standard of factual truth which transcends fashions and conventions and points of view. Trustworthy information, thus obtainable, is by no means all that men have asked of reason, but it is an essential part of it, and it is with the light that it provides, which is the light of truth, that we shall be able to proceed.

There are many who concede the capacity of rational inquiry to arrive at reliable knowledge concerning "impersonal" matters of fact, but deny its jurisdiction where our interests and valuations are concerned. Reason, they believe, is essentially "disinterested," while all valuation is the expression of an interest or bias. They are right at least in this: that the use of reason required to organize and harmonize our interests from the standpoint of a valid ideal differs in important respects from that which suffices for our knowledge of events. And if the work of human reason was once for all to be identified with the use to which it is put in factual inquiry, we should have to say that estimates of worth are sub- or super-rational and thus exempt from the discipline of rational evaluation. This identification, however, which is currently fashionable under the name of "positivism," proves radically misleading when applied to the practical situations in which we have to discriminate those among our claims and preferences that are just and reasonable from those that are not.

Part II, on Practical Reason, is devoted to a study of the criteria in terms of which such discriminations can rightly and reliably be made. We shall not here be attempting to rationalize our actions by imposing an antecedently accepted stereotype of rationality on conduct to which it is inappropriate, but rather to find out what men of good judgment and good will have meant when they appealed to right reason as a guide of conduct. We shall find that practical reason, thus interpreted, makes very good sense indeed, while much that is best in human experience makes sense only from the standpoint which such a standard provides. The rational use of ideals in the organization and evaluation of conduct is thus justified in its fruit, which is moral wisdom. If those who deny the authority of reason have meant to say that in this usage it cannot perform what it promises, or that there is some other or better way of judging the worth of conduct than that which it provides, we can show that they are mistaken, because they have failed to understand the good of which human nature is capable, and to which, when it achieves self-knowledge and self-mastery, it is addressed. Ideals that rightly estimate this good and direct our efforts toward its attainment are not all that men have understood by reason, but they are an essential part of it, and it is with the guidance they provide that enlightened conduct can proceed.

Part III will bring us squarely up against the difficulties of applying rational ideals in the determination of social policy. There are plenty of hard-headed men who are ready enough to agree that the issues of factual inquiry and "abstract" morality are proper subjects for rational adjudication. They maintain, however, that in dealing with the "realities" of the political and economic struggle for power, reason can have but a very minor place. Principles of justice may have a certain ideal cogency, but they manifestly do not govern the affairs of men, and the group or nation which puts its trust in them will assuredly be defeated. The inefficacy of reason as a factor in history and in social behavior seems an obvious fact to many of our contemporaries, and it is by the facts, not by our wishes or ideals, they believe, that a "realistic" policy must be determined. We shall need to have our wits about us at this stage in our inquiry, for the opponents of reason in social action are vociferous and well-entrenched. Yet if we refuse to be overawed by their "realities" and are prepared to examine them in their bearing upon policy-making, we shall find them less formidable than they at first appear. For intelligent social action rightly "faces" existing conditions, not by setting them up as "realities" to which all future conduct must conform, but by using them as the means for changing the world in the direction of that which is humanly desirable and attainable. Apart from an informed judgment of their bearing on an attainable good, the facts which stand as the present conditions of effective action have simply not been sufficiently understood, and those who venerate them as the final limits to human aspirations are the victims of just this lack of understanding. It is our purpose to make out, if we can, within the context of effective action, the criteria by which desirable and attainable goals of social policy can be reliably distinguished from ideals that are merely fantastic, and from "realities" that are no deeper nor more profound than the short-sighted cynicism of those who take their stand upon them. The rational use of matter-of-fact knowledge and ideals in the determination of social policy justifies itself in its fruit, which is enlightened and constructive action. If those who profess to deny the authority of reason mean to say that in this use it cannot on fair trial perform what it promises—or that there are other and better ways of deciding the social issues on which it provides a basis of enlightened judgment —we can show that they are mistaken. Nor shall we need for the demonstration any other facts or "realities" than those that display themselves in the course of history and human behavior, when these are seen, as they should be, not only for what they are and have been, but for what, with intelligence and good will, human effort can make of them. Nowhere is constructive rational insight more needed today than in just this field, and nowhere have we more to hope from its disciplined use. Such constructive intelligence is not all that men have asked of human reason; but it is an essential part of it, and it is only by its effective application that social idealism can be translated into enlightened action.

Yet even when—and if—it is granted that rational criteria and procedures work well in these special areas of human activity, there will still be those who hold that on basic or ultimate issues they are bound to fail us. For we must, they say, base all our reasonings on premises, prejudices or preconceptions which are "finally" beyond the reach of rational examination. Even if we choose reason as our guide in life, that choice itself will be an arbitrary one, since to justify it as warranted by reason would be already to assume the right of reason to legislate on such decisions, and thus to beg the question. Our final commitments are sub- or super-rational, and it is on them that all the rest must "in the end" depend.

So runs the argument, and it has had its implications far beyond the limits of academic debate. If all really basic beliefs are arbitrary, how—save arbitrarily—are we to choose between the faiths, dogmas and superstitions which compete for our acceptance? By what right, indeed, is any one among them to be called a "superstition" at all? It may seem groundless, to be sure, from the point of view which we have elected to adopt, but it has its own point of view, "ultimately" no more arbitrary or groundless than our own, and its own philosophical self-justification, not in the reasons that support it, but in the claim it makes that here no reason is necessary and none would be in place. This, as Thomas Mann somewhere remarks, is the last fine fruit of current irrationalism, a superstition with a philosophy and, as we should add, a philosophy in which the distinction between superstition and its opposite can no longer intelligibly be made. Nor should we be much surprised at the uses that are made of this doctrine. The "ultimate" that transcends all rational distinctions is, as Hegel properly observed, the night in which all cows are black. It is, in consequence, good cover for much that would not bear inspection in the light of day.

Before we are too deeply impressed, however, by this portentous linkage of the ultimate and the arbitrary, the profound and the obscure, we shall want to make use of such light at least as we can get on these purportedly dark matters. Hence, in Part IV, we shall ask what it would be like to be reasonable about allegedly "ultimate" commitments, and what, in contrast, it would mean to make them arbitrarily. We shall find, I think, that, however it may be in "ultimate reality," in human experience there are many ostensible "ultimates" and many are their prophets, each claiming access to a special revelation which only the elect can understand—and, on the strength of this, an authority to which the non-elect must piously submit. And we shall find, moreover, that there is a rational discipline which wise men have long practiced in adjudicating such claims—the discipline of philosophy. It is not an easy discipline, nor one whose claims are widely honored in many circles today. But it is none the less of quite basic human significance. What it demands of those who practice it are clarity about the preconceptions in terms of which thinking about ultimate issues is carried on, comprehensive sanity in testing all claims made by reference to the total area of relevant human experience, and intellectual and moral responsibility in the acceptance of doctrines professed as commitments by whose consequences the thinker is prepared to stand in the whole enterprise of significant thought and action. It will not be difficult to show that the reference to such a standard does distinguish claims to "ultimacy" and "finality" which can *in this way* be reasonably sustained from those which are incoherent and half thought out, willfully narrow or blindly one-sided in the aspects of experience to which they limit their concern, or irresponsible in their refusal to accept the consequences of their own doctrines when these conflict with the special interests in whose behalf they were invoked. Philosophy, thus understood, is simply the integrity of thought in its determination to carry through and to stand by to the finish the work of rational discrimination and sound judgment which is its specific and essential contribution to human life. We shall find, I believe, that reason in this usage is justified in its fruit, which is that philosophy which, as the motto of a learned society well reminds us, is, or ought to be, the guide of life. If there are those who profess to show that reason in this usage cannot perform what it promises, or that there are higher grounds on which its conclusions can rightly be set aside, we can show that they are wrong. Nor shall we need for this purpose any esoteric appeals to an otherwise undiscoverable "reality." We have no such reality to defend and no super-rational authority to speak in its name. All we ask of those who have is that they tell us coherently what they mean by it and show us how, consistently with what we know to be true, excellent and humanly useful in other and humbler fields of experience, its claim to credence and authority can be made good, and our lives enlightened and enriched by its acceptance. If they can meet this request, they will have justified their insight rationally, that is, philosophically, in the way which is appropriate to the adjudication of ultimate issues. If they cannot, if their doctrine retains its cogency only while we are forbidden to understand it, or can maintain itself only by the arbitrary exclusion or distortion of much that we know with good reason to be true, excellent and of good report, then it is not a competing "ism" of ours that condemns it. It is condemned by the whole continuing, constructive work of human reason, against which it is an offense and which today, as often in the past, it has gravely menaced.

But we have not yet satisfied our skeptical critic. He will have a final question to ask and we shall be ready, now, to give him a final answer. Even admitting that we have found a way in which it is possible to be reasonable on ultimate issues, have we really settled the matter? May not a man still be unreasonable if he chooses? He may indeed, and many will so choose, whatever this book or others like it may say on the subject. And how, for such a man, is the cogency of rational standards to be made out? It is not, so long as he remains in that position, to be made out at all. Unreason, stupidity and sheer willfulness are as much parts of our world as earth-quakes, typhoons, and other natural catastrophes, and are not to be reasoned out of existence by argument. An appeal to reason is addressed, inevitably, to those who are capable of understanding it, that is, to those who have already some disposition to guide their conduct by rational standards and some capacity to do so. Our current difficulty is this: that in many minds this disposition is weakened, and conduct based upon it confused and frustrated by a failure to see what the relevant standards are and how the claims they make upon us can reasonably be defended. This failure, moreover, is in many cases not due to original sin or inherent incapacity, but is rather a result of the acceptance of initially plausible and widely disseminated theories which, if true, would give ample ground for both doubt and confusion. It is our purpose to set against these theories an account of the uses of reason which will remove the sources of confusion and doubt and thus enable those who want to make good use of their powers of rational discrimination to see more clearly what they are doing.

Nor need we suppose that this is an affair with which only a special sect or professional class of "thinkers" is concerned. Most men use their rational powers where they can see the sense of what they are doing, and would willingly use them to better purpose if they saw how and where to do so. Indeed, as John Locke remarked, even the enemies of reason seem to follow its principles where they can. "I find every sect, so far as reason will help them, make use of it gladly; and, where it fails them, they cry out, 'It is matter of faith and above reason.'" It is our task to show that, with good sense in its interpretation and application, reason does not fail us, and that it is our human business not to fail in the use we make of it.

CHAPTER I

THE RATIONAL USE OF IDEAS IN THE PURSUIT OF TRUTH

"Say first, of God above or man below,
What can we reason, but from what we know?"

Pope's question is a reasonable one. The play of ideas may start from guess, or postulate, or fantasy, and reach logically warranted conclusions concerning the structure of these ideas, and their implications. But when we wish to use ideas rationally to extend our knowledge of what exists—whether it be God, the world or ourselves—we must start from what we know and be guided by it. And not from what we *think* we know, merely, for this, in times past, has frequently proved to be mistaken, and the theoretical superstructure built upon it correspondingly insecure. We must start from what we *really* know, what stands the test of critical inspection as authentic and trustworthy information concerning the objects, events or persons to which our beliefs refer and about which they intend to be true. Reasoning may have loftier and more speculative objects than the gathering of reliable information about what exists, or has occurred, or is likely to occur under assignable conditions, but it is on the basis of such information that it proceeds toward them if its procedure is reasonable and judicious. The capacity, therefore, to secure relevant information, to judge reliably of its authenticity, and to use it intelligently in further inquiry, is essential to the right use of reason in human affairs.

What, then, do we really know in such fashion that it can reasonably serve as the sound informational basis for our further ideas and beliefs? This would seem to be the next question to ask, if we are to be clear about the reasonable ordering of our beliefs and the rational grounds for our acceptance of them. The answer given to it will be important in our further thinking. For, as Spinoza rightly held, the truth as known is the norm or standard by reference to which we judge both what is false and what is true. Our minds may on many issues be as open as any disciple of experimental logic thinks they ought to be, but at some points and on some questions we must make up our minds if we are to have any basis for distinguishing the credible from the fantastic, the reliable from the merely conjectural, or the properly experimental from the wrongly dogmatic and misleading. If we are wrong about these distinctions the whole area of significant experience will be narrowed or confused, accordingly. If, for instance, we are so short-sighted as to reject as incredible or meaningless any belief that refers to objects not open to direct inspection or, in a more modern version, not "real enough to be kicked," we shall find the world a simple place indeed, and shall have a very short way of dealing with those who thought they could discover more in it than was in this way reachable by their eyes or feet. It is a further question, however, and a pertinent one, whether this simplicity is a trustworthy criterion of the reliability of beliefs about the world or merely a reflection of the crudity of the proposed method of testing them. Yet a line must be drawn somewhere; the capacity of some of our contemporaries to swallow new ideas, from whatever source derived, so long as they seem fashionable, or elevating, or emotionally congenial, resembles less the broadmindedness of the sage than the indiscriminate credulity of sheer mental confusion. The truth that we already know provides the standard to which we must refer the more dubious claims that compete in the intellectual marketplace for our acceptance. It must provide a central citadel of sanity to be used as a base of operations for our further survey of the surrounding world. That world itself may indeed be unimaginably vast, and, if we are wise, we will not try to reduce it to the limits of our imagination. But what we do not know about it cannot serve as evidence of anything, not even of its vastness; it is from the standpoint of the best we know that we must judge of its nature. What then do we really know?

This question, of course, is that to which the theory of knowledge has traditionally addressed itself. The method I propose to follow in answering it, however, differs in some respects from that which has been traditional, and since the reader will have some acquaintance, either direct or derivative, with that tradition, it will conduce to our common understanding if I say at the outset what that difference is. *Prima facie* it would seem that the way to find out what we really know would be to trace more questionable knowledge claims back to some ultimate assurance that is quite certain and indubitable, not in the sense merely that we *feel* quite certain about it, but by reason of the fact that when we subject it to the closest possible critical scrutiny we see that, in this instance at least, we cannot possibly be mistaken. This is the method the theory of knowledge has traditionally followed. It assumes that the alternative that applies to our more ordinary beliefs: this seems to be true but it may be mistaken, is not open in such cases. If a principle is so transparently clear, simple and evident that there is simply no way in which we can go wrong about it, then our knowledge of it is beyond all possibility of significant doubt. If an object of experience is so directly present and open to inspection that what we say of it is a mere report or register of what we immediately see, then the statement is, once more, transparently true, and the assurance of it logically beyond dispute. If a belief is so central to the rational organization of experience that to deny it is to leave nothing standing—so that in this instance the alternative is simply "this or nothing"—we have, again, no meaningful choice. We cannot, consistently with the rest of our experience, make sense of its rejection, and so it stands secure and inescapable. These, of course, are only some of the directions in which wise men have looked for the *ultimate* foundations, themselves unshakable, on which human knowledge could rightly be built. It is not my purpose to examine them here, except to indicate my own reason for taking a different course.

That reason can be simply stated. Whatever their initial plausibility, and great as has been the genius of those who have explored their implications, none of these theories has been able to prove its worth as a sound basis for further discriminations of the genuine from the spurious in knowledge, and thus as a reliable guide in the rational organization of human beliefs. They represent ostensibly impregnable positions to which a controversialist may retreat when he wants infallible security in belief, but he purchases such impregnability, or the dialectically formidable appearance of it, by withdrawal from the world in which the work of getting reliable information on matters of human importance goes on. His "citadel of sanity" becomes a beleaguered fortress, beset on all sides by those who wait to catch him venturing out into commitments that he *might* be wrong about and, hence, does not infallibly know to be correct. And if he does not starve to death mentally inside it, it is largely because he has learned to live on very little. A few crumbs of certainty are enough for him, and even these, if his opponents are right, are so tainted with dubiety that they ought to give him mental indigestion. The conclusion to be drawn from the history of such ventures and, on the whole, the conclusion that has been drawn by those more interested in the pursuit of knowledge than in the defense of incorrigibly ultimate beliefs is that if this is what "really knowing" amounts to, then we really know very little indeed, and what we thus know is of little use in the direction of inquiry and the testing of belief in those investigations, e.g., the sciences, on which we must none the less depend for most of our reliable information about ourselves and our environment.

This conclusion, though natural enough in the circumstances, is unfortunate in its implications. For if authentic knowledge rationally requires a basis in what we *really* know, and if no such basis is to be found, or, when found, reduces all that we must elsewhere take as authentic and credible to the level of mere opinion, working "fiction" or animal faith, then it looks as though the foundations of reasonable belief had been undermined. It is, as we said, in what we actually know that we seek the standard of reasonable belief. When no ultimate standard proves available we go on believing, none the less, for man is a believing animal. But our belief now has a makeshift, hand-to-mouth sort of basis, and we are uneasily aware that the methods we have to use in exploring the world are not really respectable, while the ultimate cognitive respectabilities, even if the epistemologists could agree about them, would be of no use to us. Some considerable part of the intellectual instability of our time with its attendant distrust of reason is due to this awareness, and if we are to deal with it rationally, we shall need to find some way out of the quite genuine difficulty which is its source.

What is that way out to be? I might proclaim some new (or old) set of ultimate certainties and invite the reader to join with me in their dialectical defense against all comers and, with whatever energy we had left from this exacting task, in the construction of a system of the world on this meager basis. But we should have to derive our notion of what this world was to be like from information borrowed from the fallible and "ultimately" dubious procedures of factual inquiry, and we should end, I am afraid, only by biting the hand that fed us and affirming once more that, since factual inquiry does not conform to the criteria of certainty we had set up, it is "really" not knowledge at all but mere opinion.

The discrepancy between the demands of such epistemological criteria for "really knowing" and the tests and procedures available for finding out about the world around us would thus once more be exhibited, as it often has before. But what of it? Does it prove that the informational basis for our beliefs is rationally disreputable and that rational skepticism plus irrational belief—"animal faith," as Santayana has called it —is the final position to which our attempt to guide reason by knowledge is in the end reduced? Or does it rather prove that the criterion originally adopted is arbitrary and inept, since it demands of factual knowledge a kind of validation which it could not, from its very nature, secure, and which it does not need in order to do well and accurately the work required of it as the informational basis for reasonable belief in the fields within which such information is reliably obtainable?

I believe the latter answer is the correct one, and propose to prove it in the following way. We shall ask just what "really knowing" means, not as a consequence of preconceptions, our own or others, as to what such knowing *must* be to be "finally" or "ultimately" valid, but by an examination of the way in which the distinction between factually warranted belief and mere opinion, guess or conjecture is made in inquiries in which reliable information is in fact obtainable. If we find that such a distinction can be reasonably established and that what, by its tests, is "really known" is what we need to be informed about if we are to set our beliefs in order on issues of basic human importance, we shall be able to say that *in this sense* at least, which we have not stipulated merely but discovered in the context of factual inquiry, it is possible and important for us to criticize and correct our more dubious beliefs in the light of what we "really know" and can reliably depend on. We shall then inquire whether what *seems to be* reliably established by this method can reasonably be maintained as factually authentic information, in relation to all that can be found out from other sources and by other methods, about the world and ourselves. If it can, we shall be in a position to say that we "really know" it to be true not only from the standpoint of the special inquiries in which it is acquired, but from the standpoint of philosophical adequacy as well—not, of course, that it is or need pretend to be the whole truth about the world, but that it is consistent with and contributes to our understanding of what *on the whole* we find the world to be. And if, finally, we can show that it holds this position in relation to the rest of our experience, not as a makeshift or merely superficial source of knowledge, to be revised and shunted about to meet the "deeper" or more metaphysical demands of our nature, but rather as a norm or standard to which even our "deepest" beliefs should conform, in so far as they concern the facts and issues to which it is relevant, we shall have good reason to call such knowledge "ultimate" for us, not as inside information on "ultimate reality," but as a criterion for the accuracy and credibility of beliefs that require an informational basis, and can sometimes secure it.

If it is then maintained that what is thus established as "really known" is not what the epistemologists have often had in mind, and hence is not a case of "really knowing" or infallible certainty in their sense, we shall agree, and inquire again, what of it? Abraham Lincoln was not a good president by canons of respectability applied to him when he first arrived in Washington, but he did a very good job for his country, none the less. If, however, the critic goes on to maintain that reliable information not "really known" in the epistemologist's sense has therefore something wrong with it—that it lacks a kind of support, guarantee or validation that it ought to secure before it gains our rational credence—we shall have good grounds to show that he is mistaken. In this context the function of what we know is to provide a factual basis for inquiry and for the rational organization of beliefs. In so far as it provides that basis reliably and well, it lacks nothing necessary to its validity, and needs no further warrant than can be provided by its confirmation in the inquiry through which its factual authenticity is discovered.

The relevance of this conclusion—which, of course, has so far only been proposed, and has yet to be established—to the central problem of this volume will be obvious. Profound and learned men from time to time announce that we (and they) *really know* nothing about the real world and that even our best authenticated ideas are but "bright pictures" or "human fantasies," forever inadequate to the nature of the "Reality" they purport to disclose. Such statements may have a good and useful meaning, and sometimes, though by no means always, they do. But when they are taken as proof that human ideas are not, on their own level, and with respect to the factual subject-matter with which they are concerned, sometimes both true and known to be so in the sense in which knowledge of matters of fact can be distinguished from mere opinion, these pronouncements are thoroughly misleading and confused. And when, further, this supposed incapacity of factual knowledge to reach the "real" world is used to bolster the claims of those varieties of sub- or super-rational illumination whose devotees have always been eager to settle factual questions in terms of their own "demands" as to what must have happened, or be going to happen to satisfy their preconceptions and justify their hopes, the case against reason appears in its most ostensibly profound and cogent form. It is our purpose to provide a statement of the nature of the rational cogency of reliable factual information which will remove the ground for such confusion, and help those who wish to enlighten their beliefs by known or knowable truth to see more clearly what they are doing and how they can profitably proceed.

The World We Perceive.   The contrast between mere ideas and their relations on the one hand and substantial matter of fact on the other is central to the common sense notion of a world we find and do not make, a world to which our ideas must conform if they are to be factually true and information-ally reliable. And while common sense has had some very hard things said about it by sophisticated critics, it has the advantage, when it is about its own business, of being both common (that is, publicly sharable and testable) and sensible, which is more than can be said of many of the theories that the critics seek to put in its place. We shall do well, therefore, to start our inquiry from its standpoint, and see how far we can go with it. What is the world we find ourselves living in, the world which, to adapt a famous saying of Bishop Berkeley's, we need only open our eyes to see? The full answer to this question would require all the knowledge that men, starting by opening their eyes and looking, and proceed-ing by using their minds to inquire, and their eyes and hands again to test their ideas, have been able to accumulate, and all they may still accumulate by the further use of their senses and their minds. Fortunately we need not here under-take so full an answer. For whatever else or more this world may prove to be, it is at least the familiar world that we see with our eyes and handle with our hands, the world in which we move about and greet our friends and live and work to-gether. It is also the world in which we do our thinking, and what we can observe of it provides the clue and the test for beliefs about its more remote and perceptually inaccessible areas. We can construct in our minds a more intellectually coherent world, and wish for a more emotionally satisfying one, but in so far as our wishes and our intellectual construc-tions claim informational accuracy with respect to what is actually going on, or has occurred, or is likely to happen in this world in which, for better or worse, we find ourselves, they must meet the test of truthfulness by agreement with what we find this world to be when and in so far as we are able perceptually to observe it.

It is for this reason that the appeal to *experience*, to what we find when we actually observe things at first hand, as distinct from what we might antecedently think or desire them to be, has so important and honorable a place in the history of critical thought. The empiricists have been pre-eminently the *fact* men, where "fact" is simply something that is found to be so in tested experience, and their function has been to insist on the informational primacy (for reasonable belief) of what is thus discovered, whether we like it or not, and on the primary importance, for such discovery, of accurate observation through the senses, of what is going on around us. So far they have been plainly right, and we shall be on their side in all that follows. Nor is their doctrine a trivial or merely obvious one. There are indeed truths that a man need only open his eyes to see. But to open one's eyes and see what is there to be seen, honestly, accurately and without the bias of preconception, prejudice or tradition, is an intellectual, and not merely a physiological, achievement. The ability to *learn* by experience, that is, to derive ideas from what we observe and to correct beliefs in terms of what is found to be the case, is the most basic factor in our intellectual progress, when such progress actually occurs. And it involves as its precondition the capacity to see and report what happens in just those cases in which what happens does not agree with antecedent ideas, but stands in contrast to them as mere stubborn matter of fact, *to be* taken account of but not, as it stands, either "rational" or pleasant. It is no wonder, then, that modern philosophers have so often stressed the value of experience and tried to make it the standard for all thinking that pretends to informational accuracy concerning the world and ourselves.

But what do we *really* experience? What is the final and ultimate "given" to which our ideas have added nothing and about which, therefore, we cannot possibly be mistaken? In attempting to answer this question the empiricists have often traveled far from the path of fruitful inquiry. For the reasons given in the preceding section we shall not follow their example. "Experience" in epistemological controversy may mean anything or nothing, and there have been appeals to all sorts of experience—"inner" or "outer," scientific, aesthetic or religious, fallible or infallible—for all sorts of purposes. What we propose to ask instead is what we experience, or are aware of, when we are observing the world perceptually, by seeing, hearing, smelling or handling the things in our more immediate bodily environment. This is *one* of the ways, at least, in which we find out, by observation, what is going on around us, and guide and correct our ideas by what we find. If we can see how experience functions in this capacity as a source of reliable information, we shall have a solid basis on which to proceed. Without it, wandering in the mazes of phenomena, sense data, impressions, and their like, we should never even get near to our subject.

There are three things about the process of perceptual observation, critically considered as a source of reliable information about ourselves and our bodily environment, that deserve special attention. First, this process, considered as a source of information, not merely as a physiological event, is fallible. Second, it is corrigible, and it is in the process of correction that the difference between reliable and unreliable information is reasonably made out. Third, it is quite ultimate for us as a source of information about the world, since there is no other or better way of finding out what we learn by its means. And what we learn in this way maintains itself, under philosophical scrutiny, as trustworthy information to which belief in other fields, so far as it refers to the same matters of fact, ought reasonably to conform.

First, perceptual observation is fallible. I use my eyes and my hands in observing objects in my bodily environment, and what I observe in this process is what is going on in the world, not what is going on in my body or in my mind when I observe it. And I observe such objects as they look, or feel or smell, under the conditions in which I can observe them; that is, in the relations in which they stand to me at that time. I can see objects under a variety of conditions, with the aid of a microscope or through blue spectacles or when I am so drunk that I cannot make out what they are. But I shall never see objects when I am not seeing them, or think of them when they are not objects of my thought. It has sometimes—rather oddly—been argued that this is proof that I am not "really" seeing them, or at least not seeing them as they "really" are. On the contrary, however, to see things as they look is evidently and naturally the way to see them, no other or better having yet been devised, and if what they "really" are is at all relevant to what as observable objects they are found to be, then it is through just this process that what they really are must be disclosed. It is quite true, however, that things, as thus observed, are not always what they seem. What looks to be a man may prove on inspection to have been a shadow, and the pink rats of drunken experience and epistemological controversy have no local habitation in my bodily environment, though under some conditions they seem to some people to be there. Hence, I must learn to look carefully, and to look again, and to guide my looking by the lessons of past experience, both my own and that of others as reliably reported to me. There is, however, no mystery about this. What we observe are objects and events in our bodily environment as they appear under the conditions in which we *can* observe them, and what they really are, in this context, is what they reliably prove to be on further perceptual inspection. The "reality" thus achieved is not, of course, thereby certified as a satisfactory object for metaphysics, and it is not in that light that we are here considering it. It is, however, a reliable and quite indispensable source of information concerning our bodies and the world they inhabit, and neither science nor enlightened practice would be able to stir a step without it.

Hence, secondly, perceptual observation is corrigible, and it is in this process of correction through further and more careful observation that the distinction between what is reliable in it, as information about the world, and what is unreliable appearance is reasonably made out. Those who seek to find in a single instance of such observation the infallible certainty in terms of which alone they can distinguish *real* knowledge from mere opinion, will stare fixedly at the object until it becomes transparent, and all they are aware of in it is what they *can* thus be certain about: the shape or color or feel of it which would be there even if they were drunk or dreaming, and about which there is, as they keep on telling themselves, "no reasonably probable shadow of doubt, no possible doubt whatever." The trouble is that while they will then know *something* certainly—unless, as their critics allege, they have been in error even here—what they know will no longer be a material object but only an impression, or sense-datum, which is not itself an object of perceptual observation at all, or a part of the material world. How to get from such disembodied fragments of epistemologically infallible experience to the outdoor world of men and events is a further problem, but for us a quite gratuitous one. The kind of criticism and correction that perceptual observation requires presupposes no such unprofitable quest for certainty. There are other means of correcting the illusion of the drunkard than that of retreating to a world so tenuous that there is nothing left in it that even a drunkard could be mistaken about. There is the process by which the sober man, or the drunkard when he becomes sober, learns, by observation, what sort of world he lives in. No single observation here is infallible; about any one the question can meaningfully be raised as to whether what is observed is, in fact, what it appears to be. Fortunately, however, while the question can be asked, it can also, sometimes, be answered beyond all reasonable doubt. The process of answering it, reasonably, is the process by means of which ideas are used in the pursuit of truth about the nature and behavior of the world of bodies of which our own bodies are a part. The aim of the rational criticism of belief on this subject is not to halt inquiry at the point at which we claim to know so little about the world that no question of error can arise, but to carry it through to a point at which we know enough to distinguish what is permanently reliable in our observations from what is random, superficial and misleading.

And, thirdly, this process of criticism is sufficient to show that, in the rational ordering of our beliefs, perceptual observation, as a self-correcting process, has a quite ultimate and fundamental place. We know that there is a world of bodies, because we perceive it, because we open our eyes and our minds to find ourselves involved in it and capable of learning the lessons it has to teach. If we did not know it in this way, it would be quite futile to try to "construct" it from private sense data, or deduce it from the necessities of speculative reason, or postulate it as the area in which our duty is to be done. Such constructions, postulations and deductions are familiar enough, but all are shamelessly parasitic on the information which perceptual observation provides about the kind of world we actually live in, the world to which, after many wanderings, their speculations somehow bring them back. There may, as we have said, be much more in the "reality" to which they aspire than perceptual observation can disclose, but there cannot be less. Unless this "more" can be understood along with what we find out perceptually, and interpreted in conformity with its veracious and reliable testimony on the subjects with which it is competent to deal, the doctrine that reports it must remain suspect. What can we reason, but from what we know? And *part* of what we know—or have reliable information about—is the observable nature and behavior of objects in our bodily environment. The use of reason in the acquisition of this information, and the use of this information as a criterion for the credibility and authenticity of further beliefs to which it is pertinent are not the end and sum of human wisdom by any means. But they are somewhere near the beginning of it, and no theory, however exalted its pretensions, which ignores or falsifies their findings, can stand the test of rational examination.

The Informational Worth of Scientific Inquiry. We have so far neglected the most serious charge that can be brought against the "reality" of the world we perceive and the veracity of the information derived from perceptual observation concerning it. The sciences, with physics as their leader and model, and mathematics as their method, are alleged to have carried us far beyond the limits of such observation and to have shown in the process that the external world is quite different from what we perceive it to be, and that our perception of it is consequently unreliable. We now have the means of understanding this contention, and discriminating what is true in it from what is confused and misleading. It is true, of course, as every schoolboy is supposed to know, that the world as physics describes it is different in essential respects from what we see when we open our eyes and inspect the objects in our neighborhood. If the schoolboy, or his elders, still lack this information, they are here referred to such classic expositions of the queerness of the world of physics as that provided by Sir Arthur Eddington in *The Nature of the Physical World.* Tables that lose their solidity and prove on analysis to be "mostly empty space," electrons that escape the laws of old-fashioned physics in their indeterminate, or at least unpredictable, pulsations, and space and time of unpicturable complications are among the more striking denizens of this scientific wonderland. If the reader is tempted to exclaim, as did the sensible Alice in a somewhat similar situation, "curiouser and curiouser," we can hardly blame him. And if Sir Arthur's oddities are by this time a little out of date, there will no doubt be others, no less surprising, to take their place. The world does indeed seem to be full of a strange variety of things, and those who have antecedently made their familiar perceptual environment the measure of its possibilities are pretty certain to be surprised at what the scientific explorers have to tell them.

In our discussion of perceptual observation, however, we did not claim that what such observation can tell us is all there is to know about our physical environment. The world, as we said, may well be more than what we see and hear and touch discloses it to be, *but it cannot be less*. It is at that point, and only there, that we need criticize the reports the speculative physicists are pleased to give us. For these reporters seem to suggest that, because what we observe is not the truth they have discovered about objects and processes beyond the range of ordinary observation, it is in consequence not really the truth about the objects we observe and their observable behavior either. They reach this peculiar result not by scientific analysis, but by a familiar and quite wrongheaded sort of philosophy—that which identifies "the external world" with the object of their preferential interest and concludes that whatever is not *this* reality is not "really" what it purports to be at all, that the table on which I rest my weight is, in consequence, not really solid, and that the information I derive from perceptual information concerning it is therefore mistaken. There is a mistake here, surely, but it is not our mistake or that of common sense about its observational business. The solidity of the table that I can handle, rest my weight on, and observe in its physical behavior, when, e.g., it proves substantial enough, used as a battering ram, to break through a door, is not disproved by the fact that when Sir Arthur explores the electrical charges which he takes to be the elements in terms of whose structure and behavior the laws of physics are most simply and usefully stated, he finds no such solidity. It was not about the space between electrons that I was talking when I said the table was solid, and it is not about perceptually observable and verifiable solidity that he is talking when he reports the physical relations of electrical charges to each other. If he supposes that it is—and it is only on that supposition that his theory can be understood as casting doubt on the information supplied by perceptual observation—that does not prove that the world we see is not verifiably what, under reliable conditions, we observe it to be. It only shows that eminent scientists, when they interpret their findings philosophically, do not always know what they are talking about. And while this may be disheartening to the inexperienced, who still regard the physical scientist as a philosophic seer, it is not, for those who survey the history of ideas, any longer surprising.

The point here at issue is important. For it is on the basis of perceptual observation that the scientist proceeds in his own inquiry, and it is in terms of perceptual observation, of what can be seen on a dial, or a photographic plate, or through a telescope or microscope, that the factual veracity of his theories is tested. A laboratory and what goes on in it are as much a part of the world we perceive as any other visible and tangible object, and those who inhabit it have quite as much need as the rest of us for confidence in the reliability of their observations of what goes on in their observable environment. If the theories of physics really did cast doubt on the informational reliability of perceptual observation, they would cast doubt also on their own empirical foundations, and we should then have to ask what good reason there was to suppose that what they said was factually correct, or that Eddington's wonderland has a closer relation to what actually happens in the world than that of Alice. This would not greatly disturb Sir Arthur; for, like other mystics, his philosophic interest is not so much in articulating the rational order of our knowledge as in undermining it for the sake of a faith that not only transcends knowledge but negates its more specific content. But it is disturbing, and rightly so, for those who seek to set their beliefs in order in the light of the best knowledge available, and want good reasons for believing that conclusions advanced as authentic information about the nature and behavior of physical objects are true, i.e., that what they report is in fact the case.

The fact is that a study of the results achieved by scientific inquiry, in the context of research in which that inquiry effectively and reliably proceeds, provides a basis not for doubt of the genuineness of what we perceive but for wonder and delight at the way in which the human mind has been able to use the information thus acquired as a clue to what is going on elsewhere, and to extend its knowledge of the world accordingly. The rational use of ideas in the pursuit of informationally reliable truth is here seen at its best and clearest. There are many critics of many sects who have sought for one reason or another to discredit the findings of the sciences, and to prove that their own more esoteric and inspiring methods provide a better means of access to the world of Reality. There may be some sense in which some of these claims are significant and true; we shall return to them at a later stage. But in so far as they are intended to discredit the informational reliability of the findings of the sciences with respect to what has happened, is happening or is likely to happen in the world around us, they are thoroughly mistaken. One has only to compare what has been found out about the functioning of the human body, or the chemistry of foods, or the nature of light, by scientific inquiry, with what was believed on these matters before the sciences developed or has been contributed to our knowledge of them by other means of inquiry—Bergsonian intuition, say, or authoritarian revelation, or "thinking with the blood"—to see how the cognitive authenticity of scientific inquiry is established. "Science" as metaphysics, religion or social gospel has grave defects, but scientific inquiry, as a means of finding out what is going on beyond the range of direct observation but in the world in which we live and whose order of events we must know if we are to live securely, is a cognitive instrument which has proved its worth beyond all reasonable doubt. It is our clearest example of reason in operation, of ideas at work in the pursuit of knowledge, and those who profess to doubt that "mere human reason" can tell us what the world is like are herewith referred to it for information, not on high metaphysical ground, but because there simply is no better way of finding out what is thus discovered about the world, and no good reason to doubt that much of what has been found out in this way is substantially and reliably correct. If this does not satisfy such doubters, it will not be because the information is unreliable but because they were not looking for information but for something else, for comfort or inspiration or spiritual peace. These are great goods and supremely worth seeking, but they do not take the place of reliable information, nor can they supply it. To condemn one good because it is not another is more petulant than profound. There is a large measure of that kind of petulance in the pseudo-profundities of the rivals and enemies of scientifically ascertainable truth.

It is not my purpose or responsibility to summarize here the content of scientific knowledge, or the procedures by which it is acquired. Its methods of observation, hypothesis and verification have many times been described, and I have nothing to add to them here. The history of the sciences provides the best and most enlightening account we have of the way reason operates in using ideas to extend human knowledge to remoter matters of fact, and in using facts thus discovered to correct and amplify the ideas without the use of which they would not have been found out. In the self-correcting process of inquiry theories guide observation to events that unaided observation had never seen, while observation gives the basis for new theories which mere theorizing could not have established. And therein is the Kantian dictum fulfilled that concepts without percepts are empty, and percepts without concepts are blind, while the effective cooperation of percept and concept, observation and idea, constitutes empirical knowledge. This cooperation, as we have now learned, is not something that happens in the same way always, with predetermined categories stamping on an indeterminate material the form of their own antecedent rationality. What we observe has an obdurate and quite determinate nature of its own which often shows that previously held theories, which constituted in their time the canons of "rational" explanation in the sciences, are limited, biased and defective. The work of reason here has consisted, not in the explaining away of recalcitrant facts so that the ceremonial "rationality" of antecedent preconceptions may be maintained at all cost, but in the development of new theories, frequently shocking to traditional preconceptions, which include the facts discovered in a new, though perhaps more subtle, order and thus advance our intellectual mastery of events. To see this working adjustment clearly gives a better solution to the old puzzle about the respective claims of "fact" and "theory," "reason" and "experience," than much training in epistemology can provide, and the history of the use of rational ideas in the development of the sciences is, in consequence, the best possible foundation for a sound theory of knowledge. For this, though again not the sum and measure of all we claim or desire to know, is what knowledge is like in a case where it can reliably be identified, and to see how reason functions here is to see it as it is, not merely as its defenders or its critics would like it to be. Thus seen, it needs no higher warrant or validation than that which its own further operation in tested inquiry can provide of the informational accuracy and adequacy of the results achieved by its means. Those who participate effectively in this inquiry and those who make its results available in the various activities to which they are pertinent are doing the work of human reason. Auguste Comte's inclusion of Newton and Galileo among the saints venerated in his religion of humanity has been a source of amusement among the devotees of older and better established religions. And we may well smile at its simplicity. It is not as saints of a new religion but as collaborators in the humanly excellent work of rational inquiry that they merit our gratitude and respect. But that work is a great one, and the body of knowledge to which they contributed endures and grows. We do well to honor them.

The Uses of Abstraction. There is, however, an obstacle in the way of this interpretation of scientific knowledge as reliable information, which has greatly impeded understanding in the past and will continue to do so if we cannot find the means to remove it. Those who are familiar with popular expositions of the findings of physics and astronomy, or with the speculative elaborations of them, will know that we are confronted in such accounts not merely with valuable information about both perceived and unperceived objects, but with a "world of physics" at once ghostly and menacing, inhabited by abstract, purely metrical entities—an "unearthly ballet of bloodless categories," with no place in it for the things we know best and value most in our own experience. If this is the truth about the world which the sciences discover —the "world of description" as Josiah Royce termed it— then all we care for most seems to fall outside it. And in order to defend our concrete world of sounds and colors and emotions—the "world of appreciation"—from its blighting influence it has been felt necessary and reassuring to insist that the "world of physics" is a *mere* abstraction, or symbol, or mental construction, undeniably useful for the special purposes of scientific inquiry, but not to be compared in concreteness, and hence in reality, with what we see and feel and enjoy at first hand. An abstraction, after all, is nothing *real*, and those who "reify abstractions," or confuse the symbolic entities of physical theory with the realities of direct experience, are "misplacing concreteness" in an inexcusable way. So runs the tale. It has been told many times and been a comfort to many.

There is, as always in such cases, some truth in it. The world, as physics describes it, does seem to have a curious emptiness of qualitative being; the objects and events in it, characterized merely in the terms that physical description finds appropriate and convenient, lack full-blooded vividness and potency; they seem to be in Whitehead's striking phrase "vacuously actual." It is further true that this qualitative vacuity is properly to be interpreted not as a clue to what such objects are in their own intrinsic nature but rather as a consequence of the only way in which we are able to describe them. Our knowledge of our more immediate environment, especially of that part of it with which we can enter into social relations, is, as Eddington happily expressed it, "intimate knowledge." Our pleasures and strivings enter into it; it is colored by our moods and hopes, and is thus a theme for aesthetic delight and poetic interpretation as well as for factual description. Of objects and events more remote from our human scale and situation we know only what we can find out about them, and we seem to be in a position to find out, reliably, only those properties which are ascribed to them in order to regularize the order of physical occurrence. If I could enter into sympathetic social relationships with an electron, I might discover in it a richness of meaning beside which the equations of electro-dynamics would indeed seem empty and incomplete. The fact is, however, that attempts to discover what electrons are like by sympathizing with them, or feeling their feelings (if any), have so far been singularly barren from the standpoint of reliable information, while the more impersonal exploration of their behavior as electrical charges has been productive of knowledge which has justified itself, in its informational reliability, in further inquiry. We know the world, it must be repeated, in terms of what we can find out about it, and where what we can find out is incomplete, it is the part of wisdom to realize that the resulting "vacuity" in the world thus known reflects the limitations of our knowledge, not an esoteric kind of "reality" enjoying in its inner nature the "abstract" being of incompletely specified actuality. We know more about the objects we are intimately related to than we do about those concerning which our sole reliable information is that supplied by astronomy and physics, and to deny the genuineness of what we intimately know because science can find nothing corresponding to it in events occurring in the interstellar spaces would indeed be an unpardonable error of "misplaced concreteness." It was against that error that philosophers at the end of the nineteenth century—Bradley, James, and Bergson for example—protested, and their protest was an expression of and a contribution to philosophic wisdom.

So far so good. But there are two essential qualifications to be made if we are not to slide from a half-truth to a damaging mistake. It is because the philosophers failed to make these qualifications that their theories chiefly contributed not, as they should have, to a more exact and critical understanding of the uses of reason, but to the anti-intellectualism of which we are only now experiencing the full effects. The first is this. Incomplete knowledge is not the full and adequate knowledge we should desire. But it is none the less genuine knowledge as far as it goes, and if it is all the knowledge we have, it is rightly authoritative for belief about the objects whose behavior it reports until such time as better and more accurate knowledge is available. A detective who can identify the criminal he is hunting only in terms of a back view of him by the only witness at the scene of the crime, the incriminating cigarette case he left behind, and a voice heard over the telephone in the dead of night, can hardly be said to have "intimate knowledge" of the man he is looking for. If he were to regard the criminal as a denizen of the "world of detection," possessed only of voice, cigarette case and a disappearing rearward aspect, he would indeed be misplacing concreteness in a rather odd way. But if he were to say, on the other hand, that he *really* knew nothing about the man, and in consequence to treat what he did know as negligible, he would be just as mistaken, and on a more practically important issue. Especially would this be true if what he did know were enough, when judiciously interpreted, to make the identification required and solve his problem, though not, to be sure, the further problem of the real, deeper and ultimate nature of the criminal, which only those who loved him best would know, but which might none the less be singularly unreliable for the purpose of establishing the matter of fact in question.

In the rational use of ideas in the pursuit of truth we do not deal with "abstractions" as a queer kind of objects in a world of their own, but with objects and events in the world around us abstractly, that is, incompletely, characterized and with what can be found out about them in terms of their known characters and behavior. To know of an animal only that it is a cow and not an ape or a tiger is to know it very incompletely. We must not, as the semantically enlightened love to remind us, suppose that we are here dealing with an individual that is just *cow* and nothing else, or with the word "cow" turned into a thing by verbal magic and causing all manner of linguistic disorders in those who, without benefit of Korzybski, fall prey to its insidious spell. If anyone is tempted to believe anything so foolish he may now read, e.g., Stuart Chase and see the error of his ways. But to know of an individual that it is a cow, is to know *something* about it, and if we can profit by that knowledge to enlighten our further relations with it—to behave toward it in a way appropriate to a cow and not to apes or tigers—we have used our intelligence fruitfully, as we should not have done if we had employed our time in the sapient observation that the word "cow" is only a word, the abstraction only an abstraction, and that "cow^1 is not cow,^{2} and cow^2 is not cow^3." [1] The more we

[1] See S. I. Hayakawa, *Language in Action*, p. 158ff.

can find out about an animal from knowing that it is a cow without requiring the kind of intimacy with it that only those who truly love it, and for whom the difference between cow [1] (Bessie) and cow [2] is of unique importance, can possess, the greater will be our intellectual mastery of events. The range of our intimate knowledge is necessarily limited, while the area in which it is important to have *some* knowledge about what is happening is very wide. The use of abstractions is therefore essential to the progress of knowledge. It is not surprising that we know so little about the "world of physics" when the limitations of our sources of information are considered. The amazing thing is that we know so much, and that what is thus discovered stands the test of application and confirmation in the familiar world of macroscopic objects around us. This is knowledge gained by the use of abstractions. We should never have had it if instead of finding out what can be discovered about the physical structure of the world, in so far as it is relevant to and verifiable in the events we can observe, we had restricted ourselves to the study of objects with which we can be socially intimate or poetically inspired. Nor is there any method yet devised by poetry or social sympathy or metaphysical intuition of securing more accurate or reliable information on the matters concerning which it reports. The disparagement of "merely abstract" knowledge *may* be only a cautionary warning against the clumsy or naïve use of indispensable intellectual instruments, but it tends to develop into a thoroughly pernicious attack on human reason itself. For in this world, at least, we know in part; and it is by the rational *use* of abstractions to characterize accurately though incompletely the objects and events that concern us in the surrounding world that our knowledge is effectively increased.

There may well, once again, be realities in the world that such methods cannot disclose. If intuition, or mystical illumination, or speculative imagination, can find a way of getting us in touch with such realities—a way which does not negate or disparage what we already know but enlightens and completes it—we shall be glad to hear what they report. But there cannot be less, and those who can proceed to their special revelations only by relegating "mere" abstractions to the limbo of "mere" appearance or illusion do not deserve our credence. What we can find out about the world by factual inquiry is not all we should like to know, but, in the field of its reliable application, it is the best we have, and nothing less than that is good enough.

The second qualification follows the pattern of the first. The rational use of abstractions in inquiry is not just a matter of leaving out something or other. It is an affair of knowing what, for certain purposes and in specific contexts, can properly be left out because its presence makes no difference, or no difference that need be taken account of, in the processes under examination. There is great virtue in all rationally ordered activity in knowing what to leave out, in discriminating the relevant from the irrelevant, the things that make a difference from those that are negligible in the situation with which one has to deal. It is by the rational use of abstractions that we make these discriminations, and much knowledge of the world and of ourselves is needed if we are to make them well.

There has been a tendency in recent times to hark back regretfully to the "concreter" physical theories of an earlier age, in which all manner of humanly familiar potencies and appetites were thought to pervade nature and to influence the course of natural events. When Laplace—if the familiar anecdote is authentic—answered Napoleon's query about the place assigned to Divine Agency in his "Celestial Mechanics" with the observation, "Sire, I have no need of that hypothesis," he seems, by comparison, to be taking a dull, prosaic, almost poverty-stricken view of the matter. Yet the fact remains that Laplace knew something about the movements of the heavenly bodies that his animistic predecessors did not, and something that later astronomy has not corrected or set aside. What he knew was not, of course, that no Divine Agency exists, but rather that whether it exists or not, its agency need not be taken account of in describing the stars in their courses and predicting reliably what their future course is to be. This is not in the least a confession of ignorance—it is a profession of knowledge of the relevant cause factors in the problem at hand which is, surely, not less humanly excellent than addiction to more emotionally congenial theories for which no comparable substantiation is available. It is noteworthy that even those who look down on this type of analysis and description as superficial, or trivial, or a mere abstraction in comparison with their own more privileged means of access to the ultimately real, none the less depend on it for information concerning the matters with which it purports to deal and have, apparently, nothing better or more reliable to put in its place. Hegel did, to be sure, deduce from the necessities of Absolute Reality the number of planets that there must be in the heavens—that number agreeing conveniently with that which astronomical research had so far been able to discover. But when a new planet swam into the ken of the watchers of the sky, it was the Hegelian dialectic that was adjudged to be in error—even by devoted Hegelians—not the mere abstractions of astronomy, which had predicted the new phenomenon, and told men where and when to look for it. This is a prosaic, informational consideration, but it is precisely with that use of reason that eventuates in reliable information that we are here concerned. And what we have a right to conclude, I think, is that the use of abstractions in such inquiry in no way discredits the truthfulness of the results achieved, provided always that these results are understood in the context of inquiry, as a report of what can be found out by reliable methods, not of the complete or inner reality of the world as a whole, or of its metaphysical con-

ACADEMY OF FOOD MARKETING
LIBRARY
ST. JOSEPH'S COLLEGE
PHILADELPHIA, PA. 19131

stituents. We can say further, that it is precisely by the intelligent use of abstractions that we order and extend our knowledge in fields where "intimacy" of a more personal sort has so far not been achieved, or, at least, has not reached the level of articulate expression and communicable knowledge. In these fields the alternative to "abstraction" is not something cognitively richer and more concrete, but the mental confusion in which thought ceases to be selective through its incapacity to make essential discriminations. A human skeleton is for biological purposes an abstraction and a somewhat uncanny object to encounter in isolation, but even the mystic would be hard put to it to get on without his own vertebrate structure. Thought, too, has a skeleton, and hence a backbone, and those who know something of its anatomy (though skeleton [1] is not skeleton [2] to be sure) have acquired a measure of understanding for which there is, so far at least, no satisfactory substitute.

The Limitations of Science and the Movement of Thought. Why is it, then, that the progress of scientific knowledge has so frequently been interpreted as a menace to human value? Why have zealous and well-intentioned men devoted their best intellectual efforts to a portrayal of the limitations of science, as though it were peculiarly reassuring to know that there were still some areas of experience into which the systematic and self-critical quest for reliable factual information has not penetrated, or, perhaps, that are forever barred to it? Is it good news that there is much in the world that we have not found out about, and quite possibly never shall? There is, to be sure, great comfort in ignorance, where knowledge would be disturbing to established ideas. But there is more to the criticism than that, and, in the long continued battle between the protagonists of science and its critics, by no means all virtue and wisdom have been on the former side.

The justification of a scientific theory, we have said, is to be found in its capacity so to articulate the structure of a particular subject-matter that with its aid the scientist will know where to look for the experiences that will disclose the nature and predictable behavior of the objects and events with which he has to deal, and thus will serve as sources of reliable information concerning them. It is in terms of his theory that he distinguishes the relevant from the irrelevant, the significant from the insignificant, the objective from the subjective. But which theory is thus justifiable is itself something to be found out in the course of inquiry. There was, for example, no antecedent reason to suppose that a good physical theory could not, like that of Aristotle and his medieval followers, be based upon the nature things possess, as wet or dry, hot or cold, light or heavy and the like. These *might* have proved to be the most significant of all the physical properties of bodies, in the sense that, in terms of them, the order of physical happenings could reliably have been predicted and the way opened for further inquiry which would have confirmed the initial assumptions and extended our knowledge of what is going on in the world beyond the range of direct or unguided observation. And if they had proved thus reliable, the theory based upon them would seem today an excellent and uniquely rational theory, while those who, like the early atomists, looked to the atomic structure of bodies for the clue to their physical behavior would be regarded as the most extravagant of theorists and scornfully called "philosophers." The rightness of a mechanical physics was something that had to be *found out* by the nature of its functioning in the context of inquiry in its capacity to disclose the physical structure of the world itself, in the only way it can be disclosed to the human mind, through the rational use of ideas which prove their validity in the truthfulness of the knowledge which, under their guidance, we are able to secure. And its rightness was established only where it did so apply, and within the limits in which inquiry was then working. If mechanical laws prove insufficient for the description of electro-magnetic events on a sub-atomic scale there should be no great surprise at that. We are still finding out about the world and there is no advance guarantee that what is found will be a simple extension of the pattern of what we already know.

There is, however, a very human tendency to assume that such will be the case, not merely in the sense that what is still to be discovered will be compatible with what we already know, but in the sense that the pattern of our present knowledge, its leading ideas and discriminations of relevance, can be applied without modification to any further subject-matter with which we have to deal. This has not proved true within the sciences themselves, and the excited reports of a "revolution" in the notions of space, time and causality in physics a few years ago are the layman's evidence that scientists can broaden and subtilize the categories with which they work as their work proceeds, and can extend their knowledge of the world accordingly. Such a development is upsetting only to those who had misunderstood the rational use of ideas in the first place, and had therefore attached to particular conceptions of limited applicability a finality that did not properly belong to them. It is, in fact, a major triumph for reason that it can thus proceed and can vindicate itself, not by conformity to old ideas but in its capacity to develop new ones when the progress of inquiry demands them. Thought moves, and ideas develop, and it is in what it achieves in process of movement and development that the justification of our thinking is to be found. There are many ways in which you can use a good scientific idea, but it does not make a comfortable resting place for a tired mind or a fixed pattern for the growing body of our knowledge. It is not surprising, therefore, that those who have tried to use scientific theories in either of these ways have been disappointed.

The pertinence of these observations to our previous problem about the urge to "limit" science can now be indicated.

Modern science developed first and has won its greatest triumphs in astronomy, physics, chemistry and, more recently, biology. The theories developed in these sciences are not *a priori* statements concerning the structure the world must have in order to be a proper subject for truly scientific inquiry. Neither are they mere descriptions of what anyone could find out by opening his eyes and noticing what is going on in the world around him. They represent substantial discoveries of what can be observed by those who know where to look for the significant phenomenon and what can be found out when such phenomena are used as clues to the further order or structure of events. As such, they are among the greatest of man's intellectual achievements. But, quite naturally, and properly, they reflect the nature of the subject-matter from which they were derived and our means of finding out about it. *It may be* that factors in experience that have proved irrelevant or misleading in physics will equally be so in sociology. Atoms do not appear to be guided by purposes, or inspired by ideals. It is, therefore, proper for the physicist to ignore such considerations in his inquiry. He has found by patient investigation that, like the flowers that bloom in the spring, they have, for his purposes, nothing to do with the case. Does it therefore follow that human purposes have "really" nothing to do with human behavior, or that it would be unscientific in psychology to take account of factors in behavior for which a chemist would properly have no use in his somewhat different inquiry? When the question is put in this way the answer seems obvious. What is pertinent to a particular subject-matter is something *to be found out* in the inquiry which has reliable and adequate knowledge of that specific subject for its goal. A new effort of understanding and rational discrimination is needed for each new problem and, as Bergson has well said, there is no faculty of intelligence, not even that labeled science, which enables us to pass judgment on specific sorts of objects and kinds of process without having studied them.[2] A consideration of human preferences may well be irrelevant when it is astronomy that we are studying, but it is not equally irrelevant when it is human preferences and their reasonable organization that constitute our problem. Yet, if we identify reliable knowledge with "science," and "science" with the sciences so far most adequately developed, we may reach a similarly misguided conclusion by a slightly more devious route. "Science" has nothing to say about, e.g., justice. Rational knowledge is confined to what science says, and does not go beyond it. Therefore rational knowledge has nothing to say about justice. This seems to be a mere generalization of "scientific method," and as such admirable. But what it does in effect is to rule out *in advance* as irrelevant, or not proper subject-matter for rational treatment, certain aspects of human behavior that are seen by those who try to understand it at first hand, to be relevant and even essential to an adequate understanding of its nature. To such men the progress of "science" often seems to mean the progressive impoverishment of experience, in the very areas where we have our fullest evidence of what is going on. Hence, to set up limits beyond which science is not to pass is for them a way of protecting the specific content of their subject-matter against a reductive analysis which would distort its nature. Their antipathy is not, for the most part, to the acquisition of reliable information but to rules of interpretation arbitrarily imposed on a subject-matter to which their relevance has not been made out.

The controversy that thus arises is of a typically unrewarding nature. Those who value the use of reliable methods of inquiry without fear or favor, and who rightly see in the procedures of the natural sciences a preeminent example of what such methods can achieve, have a very strong case indeed. And among their opponents are many who oppose the progress of inquiry because they are afraid of truth and dis-

[2] H. Bergson, *La Pensée et le Mouvant*, p. 105.

trust its influence. But, equally, those whose primary concern is with human behavior and its adequate understanding, and who have seen the confusion that can be wrought by "scientific" theories which, borrowed from physics or biology, are applied with self-righteous naïveté by would-be Newtons, Darwins and Einsteins of sociology, have good ground for their suspicions. On one side is a "science" that in this usage is abstract not merely because, like all organized knowledge, it makes use of abstraction, but because its abstractions are, with respect to the subject at hand, arbitrary and inept. For they are applied on the assumption that we cannot reasonably take account of anything about our fellow men that would not be pertinent to thermo-dynamics or, at least, to general biology. On the other side are the spokesmen for an unorganized mass of experience in whose interpretation confusion becomes a virtue and special pleading a mark of profundity, since it is by refusing to admit the authority of reason here that they propose to correct the "abstractions" of science and return triumphantly to the concrete. The resulting situation is not a happy one.

It is fortunate, therefore, that the difficulty which gives rise to it is also quite gratuitous. There is nothing whatever in the progress of reliable knowledge in the context of physical, chemical or biological inquiry which can dictate in advance the categories in terms of which social behavior is most adequately to be understood. The matters of fact established by these sciences will of course be basic and authoritative for all further inquiry. And in so far as man is a physical object, and a biological organism, the findings of these sciences will apply to him as well. But their relevance to what is done in social groups where men—unlike most other physical objects and biological organisms—are concerned to act for ends they judge to be good by methods they hold to be just and right, is a further question. The demand that this question be settled in advance by reference to methods scientifically applicable elsewhere is a mark not of peculiar enlightenment but of mental laziness, or even of intellectual hardening of the arteries, a disease that manifests itself not only among ordinary mortals but even among eminent scientists when they mount the pulpit or the lecture platform and lay down principles of social justice or ethics or theology on the basis of information they have acquired about the curvature of space, the velocity of light, or the mental capacities of apes. Such information *may* be relevant, of course, but the determination of its relevance can reasonably be made only from the standpoint of the further inquiry to which the information is supposed to contribute; not from that of the science from which it was initially derived. The limits of science here are not the limits of rational inquiry to selected areas of experience, but the limits of special theories and methods to the contexts in which their applicability can be fairly established. The proof of such limitation is not, therefore, a proof that we need something else beside rationally directed inquiry to obtain knowledge of the world, but that we need to be more reasonable in our use of ideas and preconceptions *in* inquiry than we have been in the past. There is no higher mark of the rational use of ideas than the ability to criticize, revise and expand one's preconceptions to meet the specific and sometimes unanticipated structure of a world we know in part but can learn to know more fully as we proceed. If the specialists and pedagogues have forgotten this fact it is they, and not the capacity of reason to explore and understand the world, that thus betray a basic "limitation."

What, then, in summing up, are we to say of the ultimacy of the kind of knowledge of the world that can be derived from perceptual observation, and from the scientific inquiry which uses such observation as a basis for theories that extend our knowledge beyond the range of observation but are confirmed in or corrected by further observation and research? We have found no instances of infallible certainty here, and neither have we found any theories so comprehensive, concrete and final as to qualify as *the Truth* of which all further truth must somehow be a mere aspect or reflection. What we have found is reliable information, reached by methods which prove their trustworthiness for this purpose, not by being always right, but by providing the means for the correction of their own mistakes in their further and reasonable development. Such knowledge, as so far acquired, is not by any means all we want to find out, nor is it assured that all we shall later learn will leave unaltered the categories in terms of which our thinking now proceeds. What is assured, however, is that by these means we have gained indispensable information which would not otherwise have been available. And what is important for our philosophical purposes is that we have found an area of experience in which the distinction between warranted belief and groundless or arbitrary opinion can genuinely be made out. Here at least, whatever the skeptics may say, we sometimes know what we are talking about and whether or not what we say is true. This is only a beginning in the total work of human reason, but it is a beginning that is also a foundation on which we can build. From now on, when the professionally cynical, edifying or profound try to tell us that human reason is incapable of attaining truth or that what we *call* "knowledge" is *really* only irrational opinion or animal faith, we shall not be greatly impressed. If their words are being used informatively, to characterize what we can identify as factual knowledge in the respects in which it reliably differs from both faith and opinion, we can tell from what we reliably know that they are wrong. We know what authentic knowledge is like, because in these instances we possess it. And it is in the light of what we know that our reasoning can responsibly proceed.

CHAPTER II

SOME SKEPTICAL DOUBTS AND THEIR RESOLUTION

The true, as Spinoza told us, is the norm both of itself and of the false. The view of the use of reason in factual inquiry presented in the previous chapter claims to be true, and I have tried to show that the claim is justified. But it is by no means the only or even the most popular view on this subject at the present time. Men whose learning and first-hand acquaintance with the procedures of the sciences entitle them to a respectful hearing frequently reach conclusions that appear to be quite incompatible with it. If our view is true, as it claims to be, it ought to be possible in its terms to show not only that those that contradict it are mistaken, but, what is more fruitful, where and how they are mistaken, and how the truth that is in them can be clarified and preserved when such mistakes are eliminated. This is not a matter of combating one "ism" in order to clear the way for another. Each of the views that will here be examined involves an interpretation of the use of reason which ends in an apparent denial of the capacity of rationally directed inquiry to attain literal truth about the world and thus to provide a sound, substantial basis for the reasonable organization of our beliefs. This implication was not always intended by those who propounded these views, and is sometimes rejected when it is explicitly pointed out. The harm done by a mistaken theory is not avoided, however, by disavowing its consequences when they become inconvenient. Others, more consistent if less judicious, will draw the skeptical conclusions implicit in the doctrine, and in the cases we shall examine have done so with telling effect. The current irrationalism has made much use of these conclusions, and if we are to meet it rationally we must show not only that they are undesirable, but also that they are unwarranted, and that the attainable truth which they have misinterpreted provides the sufficient basis for their correction. From the standpoint we now occupy we are, I believe, in a position to do this.

Science, Truth and "Reality."   A drastic, though not untypical statement of the unhappy state of scientific knowledge today is offered by Professor Sorokin. "Decadent sensory science [by which he means the science of our "sensate culture" in its present decadent or "over-ripe" stage] even declares that it is not concerned with any true reality. It offers merely certain propositions based upon sensory observations which appear to be convenient and therefore speciously true. Such a formulation of the task of sensory science is equivalent to burying the truth, reality and science itself." [1] For, as Sorokin urgently queries, "If science is not concerned with reality, then what *is* it concerned with? What, then, is the difference, apart from expediency, between the 'as if' construct of the inmate of an insane asylum and that of the scientist? What a distance we have traveled from the conception of the truth as *adaequatio rei et intellectus* entertained by Saint Thomas Aquinas!" [2]

Bertrand Russell, in one of his philosophical phases, though not, perhaps, the most characteristic, writes in a somewhat similar vein. "Science, which began as the pursuit of truth, is becoming incompatible with veracity, since complete veracity tends more and more to complete scientific skepticism. When science is considered contemplatively, not practically, we find that what we believe, we believe owing to animal faith, and it is only our disbeliefs that are due to

[1] P. Sorokin, *The Present Crisis of Our Age*, p. 98.
[2] *Ibid.*, p. 117.

science. When, on the other hand, science is considered as a technique for the transformation of ourselves and our environment, it is found to give us power quite independent of its metaphysical validity. But we can only wield this power by ceasing to ask ourselves metaphysical questions about the nature of reality. Yet these questions are the evidence of a lover's attitude towards the world. Thus it is only in so far as we renounce the world as its lovers that we can conquer it as its technicians. But this division in the soul is fatal to what is best in man. As soon as the failure of science considered as metaphysics is realized, the power conferred by science as a technique is only obtainable by something analogous to the worship of Satan, that is to say, by the renunciation of love." [3]

The central factual content here, somewhat melodramatically announced in each case, is that the sciences have reached a point of development at which they are no longer concerned about "reality" or claim to provide information concerning it. This means to Sorokin that they are no longer concerned with truth in any sense in which the "truth" of science can be distinguished (save by its expediency) from that of an insane asylum. It means for Russell (in this mood) that science gives power but not veracity, and since those who are willing to purchase power at the expense of veracity are satanic, that science is, so far at least, on the side of the Devil, a conclusion shared by some of Russell's more recent critics.

Yet the same factual content can be presented in a very different way. Thus Benjamin Ginzburg, in his article, "Science," in *The Encyclopaedia of the Social Sciences*, stresses the character of science, as he understands it, "as a representation, or schema, for anticipating the further course of phenomena and not at all as a body of laws directly governing reality," [4] and more explicitly not, "even in its own plane, as a direct and metaphysical view of reality but only as a special and progres-

---

[3] Bertrand Russell, *The Scientific Outlook*, p. 264.
[4] Vol. XIII, p. 592.

sive approach to experience." [5] But he considers this not a disastrous deprivation through which science loses contact with the truth appropriate to it, but as an emancipation from problems which are none of its affair and difficulties which, for its own proper interest, are merely gratuitous. The urbane Crane Brinton is not merely cheerful but almost smug in his announcement that "Science makes no attempt to study or describe reality—certainly not ultimate reality. Science is not even concerned with truth, in the sense that word has for theologians, for most philosophers, and for a good many other people. . . . That discipline is based, not on faith, but on skepticism, on a skepticism which does not even worry itself over its status in the universe." [6] And Norman Campbell sums up the attitude of many scientists bluntly but effectively when he asserts that "the great development of science of the last century is intimately connected with its divorce from philosophy," [7] and hence from the problems and commitments concerning "truth" and "reality" in which that discipline is involved.

What are we to make of this? If the scientist is no longer concerned to tell the truth about the world as it really exists, but only to devise techniques which enhance the power of those who use them—whether for "good" or "bad" ends it would not be scientific to decide—we have indeed been brought by the progress of inquiry to a low intellectual and moral level. For the respect for truth is the beginning of wisdom, and nothing to be gained by the surrender of it will be worth the price. But is this really a fair or accurate way of reporting the development that has actually taken place? I think it must be evident, on more circumspect and less heated investigation, that it is not. It should be noted that Brinton, for instance, did not deny that science is concerned with

[5] *Ibid.*, p. 599.
[6] Crane Brinton, *The Anatomy of Revolution*, pp. 16-17.
[7] Norman Campbell, *What is Science?* p. 8.

truth, but only with "truth," "in the sense that word has for theologians, for most philosophers, and for a good many other people." He gives as instances the truth about a final cause, an unmoved mover, or a *ding an sich*. Or more generally, it is the truth about "reality" that is not to be attained by the method of scientific inquiry. Truths about sodium, or an eclipse of the moon, or even the anatomy of revolutions are still presumably obtainable by the methods of scientific inquiry, and indeed are better and more reliably attained when the scientist is content to describe the behavior of "phenomena" as, with the aid of an adequate theory, he is able to discover it, without attempting to square his results with preconceptions concerning the nature of "ultimate reality." Even Russell, in the same volume in which he expresses the dark views noted above, affirms that "science is in its essence nothing but the systematic pursuit of knowledge," [8] and claims that we have enough of it to say, for instance, that "the progress of biology, physiology, and psychology has made it more probable than it ever was before that all natural phenomena are governed by the laws of physics" [9]—a conclusion of some importance, as he goes on to observe. And while Sorokin proclaims the bankruptcy of sensate science with enthusiasm, he does not hesitate to use one of the most fallible of its methods, that of statistical generalization from quite meager evidence, to arrive at conclusions, in whose truth he has perhaps too generous a confidence, about the coming collapse of our culture.

It is not, then, the truth about the structure and behavior of observable objects, or about the actual past and probable future sequence of events, that scientific inquiry is held no longer to be capable of, or even interested in, supplying. It is the truth about "reality," or "ultimate reality," as more esoteric disciplines, notably theology and metaphysics, depict

[8] *Op. cit.*, pp. 132-133.
[9] *Ibid.*, p. 120.

it. And what is ultimate reality? That, as the saying has it, is a hard question, and there is remarkably little reliable information to be had concerning it. It is the object that the scholastics confidently identify as the *Ens*, which is "unum, bonum, verum," which Kant believed he had shown to be theoretically unknowable—a *ding an sich*—and which Professor Whitehead has more recently discovered to be a world of feelers, feeling other feelers and their feelings and organizing such feelings into aesthetic unities of experience which are the final concrete facts of existence. What the development of scientific knowledge has served to show is that we do not need to answer this sort of question or achieve *this* truth in order to secure reliable information on a wide variety of other subjects with which human knowledge is more proximately, though perhaps not so ultimately, concerned, and that, in fact, the progress of scientific inquiry is hindered rather than helped by the intrusion of such issues. The serenity of the informed scientist in the face of this alleged incapacity of his research to achieve "the truth" is based not on what he is skeptical about—"science considered as metaphysics," as Russell aptly puts it—but on what he is reasonably assured of, the capacity of science, considered as science, to achieve without benefit of metaphysics the kind of reliable information which, so long as it remained the handmaiden of metaphysics or theology, it somehow never got around to procuring. The emancipation of science from metaphysics, which is the basic tenet of a critical philosophy of science, is not a mark of our intellectual disintegration, but a substantial discovery about the way in which factual inquiry in specific fields can reliably and profitably proceed. This does not mean, of course, that speculative hypotheses suggested by metaphysics or theology have not been and may not continue to be of considerable suggestive value in the development of inquiry in the sciences. What it means is that the truth or authenticity of the conclusions reached by means of such hypotheses is to be determined not by conformity to canons of metaphysical ultimacy or intelligibility, but by their confirmability in tested experience and scientifically guided observation. Whether or not what is thus confirmed or confirmable is "ultimately real," by the standards of metaphysics, is a further question, which cannot, in the same way, be settled. Since it appears to be in any case so very difficult to settle, the discovery that the progress of factual inquiry in these fields need not wait upon its solution but can proceed reliably without it should properly be regarded as good news for those who, without aspiring to omniscience, are still anxious to know as much as they can of their relevant environment.

Why has it not been so regarded? For the reason, chiefly, that having antecedently identified *real* knowledge with knowledge of reality, or ultimate reality, those who failed to find in the sciences the solution of their metaphysical or theological problems went on to claim that if science is not knowledge of "reality," then it is not *really* knowledge at all. What is not *really* knowledge is then set down as mere opinion, ultimately groundless because not grounded in the ultimate truth, and, hence, ultimately not rationally better or more truthful than other groundless opinions—those of the insane, for example—which are also convenient for certain limited purposes but fail to stand the test of more stringent inquiry. And this, if true, would be damaging not only to the *metaphysical* finality of scientific inquiry, to which it does not and need not aspire, but to the factual veracity which is essential to it and in terms of which we rightly prefer it, not only to the delusions of the insane, but to the irresponsible talk of theologizing sociologists on the lecture platform. A skepticism concerning the *metaphysical* truth of science—that is, its capacity to answer our questions concerning the ultimate object of metaphysical inquiry—is a healthy sign of critical sophistication in the use of scientific methods. But skepticism concerning the capacity of science to attain factual truth in its own field and to guide its research by the truth that has been found would be intellectually demoralizing. It is fortunate that the responsible scientist does not confuse these two skepticisms in his scientific practice, or when he is about his own business. If he did, there would be little to choose between the scientific anthropology to which we already owe so much in the social sciences and the Aryan anthropology of those who think with their blood and carry the teachings of their "science" to a bloody conclusion. But while he does not confuse them in practice, he sometimes confuses them in what he says, and thus quite grievously misleads those who depend for their knowledge of scientific method on what scientists say in their more speculative moments rather than on what they do when they are about their scientific business.

If the careful reader will follow out the accounts of scientific method in which these damaging statements about the scientist's lack of concern for "truth" and "reality" and his inability to attain them occur, he will find that the context of their affirmation is that in which metaphysical commitments and pretensions are being disclaimed and in which the scientist is claiming his right to proceed with his own business without regard for them. That his own business, therefore, is not the discovery of truth, as reliable and tested information about the objects and events in the world with which he deals, could only be concluded by those who know of no methods other than those of metaphysics or theology of distinguishing factually warranted assertions from the beliefs of the uninstructed or the insane. There is such a method, the critical and self-correcting method of scientific inquiry; and those who think that the respect for truth has fled the modern world because they no longer find it expressed in the language of Aquinas would do well to become better acquainted with this procedure, and with the intellectual integrity of those who faithfully employ it.

If science is not concerned with "reality," then what is it

concerned with? Why, with the movement of light, and the growth of plants and the properties of carbon compounds and the probable effects of one sort of diet or another on human health. With these subjects, and many more. And what is the difference between what is thus found out and the "mental constructs" of the insane? Chiefly this, that what has been found out about light, and growth and carbon stands the test of factual authenticity in public and testable inquiry in a quite remarkable way. Are the objects thus discovered "real"? We have good reason to believe that they are really, or actually, or as a matter of fact, in relevant respects what they are reported to be, and that what is thus reported is, in consequence, reliable information about what is going on in the world around us. Are they "realities" of some further or more final sort? When we know what "reality" is, and how we are to detect its presence, we shall be able to judge more intelligently as to that. But this we know: whatever this further reality may be, it must be such that within it light travels, and plants grow, and carbon behaves in its own discoverable fashion. If "reality" cannot find a place for these familiar but authentic facts and the truthfulness of the inquiry that reports them, then so much the worse for "reality," and its prophets. To acknowledge this and insist upon it is neither "skepticism" nor "dogmatism"; it is responsible good sense in the ordering of our beliefs with respect to the kind and amount of evidence we have for them. It is not incompatible with the aspirations of men who love the world, but only with the claims of those who do not love the truth, whether sensory or super-sensory, when it fails to fit their preconceptions.

We should be content to leave the matter here, were it not for a further consideration, derived from this same confusion, which enters into and distorts other and better theories of the nature and truth of science. The claim that science can deal neither with "reality" nor, in consequence, with "truth" has intimidated competent critics who should not have been imposed on by it. Accepting its negative implications, and sensibly aware that scientific inquiry does nevertheless have its own distinctive sort of cogency and validity, they have tried to account for this validity without laying claim to literal truth for scientific findings, even in the sense in which, as we have seen, such truth is attainable and essential to cognitively responsible inquiry. Scientifically warranted conclusions may not be "true," it is said, but they are "convenient," or socially agreed to, or simple and aesthetically pleasing, or the like. They apply not to objects in the external world, but "ultimately" only to objects of immediate sensory experience or phenomena, though what they say of such phenomena is nothing that is true of them as such, but only of quite complicated "constructs" which, for rather obscure reasons, scientists set up in their place. All such accounts come to grief on one essential point: they are unable to say clearly what the difference is between the "convenience" that justifies a scientific conclusion and that which excuses a useful lie, or why the social agreement arrived at by the use of scientific methods has a cogency which other methods of achieving such agreement, e.g., by propaganda of various sorts, seem to lack. They cannot say this, because the actual difference consists in the fact that in the scientific case the convenience established or the agreement reached is substantial evidence of the truth of what is asserted, while in the other cases it is not. They have renounced the claim to "truth" as a distinguishing feature of scientifically warranted beliefs and are trying to set up something else in its place, where nothing else will do. This imports an ambiguity into their theories that the hostile critic is quick to see and take advantage of. As a consequence, the skeptical attack on the reasonable credibility of the sciences, while not at all justified by scientific procedures themselves, is partially justified by the account of such procedures given by over-cautious theorists who, having been frightened by philosophy in their early days, are unwilling to acknowledge anything as a fact for fear it may grow before their eyes into a metaphysical monster. This negative metaphysics colors most of the currently accepted "critical" or "empirical" or "instrumental" theories of knowledge, and helps to impair the confidence of well-intentioned men in the veracity of reliable, factual knowledge. It thus plays its part in the reaction against reason and, hence, requires our further examination.

The Linguistic Criticism of Thought. One of the most currently influential of such gospels of critical enlightenment is that which is called by its admirers "the discipline of semantics." Its aim is to correct the errors and excesses of abstract and too ambitious thought by concentrating attention on the linguistic medium through which such thinking operates, and pointing out the pitfalls into which we stumble if we forget that words are only words and proceed instead to mistake the word for the thing to which, in intelligent discourse, it refers. Its favorite maxim is "point to the referent," the object or thing in the real world about which you are talking, and its doctrine is that where no such "referent" can be found, nothing is being referred to, you do not know what you are talking about, and your pretended thought reduces to mere verbiage—"blah, blah, blah," as Stuart Chase likes to say—without sense and without an object.

This movement has its roots in a very old and reputable philosophy. To make our words precise and our ideas clear by indicating the usage in which they have a reliable sense and meaning has been one of the continuing aims of critical philosophy. When Thomas Hobbes concluded, some centuries ago, that "the light of human minds is perspicuous words," and strove with good effect to make his own words perspicuous and pertinent to the subjects with which he was dealing, he did not regard himself as introducing a new method and standpoint in human thinking, but as following a procedure normal to rational inquiry and essential to its success. It is, we should all agree, a very good thing to know what one is talking about, and it is not as common as it ought to be. Hence, any method that can help us to be more definite and responsible in our speech and thought is to be welcomed. But how are we to tell when we are talking about something real or objective and when, on the other hand, our words have no referent beyond themselves and are hence *mere* words, which it would be an obvious error to identify with things in the real world outside us? The disciple of semantics has a simple answer to this question. There is on the one hand the world that we are capable of knowing through our own experience. This is the extensional world. It is "the world of happenings about us which we know at first hand. But," as the semanticist goes on to tell us, "this is an extremely small world, consisting only of that continuum of the things that we have actually seen, felt or heard—the flow of the events constantly passing before our senses." [10] Then there is the verbal world, which is simply the world that "comes to us through words," [11] and of which we have no such direct or first-hand experience. And the simple principle of linguistic criticism from which the rest proceeds is that "this verbal world ought to stand in relation to the extensional world as a *map* does to the *territory* it is supposed to represent." [12]

In the extensional world we point to referents in a quite simple and literal sense; they are objects of direct experience and can therefore be indicated by gestures and physical manipulation, without recourse to words. The "extensional meaning" of a word is "that which it *points to* or denotes in the extensional world" and hence "is something that *cannot*

[10] S. I. Hayakawa, *op. cit.*, p. 21. I have chosen this account as the clearest, most characteristic and most widely read of the pronouncements of this school with which I am acquainted, and the one with which the reader is most likely to be familiar. It is with semantics as a gospel of critical enlightenment, not with the logic theories of Carnap and his associates, that I am here concerned.

[11] *Ibid.*, p. 22.

[12] *Ibid.*, p. 23. Italics in text.

be expressed in words, because it is that which words stand for. An easy way to remember this is ɛɔ put your hand over your mouth and point whenever you are asked to give an extensional meaning." [13] And, by contrast, "the *intensional meaning* of a word or expression, on the other hand, is that which is *suggested* (connoted) inside one's head. . . . To remember this, put your hand over your eyes and let the words spin around in your head." [14] An "intensional orientation" of thought is the habit of guiding ourselves by words alone,[15] an extensional orientation, which is enthusiastically recommended as its alternative and corrective, directs us "outside our heads" to the facts and real objects in the extensional world.

With this critical equipment it is possible to deal in a short way with many antecedently puzzling questions. In "a short study in applied semantics," Stuart Chase comments ironically on the difficulties people get into when they talk about the conflict of "government" with "business" under the Roosevelt Administration. It is obvious that they are not "extensionally oriented" when they speak in this fashion. For "in the world that we actually see with our eyes and touch with our hands, there is no entity 'government' and no 'business.' A man with a camera could not take a picture of either." [16] The student of semantics will get excited about no such bogus entities. President Roosevelt he knows, and Albert P. Sloan, and their respective doings, but "business" and "government" he cannot find. Nor, in 1938, when *The Tyranny of Words* was written, could Stuart Chase find "fascism," a word which he held to be peculiarly unreliable. "But should not one be afraid of fascism and fight against it? The student of semantics is not afraid of evil spirits and takes no steps to fight them.

[13] *Ibid.,* p. 61. Italics in text.
[14] *Ibid.,* p. 62. Italics in text.
[15] *Ibid.,* p. 218.
[16] Stuart Chase, " 'Government' vs. 'Business,' " *Common Sense,* June, 1938. Reprinted, as a model of semantic analysis, in *Language in Action,* p. 288.

... If the armies of Mussolini or Hitler invade his country, he is prepared to fight. But he refuses to shake and shiver at a word, and at dire warnings of what that word can do to him, at some unnamed future date." [17] It is all very simple. As Max Schiferl summed it up, for a Stanford Language Arts Investigation: "To make sure that the words we use deal with the world outside of us, we have only to follow the advice of Stuart Chase: Look for the referent! Be certain that the word refers to something that is real enough to be kicked." [18]

When Alice had completed her somewhat original version of "You Are Old, Father William," she was prepared to admit that it was perhaps not quite right. But the caterpillar, who was something of a pedant in such matters, pronounced the sterner judgment that it was wrong from beginning to end. I am afraid that in this matter of semantic analysis we must echo the verdict of the caterpillar. And while the interpretative vagaries of Alice were a positive improvement on the original, the critical philosophy of the semanticists is a source of serious confusion. Let us consider more closely the critical principle on which it proceeds. Our words have extensional meaning when we can point, without the use of words, to the objects within the area of our direct observation to which they refer. Unless this connection can be established their "meaning" is *merely* intensional, and we are dealing only with a "verbal world," "inside our heads," to which it is sheer superstition to attach any factual significance. Thus the factual or non-verbal significance of anything we try to say is measured by the possibility of identifying and manipulating its object or "referent" within the area of our own direct experience.

Taken literally and consistently this would mean that no individual can significantly refer to anything that he does not himself experience in this way, since, *for him*, it is a part of

[17] Stuart Chase, *The Tyranny of Words*, p. 135.
[18] Stanford Language Arts Investigation: Interpretation. Series I, p. 5.

the verbal world, that is, a world not in its own nature verbal, but having that status for him in so far as he is unable to refer to it without the use of words. Moreover, even within the range of observation, critical caution should prevail. For, as Dr. Hayakawa warns us, we are prone not only to observe what is around us but also to make judgments and inferences concerning it. And while this has its literary uses, for the purpose of accurate reporting of "the facts" it is to be frowned upon. It is with understandable regret that he observes that "In the course of writing reports of personal experiences, it will be found that in spite of all efforts to keep judgments out, some will creep in." [19]

Now philosophers and mystics long ago pointed out the goal a man would reach if he consistently refused to make factual statements, or to understand those of others, except in cases where they referred to objects he himself could refer to without the use of words. It is precisely what each of us could find out about the world if he refused to *use* his experience as evidence of what was going on elsewhere, or to employ ideas rationally in the pursuit of truth. Various artists and proponents of the immediate have described it in their fashion as a "blooming, buzzing confusion," or a "realm of essence," or a collection of sense data, or a "pure phenomenon." It is not our purpose to describe it further, for our aim is not to discover how little we should know about the world if we were in fact reduced to such inarticulate pointing and kicking as our final means of identifying objects of factually significant discourse, but how much we can learn if we use our intelligence responsibly for its exploration. The delineation of such a world is, however, a useful philosophical exercise, since it indicates what, without the use of our rational faculties, we should be aware of. Those who retreat to it in earnest in their zeal to escape the "abstractions" of articulate knowledge have left our world behind. In the purity of their

[19] *Op. cit.,* p. 47.

speechless contemplation they resemble the mystic and the poet rather than the brisk, clear-eyed reformer of Chase's imagining.

The semantic critic does not carry his critical principle to any such conclusion. He is quite ready, on the contrary, to credit the meaning and "reality" of a great deal that he has never been able to point at in non-verbal precision, and that would certainly never have been found out if men had restricted their factual survey to a report of what could be identified in this fashion. Hayakawa claims to have learned from modern physics that Bessie, the cow, a favorite illustrative object, is a "whirl of electro-chemico-neural eventfulness," and while he was very cagey about "abstractions," like "cow," he seems to have no trouble at all in understanding "electro-chemico-neural eventfulness," and accepting it as a valid description of the concrete process from which even the familiar Bessie of ordinary experience is an "abstraction." Yet Hayakawa never saw such a whirl, nor would he have found out about it if those who explored its nature had not used abstractions, judgments and inferences which carried them very far beyond the extensional world of their own observation. So far as he, and the rest of us, are concerned, electrons are part of "the verbal world," that is, they can be referred to only inferentially and by the use of words and ideas which interpret given experience and do not merely report it. This deviation from the semantic gospel is not hard to explain. The semanticist believes that what the scientist tells him is true, and that the objects the behavior of which he reports are in "the extensional world," not because he can refer to them without the use of words, but because, starting from what he can point at and using it as evidence of things not seen, he had completed a process of inquiry which gives him good reason to conclude that such objects exist, and that what is said of them is informationally reliable and hence not merely verbal. There are, then, two quite different criteria of the factual or non-verbal character of what is asserted in statements that purport to be about the world "outside our heads." One, which the semanticist professes, is the extensional character of the objects described, as objects the relation of which to our bodies is such that they can be pointed at without the use of words or the use of reason to which words, accurately employed, can contribute. "Verbal" objects, by contrast, are those which do not admit of such designation. To say that an object was in this sense "verbal" would not imply that it did not exist, or that what was asserted of it was untrue, but only that it could not be identified by the rudimentary device Hayakawa has prescribed. The other criterion classifies objects as "non-verbal" or "parts of the extensional world" when there is good reason to suppose that such objects exist and that in characterizing them we are conveying information concerning their nature and behavior. A merely verbal world would by this standard be one in which our statements failed to refer to what exists, or is the case. This is a fair enough classification, though a rather crude one. But we here identify what we are talking about, not by putting our hands over our mouths and pointing, thus presumably substituting a "non-verbal" for a verbal reference, but rather by using experience as material for theories and theories as guides to further observations which thus become not mere inarticulate gesturings but evidence of what is happening in our physical and social environment. *In this latter sense*, to "point to the referent" is to perform the process of research, bound up at every turn with the use of theory, and hence of words or other symbols, by means of which we find out that objects of a specified sort exist and that they are in relevant respects what words, combined into significant statements, report them to be. Those who suppose that this process is reducible to observing and pointing, or even to taking pictures with a camera, must have a somewhat elementary notion of the reliable processes of factual inquiry. It is only when this latter process of identification is reduced to the former, however, that the case of the semanticists against the merely "verbal" character of the "abstractions" they criticize can be made out.

But surely, it will be said, the semanticists meant nothing as simple-minded as this. They were writing for a popular audience and hence put figuratively and shortly a view that no doubt requires further qualification and a more circumspect critical formulation. That, however, is simply not the case. On some occasions, when words and abstractions which they approve of are in question, they are indeed as ready as the rest of us to credit information which violates the canon of semantic speechlessness in the final location of its referent. But when it comes to other abstractions, of whose use they disapprove, and to the words by which such abstractions are referred to, they resort to exactly this short and drastic method of discriminating merely verbal from non-verbal significance. We have seen that Chase refused, with what purported to be semantic acumen, to be afraid of fascism—"to shiver and shake at a word, and at dire warnings of what the word can do to him at some unnamed future date." If the date could have been named as December 7, 1941, he would perhaps have been more impressed. But that is not the point here. Of course the *word* "fascism" is a mere word and by itself could harm no one. That is true of any word whatever, considered apart from its communicative and possibly informational function. The question, surely, was whether in this use the word had informational significance, whether the tendency in political affairs, which the writers Chase ridiculed were trying to call attention to by its use, was a genuine and important one, about which we should have been well advised to concern ourselves. Of course Chase would not meet "fascism" walking down the street, or be able to take a picture of it with a camera. But he could have made far better sense than he did of the behavior of men who were marching in the streets of many cities at that time, if he had been able to discern the significance of what they were doing and its probable future consequences as those men did who were able to use the term "fascism" informationally to depict the structure and tendency of a given state of affairs. To say that "fascism," or "government," or "freedom," is a mere word to which nothing corresponds that is real enough to be kicked, is to indulge in mere semantic vituperation. We cannot estimate the significance of words until we understand their rational use and have determined what, by the use of the ideas they verbalize, we can find out about the world and our relations to it that would not otherwise have been discovered. The basic defect in the semantic discipline is that it tries to estimate the meaning of words and the verbal or nonverbal character of what they report in a context other than that of their rational use and application. If the only informational function of words were that of naming perceptually observable objects, then they would lose all non-verbal significance when no such referent could be found. Where their function is to discriminate tendencies, habits or uniformities, or to call attention to possibilities nowhere actualized, they justify themselves as informationally significant when they indicate clearly what such tendencies and possibilities are and to what they are relevant. If Chase lies in wait with a camera for a uniformity or a possibility he will, I am afraid, be disappointed. But if he tries to take rational account of what is going on in the world without finding out all he can about both the uniformities and possibilities in the order of events around him he will be singularly ill-informed. He will be well-advised, of course, not to mistake a word for a thing; but if he refuses to understand or credit information about the world conveyed by the rational use of words which fail to name any object of direct observation, he will not be well-advised, nor will those who follow him.

This excursion into the critical gospel of semantics has a bearing on both our present and our future interests in this volume. When we come to deal with issues of practical reason and social policy we shall find these same doctrines at work. Those who could find in discussions of fascism only a word by which no man of sense need be frightened, will naturally make little sense of appeals to principles and ideals in political affairs, and will dismiss as mere verbiage the consideration of what ought to be a guide for moral behavior. We have now, I think, the means to see where they are wrong. Before we decide that 'justice" is only a word, or "moral obligation" a fiction, we shall want to know how those words are used in the inquiries in which they are employed, what sort of identification can be made in terms of them, and how statements that contain them are substantiated. If we can make sense of them in the operations of practical reason and make sense *through* them, of the reasonable direction of conduct in whose organization they function, we shall not be much disturbed at our failure to identify them as observable things in our environment. For we have seen that the use of words, even in the sphere of severely factual inquiry, quite transcends the designation and description of such objects and is to be understood only in the total role it plays in the use of ideas and theories in the pursuit of truth. We should expect nothing less than this when we investigate the more complex field of social action, and with this in mind, we shall not be inclined to regard such maxims as "words are not things," and "cow [1] is not cow [2]," as an adequate substitute for the contextual analysis of the uses of practical reason and the way in which its "abstractions" function to clarify and enlighten conduct and find therein their sufficient significance and justification.

Meanwhile, we have acquired the means to counter skeptical attacks on the verbal instruments of theoretical reason, in the use that is made of them in the pursuit of truth. We do indeed use words, sometimes very abstract words, in the process of rational inquiry, and we know that words are not things, nor even in all cases names of the things we observe around us, nor names of more rarefied things that occupy a realm of abstractions beyond the reach of mortal eye. But we also know, if we have had any serious acquaintance with the use of abstractions in rational inquiry, that what things are, in respect of their more general properties and manner of behavior, can be accurately stated by the use of abstract words. The things are not the words, to be sure, but what the things are, or were, or might, with proper effort, be made to be, is what the words report of them. The plainest and on the whole the best answer to the fashionable inquiry concerning the nature of the correspondence of word and fact is that of Woodbridge: the correspondence is such that we can say in words what things are,[20] and the way to find out whether and how far that correspondence exists is to find out whether the fact is what the words, when properly interpreted, declare it to be. There is no linguistic shortcut to this end which enables us to say in advance what "the extensional world" or "the facts" must be in order for us to speak significantly about them and hence to reject as mere verbiage any statements which fail to conform to such specifications. We shall be grateful to the linguists, as distinct from their "semantic" press agents, for all the information they can give us about the way language works, but we shall not expect to learn from them what only the long labor of factual inquiry in all its branches can determine, that is, what "the facts" are concerning which significant discourse is competent to provide reliable information. Informative knowledge is the fruit of inquiry, in which the perspicuous use of words plays an indispensable part. And it is by its fruit, which is knowledge, that the function of language thus employed is properly to be judged.

Truth as Social Agreement.   One of the most popular and familiar devices for accounting for the cognitive superiority of scientific findings to those reached by other methods without claiming literal informational truth about the world for

[20] F. J. E. Woodbridge, *An Essay on Nature*, pp. 217ff.

them, is to say that science deals with those matters concerning which general agreement is possible, with respect to which all observers will come to the same conclusion, and the like. Whether a conclusion thus established is "true" in any further sense, the cautious theorist refuses to say, for he is sure that any attempted answer would involve him in philosophical puzzles with which, as a scientist, he is not properly concerned. Thus Norman Campbell tells us that "science is the study of those judgments concerning which universal agreement can be obtained," [21] and maintains this doctrine, in spite of the rather drastic cuts in the sciences that must be made if they are to conform to it, precisely because it absolves him from the responsibility of saying that the sciences tell us about "the external world" or "nature," or even of assuming that nature or an external world exists. In any case there are judgments which command universal assent, and it is with these that science is exclusively concerned. This kind of theory is often supported by contrasting the agreement that can be reached concerning, for example, the dimensions of a physical object as measured by approved "operational" methods, with the diversity of opinion that exists concerning beauty, or goodness, or the nature of God. The fact to which this contrast points cannot seriously be questioned. The publicity, actual or potential, of the findings of the sciences, the fact that they can be arrived at and tested *in the open*, without recourse to special intuitions or revelations which only a special group can enjoy, is one of our major reasons for respecting their rational authority as sources of reliable information. But this fact is misstated and misinterpreted in the theory of truth as social agreement, and the confusion thus engendered has had unfortunate consequences in popular thought.

The obvious and essential difficulty with it is that it does not enable us to discriminate between the agreement which is

[21] Norman Campbell, *op. cit.*, p. 27.

the fruit of reliable and public methods of attaining truth, and that which is achieved by less credible devices. Mr. Campbell wrote his book before the rise of the totalitarian powers in Europe had given us our most vivid object lesson of the way in which agreement can be reached by the skillful dissemination of lies and the ruthless silencing of those who question them. To be sure, such agreement is not *universal*, but neither is that accorded the findings of the sciences. There are plenty of men in any community who will deny, and have denied, any scientific conclusion, no matter how well established, that conflicts with their own preferences and preconceptions. The outcry in Germany against "Jewish" science and that against the theory of the animal ancestry of man in some parts of the United States are only the most obvious of many instances that might be cited. Shall we then say that at least there is universal agreement *among scientists* on these matters, and that is what constitutes their findings as valid? But there is universal agreement among good Nazis about statements which by any scientific criterion are preposterously false. Are we simply to appeal to the agreement of one social group, as against another, and, if so, on what basis?

The answer, which C. S. Peirce was never tired of pointing out, is that the agreement that distinguishes scientific findings from others is that which is achieved by a quite distinctive method, the method of *finding out* by observation and experiment. It is, in short, the method of learning from experience, and so far from being universally agreed to in the affairs of men it is only in a limited area, and there precariously, that it prevails. Its rivals, the method of tenacity in holding on to antecedent convictions and closing one's mind to further evidence, the method of appeal to authority and the method of *a priori* reasoning from "plausible" premises,[22] have been considerably more common and more popular in the history of

22 C. S. Peirce, "The Fixation of Belief," in *Collected Papers;* Vol. V, p. 223ff.

human beliefs. And if we ask why agreement reached by this method is to be regarded as superior to the others, we cannot appeal to social agreement as the source, or as the criterion, for its validity. It is *cognitively* the best method, because it is the only one that enables us to correct our ideas by reference to what is found to be the case independently of our ante-cedent wishes and beliefs. Through its procedures, mistakes can be found out and bias corrected, and it thus provides the best possible guarantee that we are conforming our ideas to the facts which they purport to be about, that is, are finding out the truth about them. Agreement thus reached is of the utmost cognitive significance, for here the agreement is pertinent to the truth of the beliefs arrived at, and each man can profit by the experience and criticism of others to raise his own ideas to the level of the soundest available knowledge of his time. It is the capacity to lead to truth that makes the agreement significant, not the agreement that constitutes the truth.

This version of the matter helps to correct a further serious misapprehension. The illustrations used to show how simple it is to get scientific agreement on "the facts" are themselves far too simple to do justice to the situation they are intended to portray. Measuring a table with a yardstick is one thing, and a fairly straightforward one. But accepting the result of this measurement *as evidence* of the theory the scientist bases on it and with the aid of which his research proceeds, is a different matter. The skeptics who looked into Galileo's tele-scope did not differ from him as to what was proximately to be seen. But they refused to interpret what they saw as he did, and preferred, not without some reason, to attribute what they observed to a defect in his instrument rather than to accept it as evidence of a state of affairs in the heavens which, if admitted, would have created grave difficulties for theories to which they were profoundly attached. The battle Galileo and those who followed him had to fight for social agreement, or even social tolerance, of their findings, as reports of the

solar universe, was long and arduous. It was finally won, and
the profit for human enlightenment has been great. But
something like it had to be fought again in the nineteenth
century, when biology ran afoul of strongly held preconceptions; and in the social sciences we have hardly, as yet, begun
to face the issue. It is well, therefore, to remember that the
agreement that counts in science, and in the pursuit of truth,
is agreement reached by a method concerning the cogency
and desirability of which there is, outside a quite restricted
area, by no means universal or even widespread agreement.
It is a method whose continued use requires discipline and
intelligence of a high order, and which justifies itself not by
simple observations which everybody will agree to, but by
rigorous inquiry with the conclusions of which everybody
ought to agree, because there is good reason to believe that
they are true. In fact, however, they will be bitterly con-
tested precisely where and in so far as they prove inconvenient
to established interests of various sorts, and if we wait for
"universal agreement" before acknowledging their truth we
shall have a very long time to wait.

The prestige of the sciences in contemporary society is a
curiously precarious one. The wonder-working results of
physics, chemistry and biology have won for them a respect
which has, for the most part, little to do with what they actually report, or with the evidence that substantiates them.
Hoping for similar results on more humanly important issues,
the popular mind turned eagerly to psychology and the social
sciences and has, on the whole, been disappointed. Meanwhile,
confusion as to the aims of science, and confusing and irresponsible pronouncements by scientists themselves about the
incapacity of mere "science" to reach "the truth" have undermined public confidence in the rational authority of scientifically warranted statements concerning matters of fact. And
when these statements have proved, on other grounds, to be
inconvenient, there has been little scruple in rejecting them

and accepting in their place emotionally congenial doctrines which there is good reason to believe are false. So long as scientists restrict their inquiries to fields in which our emotions are not strongly engaged, and continue to produce results guaranteed "useful" by current social standards, they are not only tolerated but subsidized. Beyond these limits, however, the method of scientific inquiry has still to win social acceptance. And nothing is more essential, if this acceptance is to be won on a solid and enduring basis, than the recognition that the distinctive claim to be made for the findings of the sciences is not that they are obvious, or convenient, or socially accepted, but that they are reached by a method which gives the best possible guarantee that what they say is true, or reliably informative, with respect to the world around us. Men do not always want to see the truth, nor do they love it when they see it; but they have great need of it, and they do tend to respect it, when its claims are so presented that their cogency can be reasonably understood. Those who, in their urge to emancipate science from metaphysics, would emancipate it from its claim to truth as well are thus ill-advised in their procedure. As a way of reaching social agreement on disputed questions scientific inquiry is but one of many and by no means always the most efficacious. As a way of reaching informative truth concerning the structure and behavior of objects in the world around us it has proved superior to every other method. It claims our credence not *de facto*, as a widely accepted dogma, but *de jure* as a sound and reliable basis for reasonable belief. It is in this latter capacity that its cognitive claims are defensible and worth defending.

The Pragmatic Theory of Truth. No other group of philosophers have, in the past half-century, contributed so much to our understanding of the rational use of ideas in the pursuit of truth as have those who are called and used to call themselves, "pragmatists." Their insistence that the meaning and worth of ideas is rightly judged, not by their conformity to a "reality" set up in advance as the final standard of truth and reasonableness, but by the way they function in the context of responsible inquiry, was both revolutionary and salutary. Pragmatism did not, as its enthusiasts supposed, give us a new meaning for truth, but it did help enormously to show us where to look for the truth that is reliably attainable, and how to know it when we see it. Its emphasis on the plurality of contexts in which ideas can function significantly, and on the importance, if we would make our ideas clear, of interpreting them specifically by reference to their use and function in such contexts, is, in my judgment, the greatest single contribution to critical philosophy of our time. The title C. S. Peirce gave to his pioneer essay in pragmatism, "How to Make Our Ideas Clear," [23] is still our best guide to the nature of this contribution. The pragmatic method of contextual reference and analysis is a way of enabling us to know what we are talking about when we try to assess the meaning of "hard words and concepts" the generality of which is endlessly confusing until their use in inquiry, or any other activity to which they are relevant, has been ascertained. If I do not stop to elaborate on it here, it is simply because I have tried to exemplify it throughout this volume. I hope that it will thus, in true pragmatic fashion, be clarified by its use and justified in its cognitive fruits.

And yet, grateful as we must always be to Peirce, James, Dewey, and their disciples, there is one major issue on which their theory has been persistently equivocal in its pronouncements and seriously misleading in its influence. And since this is just the issue which looms most prominently in the popular mind when the word "pragmatism" is mentioned, we shall have to deal with it explicitly if our own position is to be understood. The principal intellectual novelty of pragmatism, in its impact on the thought of its period, was undoubtedly its theory of truth. This was generally understood as the doc-

[23] This essay is now included in his *Collected Papers*, Vol. V, p. 248ff.

trine that the truth of an idea *consists in* its capacity to bring, or help to bring, the activity in which it functions to a "satisfactory" eventuation. Ideas are significant only when they make a difference in some such activity and their validity *as true* is a function of their usefulness in furthering the ends of the activity in question. Coupled as it usually was with the more general doctrine of the primacy of practice, as contrasted with mere theory, and the claim that ideas must justify themselves, not only in the "self-enclosed" area of theoretical analysis, but in the affairs of *life*, this theory seemed to suggest that the "ultimate" ends of life are not cognitive but practical, and that it is only in so far as knowing contributes to these practical ends that its validity *as knowledge* can be established. Reduced to short and easy terms, as such theories always are when they gain popular currency, this appears as the dictum that the useful is the true, and that utility is to be judged in the widest "practical" terms—utility for life, for success, for satisfaction, and the like.

In this form the doctrine is quite untenable, and for a familiar reason. It is of the utmost cognitive importance to distinguish ideas which work for the purposes of factual inquiry, where the activity aims at the discovery of truth, and is successful in so far as it achieves this end, from other ideas which in their working contribute to success of other sorts, popular, political, economic or the like, without thereby justifying themselves as true in any usual sense of that term. The general pragmatic formula seems to apply to both sorts of working, but it is only by the first that truth, in the sense in which it is rightly distinguished from convenient fiction, can reliably be established. Did the pragmatists really mean to undermine this distinction, and to claim for ideas which work well for *any* "practical" purpose the cogency with which the term "truth" has more usually been associated? The critics assumed that they did, pointed to plenty of pragmatic dicta which seemed to support their interpretation, and found in them inexhaustible material for crying up pragmatism as an expression of the temper of the times, which undoubtedly gloried in "efficiency," "action," and "life," rather indiscriminately enjoyed, or for crying it down as a negation of all cognitive standards and all regard for truth. The pragmatists themselves denied the imputation angrily and repeatedly, and went on expressing their views in exactly the fashion which appeared to the unconverted to substantiate the charges of their critics. Philosophical misunderstandings are by no means uncommon, but a "misunderstanding" of this sort, persisting over a period of many years and cropping up again and again, would seem to have some deeper basis than mere verbal infelicity on one side or critical ineptitude on the other. It is ironical that the philosophy whose distinctive aim was to make ideas clear should have had such special difficulty in making its own leading ideas clear to those not antecedently committed to its conclusions. Whatever its causes, there can be little doubt that the contribution pragmatism might have made to clear thinking has been largely vitiated by this abiding unclarity as to its central doctrine.

Can this ambiguity be eliminated? I believe that it can, but only by taking a further step which the leading pragmatists, for philosophical reasons, have been unwilling to take. There is little doubt, I think, that when James or Dewey is thinking about the "working" of ideas in inquiry, the kind of satisfaction he has in mind is the *cognitive* satisfaction that develops when there is good reason to believe that we are actually *finding out* what the inquiry set out to discover, when, in other words, the ideas employed have vindicated their usefulness in the discovery of factual truth. Whether or not such ideas are themselves accepted as true will depend on whether or not what is found out by their means actually is (in so far as we can discern its nature) what they report it to be. Where no such informational correctness is claimed, no question of truth, in the cognitive sense, arises. Where the claim is made, the process of its testing is the process by which we find out about the world, and judge the accuracy of our beliefs in terms of what is thus discovered.

But if this, as it might be more deviously put by Dewey or more eloquently by James, is what is intended, why is it not explicitly said? For two reasons, chiefly. The leading pragmatists belonged to that unhappy generation which never recovered from its early fright of metaphysics. To say that factual statements, when properly criticized and tested, are really and literally true as information concerning what exists and has existed in the world outside us, raised in their minds the specter of an "antecedent reality" which transcends the situation in which inquiry occurs and is "finally" disclosed only by some sort of metaphysical, not by scientific, investigation. They sought to avoid all reference to such a "reality" by insisting that the real object (or aim) of factual inquiry is to reconstruct the situation in which doubt or difficulty has arisen, and to bring confused or impeded activities to a successful conclusion. In a sense, again, this is true if what the reconstruction achieves is knowledge of objects and events, some of which are quite indubitably antecedent in their existence and nature to the activity through which we find out about them, and if in consequence this activity, to the successful conclusion of which our ideas contribute, is that of securing truthful information about them. But that, of course, cannot be said explicitly without bringing up again the question of the reference of factual knowledge to objects not constructed or reconstructed in the process of inquiry, and it is this that the pragmatist wishes at all costs to avoid. Hence he says once more that the *ultimate object* of knowledge is the satisfactory completion of the activity of inquiry, without being willing to say plainly that what the satisfactory completion of this activity consists in is the attainment of literal, and not merely of "pragmatic" truth. So the ambiguity recurs, and the argument goes on indefinitely and unprofitably. For it could only be resolved unequivocally by admitting a factual reference which the pragmatist holds to be philosophically dangerous or by denying the distinctive cognitive status of inquiry, which he knows to be essential to any accurate account of the work of thought. Thus, in trying to get rid of "reality" he has compromised the status of truth, and this central instability in his theory renders all his further theorizing insecure.

This unfortunate outcome is both unnecessary and undesirable. It is unnecessary because, as we have seen, the claim to literal knowledge of the world *as it is* need involve no such dubious commitments. The "reality" which true knowledge, on the level of factual inquiry, discloses, is simply the nature and behavior of the objects and events in the world around us, in so far as these can be found out by methods of reliable inquiry, the very methods to which the pragmatists are, in practice, most addicted. Such knowledge makes no pretension to *metaphysical* ultimacy, that is, to preferential status as information concerning what is metaphysically "ultimate" or "final," or completely real; it claims only to be an accurate account of what has happened, is happening, and is likely to happen. And that claim can sometimes be made good on the level of factual inquiry itself. To say this plainly would not, so far as I can see, involve the abandonment of anything in pragmatism that is worth preserving. It would, however, involve a final break with antiquated philosophical preconceptions from which the pragmatists, in spite of heroic efforts, have so far been unable to free themselves.

The present situation is undesirable from the standpoint of the very causes the pragmatists seem to have most at heart. Instead of outflanking their epistemological enemies by their devious procedure, Dewey and his followers have put themselves in a false position, which enables their critics to pose, with some plausibility, as the righteous defenders of truth and to denounce as relativism and skepticism what is soundest and most enlightening in the pragmatic method. The contextual specification of the meaning and use of ideas is in fact an expression, not of disregard for truth, but of regard for the conditions under which the difference between truth and falsehood can clearly and responsibly be established. The intellectual alternative to it is literary, philosophical and theological loose talk, in which the appearance of profundity does not compensate for the absence of intellectual content and a decent respect for the conditions of accurate thinking and speaking. The case for contextual clarity in analysis would be greatly strengthened if its divorce from pragmatic unclarity about the nature of truth were made final and complete.

The second reason for the unwillingness of the pragmatists to take the step that I have recommended can be more briefly dealt with. Pragmatism in its early days was a philosophical expression of a much wider popular movement—the demand that thought, and thinkers, be brought down from the well-known ivory tower of academic and speculative aloofness and put to work in the affairs of men. There was much in this demand that was just and discerning, and those who, like Dewey, have not only preached but practiced the doctrine that ideas can exercise a liberalizing and liberating function in human conduct are the sages of their own generation in American thought and the inspiration for ours. But the fruitful use of valid theory for the ends of enlightened practice is one thing; the identification of theoretical validity with practical utility is another. Whether it was intended or not by its authors, the latter is the doctrine which has gained wide currency as the teaching of pragmatism. And where it prevails, there will always be impatience with those who insist, as I have done, that the proper goal of factual inquiry is the discovery of what is the case, and that this is by no means to be equated with what on other grounds and for other purposes it might be useful or inspiring to believe. This attitude is understandable, but I do not believe that it is judicious or wise. For of all the contributions that theory can make to practice none is so excellent or so essential as the provision of reliable information on matters of practical concern, where "reliability" is determined not by practical utility for some further purpose but by the evidence that what is asserted is in fact the case. If we are to act intelligently we must know what we are doing, and no other theory is so dependably helpful for that purpose as that which there is good reason to suppose is informationally reliable. The vindication of such reliability, therefore, is by no means opposed to the ends of enlightened practice, but is in fact essential to any rational estimate of their nature. In reaffirming, in this sense, the intellectual rights of theory we may not be pragmatists, but we shall be practical none the less.

"Dogmatism" and Culture.   At this point, and in concluding our survey of the cognitive claims of factual knowledge, it will be advisable, I think, to deal with a fairly general sort of objection to our position which the reader may for some time have been feeling and which expresses, in any case, a very widespread contemporary attitude. We have had much to say of what we *know*, and of "the truth," as though it were something we possessed and could take a stand on, and we have criticized other views which profess a basic skepticism concerning such knowledge. But is this, the objector will ask, a truly profound or philosophic view of the matter? Have not the wisest men always stressed their ignorance rather than their knowledge, and spoken of their best knowledge as the merest fragment compared to the vastness of the world to be known? We know in part, and we must forever be on our guard against the temptation to make our finite thinking the measure of a reality, that in its inner, total or absolute nature transcends the categories of human understanding. Even what we think we know is, in the progress of science, subject to constant revision and correction, and

no "fixed" or "final" opinions concerning it seem legitimate. The claim to literal knowledge, under such conditions, will almost inevitably seem "dogmatic"; and "dogmatism," for our generation, is the gravest of intellectual sins. When Dr. Thomas Briggs, of Teachers College, Columbia University, set out to discover "pragmatically" what it means to be a cultured person, by asking his classes, and a selected group of men whom his classes selected as cultured persons, whether a cultured person was in their view (along with 97 other suggested traits) "dogmatic and assertive of his opinions," 96 per cent answered in the negative.[24] It was found, on tabulation, that no other trait among the 98 listed was so widely regarded as incompatible with genuine culture.[25] Whether, as Dr. Briggs believes, this tells us something important about "the concept of culture," as enlightened pedagogues ought to understand it, or whether it merely tells us something about the prevailing state of mind at Teachers College and among those of whom Teachers College students approve, is a further question. It is, in any case, with the state of mind that we are here concerned.

Yet while the reader may have felt some such objection, he will also, if he is an attentive and understanding reader, have seen the proper way to deal with it. For we have not, in any claim yet made for knowledge, professed to know the inner, total or absolute nature of "reality" whatever that may be, or claimed that the use of reason here defended is adequate to any such undertaking. It is precisely by adopting a view of reason which discriminates its reliable achievements from the more questionable pretensions to which the doubter takes exception that we have been able to reach an affirmative and constructive conclusion. Our ignorance of the unknown is indeed both vast and impressive; but our knowledge of what can be known is none the less of quite central

[24] Thomas H. Briggs, *Pragmatism and Pedagogy,* p. 90.
[25] *Ibid.,* p. 109.

significance in the rational ordering of our beliefs. For while it is true that we often must revise our opinions and theories, and that the readiness to do so is a great intellectual virtue, it is no less essentially the case that such revisions, if they are reasonable and not merely random, are made on the basis of tested information, on what has been found out by the use of reliable methods of inquiry. And, as Emile Meyerson, the greatest of the historians of science, has pointed out, an old theory is never surrendered except for the sake of a better one—a new account of things which better harmonizes the ideas with which we operate with the structure of the world to which those ideas are found in striking measure to apply. We proceed into the unknown, to be sure, and must not prejudice in advance, by our limited ideas, the nature of what we have yet to find. But we proceed with instructed minds, on the basis of what we so far have discovered, and we shall correct this only when we have found out something else, better attested or more adequately understood, which justifies us in making the correction. Lacking such standards for the evaluation of evidence, the openness of mind which is prepared to welcome sense or nonsense, half-baked "ism" or soundly based hypothesis, with equal friendliness, provided only that it be new and fashionable and "stimulating" to an ill-furnished mind, reduces to sheer intellectual irresponsibility. I am not clear as to what the group at Teachers College meant by "dogmatism," but if they meant by it the refusal to accept with an "open" mind theories which, on the evidence available, are flimsy, superficial and ill-conceived, then I am quite sure that they were wrong in their estimate. For such "dogmatism" is a principle of sanity from which even advanced educational circles could greatly profit. That, in any case, is the only sort of dogmatism to which the view here defended commits us, and there is much virtue in that commitment.

There is always room for critical caution concerning the

claims of thought, but there is also in these days a genuine need for rational integrity and self-respect concerning them. For what is the "correspondence" of thought with "reality" that is supposed to be required to vindicate the veracity of our knowledge? What could it be, if it is to be pertinent to the kind of thinking by which our knowledge is actually extended, but the evidence that what is found to be so in reliable inquiry is so? The vindication of our knowledge that a molecule of water is made up of two atoms of hydrogen and one of oxygen is to be sought in something we have found out about water, not about either "knowledge" in general, or "reality," namely that molecules of water are in fact thus constituted. The rational use of ideas in the pursuit of truth, thus tested and criticized, *is* the "correspondence" of effective thought with the "reality" to which it is addressed—not a metaphysical demonstration that the world *must* be "in the end" what we antecedently supposed or desired it to be—but working evidence that what goes on in the world can be found out in rationally directed inquiry and that what is thus found out, though corrigible in principle, is, in particular instances, established beyond all reasonable doubt. There can be no good reason to doubt that the belief that water is made up of hydrogen and oxygen corresponds to reality in the only manner required for its rational vindication until there is reason to suppose that water is not in fact analyzable into hydrogen and oxygen in the manner specified. If and when such reason ever develops it will be on the basis of something that is found out about water, not about the general incapacity of finite intelligence to encompass reality as a whole. Until such time, in the light of what we do know, the belief is entitled to our rational credence. That is our warrant of its truthfulness, and it is in its capacity to achieve such truth that reason finds its primary, and essential, justification.

CHAPTER I

THE CONTEXT OF MORAL JUDGMENT

The Meaning of "Practical Reason." " 'Tis not contrary to reason to prefer the destruction of the whole world to the scratching of my finger." In these words, and others of similar import, David Hume summed up one of the most important and one of the most disturbing of the doctrines we owe to the development of modern critical philosophy. All of its puzzle, and much of its influence, are due to the fact that it states a substantial truth in a provocative and misleading way, and thus lends to what would otherwise seem to be an indefensible conclusion the support of apparently irrefutable evidence. Is it true or false? The answer depends on what it is understood to say, and that, in turn, on the meaning assigned to the term "reason." If you limit the operations of the mind properly described as "rational" to the tracing out of the implicative relations of ideas, and causal inferences concerning matters of fact, then it will follow that reason, thus employed, can discover nothing in the things it deals with to correspond to what we call their values. It is only when you turn from the object to the subject and survey, not the properties of things themselves, but the "relish" with which they are experienced and enjoyed, that a basis is found for preferring one to another—even if the one be the scratching of a finger and the other destruction of the world. But this "relish" is an affair of feelings and desires, or, in proper eighteenth century terms, of "the passions" and it is these, therefore, that determine what is good or bad, so far, at least, as "good" and "bad" have an empirically discoverable application. "Reason," identified as above, can tell us whether our estimates of value are logically consistent, and inform us concerning the causal means best suited to further the ends we have in view. The means are properly judged as good, however, only if the end is good, and on this point "reason" has no jurisdiction, for "ultimate ends recommend themselves solely to the affections," or, as a more modern version of the same doctrine would say, to the primary "drives" which determine what the organism desires and on what conditions it can be satisfied. And since the means derive their goodness only from the end they serve, we can see why Hume should conclude that, in the field of morals, "reason is and ought to be the slave of the passions."

What this doctrine says that is true, and will stand the test of critical inspection, is that things are discoverably good or bad, not in their intrinsic characters, but in their capacity to satisfy interests and desires. In Hume's famous instance you may search the geometric properties of a circle as you will, but you will never discover its beauty until you consider it as an object of enjoyment, in its capacity to please aesthetically those who contemplate it. It may be the case, as Miss Millay alleges in a well-known sonnet, that "Euclid alone has looked on Beauty bare," but we shall have to modify the Platonism of this dictum to add that it was not in his capacity as a mathematician that he made this observation. Those less enamoured of the charm of circles than Euclid and Miss Millay can understand the same propositions of geometry and use the same "reason" in exploring their implications. To ask whether, in addition to the beauty that is thus variously enjoyed by appreciative beholders, there is a "real" beauty which inheres in circles quite independently of their capacity to delight aesthetically those who enjoy them—or would enjoy them if their tastes were "developed" in that direction—is to ask a question that we have no means of answering and had better, therefore, leave to those whose interest is literary or edifying rather than philosophical. The value, at least, that *we* find in things and persons is a good that answers to an interest in ourselves, and every command of practical reason, no matter how exalted its pretensions, is cogently addressed only "to whom it may concern." To say, therefore, that reason in morals is "the slave of the passions" *may* mean simply that it is concerned with objects which satisfy desire, and that it is only as affording such satisfaction or capable of doing so that their goodness can responsibly be made out. And, as it is the business of reason, in its practical application, to serve the good, it is *in this sense* its business to serve "the passions" and contribute to their satisfaction. *Apart from* such concern there is no "reason," in the nature of things, to prefer the scratching of a finger to the destruction of the world—or anything to anything else—for the ground of preference, in the possibility of attainable satisfaction, cannot, on this basis, be made out.

But if there is thus a sense in which Hume's statement is true, there is another and no less important one, in which it not merely seems to be, but actually is, false. The burden of the message of the great classical moralists, Greek and Christian alike, was that reason ought not to be, and in a well-ordered life is not, the slave of the passions, but rather controls and directs them to a good, which, apart from its normative influence, they would not have been able to achieve. Did Hume really mean to deny this, as his disciples have denied it since his time? The answer, as in most cases where we are dealing with confused thinking, must be yes and no. As a humane and judicious man he knew how to value what he called the "disinterested" passions, and much of what had traditionally been said of the authority of "reason" in conduct could be restated in his terms, with sympathy taking the place of "reason" and calculation, on a utilitarian basis, operating to liberalize conduct and add foresight to benevolence in a way which, if his terminology did not discourage it, we should naturally describe as rational. Yet the shift in terminology made a real difference, none the less, and one whose effects are still observable. Men do want *ultimate* reasons, and *final* sanctions for conduct, and if they come to believe that there are none, and that the final basis for all our standards of excellence is to be found in "arbitrary" preference and "irrational" instincts, or drives, or will to power, they will be inclined to see in that belief the excuse for arbitrary preferences and irrational claims of a much less innocent sort. There *is* a context in which an arbitrary or irrational action is a wrong action and in which reason is not just an *ad hoc* instrument for finding means to satisfy desires in themselves beyond the range of rational criticism. To suppose that in its use *in this context* the authority of reason was in any way compromised by the Humean discovery that what we are here being reasonable *about* is our desires, and the conditions for their satisfaction, is a mistake, and a disastrous one. Yet it is a mistake that is easily made, once "reason" in general is identified with "reason" in its purely theoretical use, and, in consequence, what is not in *this* sense an affair of reason is handed over to the jurisdiction of "passions" with whose ultimate demands and preferences *mere* reason has nothing to do. Hume, who was in some respects the Bertrand Russell of his time, was at no pains to divorce his theory from this unhappy implication, and later empirical thinkers, encouraged by the prestige of the sciences to limit the properly "objective" and respectable use of reason to the methods of inquiry employed in the physical and social sciences, have for the most part followed in his footsteps. In this way, and with this dubious philosophical benediction, we reach the dichotomy of a reason which has nothing to do with "values," and "values" which, in their *ultimate* basis in non-rational drives, have nothing to do with reason. What it can then mean to be reasonable about values is a further problem to which busy scientists could hardly be expected to give a well-thought-out answer or their popularizers and publicists to take quite seriously. Science, after all, is remaking the world, and will doubtless get around to values in time, if they turn out to be really important.

Philosophers, on the whole, were more far-sighted than this. They saw the necessity, if we are to make sense of morals, of making clear the sense of "reason" in which it properly claims practical authority. The "reason" thus employed will be something other than the purely theoretical faculty which Hume recognized, and its claims will be without cogency save for those who acknowledge the good to which it is directed and the obligations entailed in the pursuit of it. But it will be *reason,* none the less, as distinct from groundless preference or arbitrary demand, and it will be in the name of principles rationally defensible that it speaks. Granting that theoretical reason, dealing with events in space and time in so far as these are causally understandable and predictable, provides no ultimate answer to the question "what ought I to do?" the philosopher therefore looks for further light to *practical* reason, and reaffirms, with its sanction, the truths which he finds that morality requires and science cannot supply.

It was in such terms as these, of course, that Kant, in his great *Critiques,* solemnized the divorce of theoretical and practical reason, thus summing up the results of one period of scientific and philosophical thinking and setting the problem for another. His contribution was a great one. By insisting that there are problems for reason outside the limits of the categories of Newtonian science and, as he thought, of theoretical reason, and that we must look for their solution to the context in which men acknowledge rights and duties, in which, specifically, they appeal to reason in justification of conduct and try to be rational about it, he accurately located the practical use of reason and the area of its significant application. More than that, he formulated some of its basic principles in a way that has not been bettered since his time. But the subject with which he dealt was an uncommonly slippery one, and it cannot be said that he freed it satisfactorily from the confusions he had inherited, or failed, for that matter, to add a few of his own.

For what is this "reason" that is somehow more than reason in its theoretical use? Long before Kant's time there had been prophets to proclaim that the heart has reasons that reason knows nothing of, that the highest reason is to scorn the claims of reason, and the like. And it was Kant himself who said that he had circumscribed the domain of reason to make way for faith. The romantic philosophies of the nineteenth century are sufficient evidence of what can happen when the claims, not only of theoretical reason, but of elementary good sense, are superseded by the deliverances of "higher reason" for which the heart alone can speak, and which only truly *spiritual* men are qualified to understand. The chief function of the notion of practical reason in the period from Kant's time to our own has been to justify as "reasonable" in a deeper or spiritual sense conclusions about the world which, apart from its pronouncements, there seems no good reason to believe. Even Santayana in a poetic moment assured us that "it is wisdom to believe the heart," and his colleague Royce got around some rather curious twists in Hegel's *Logic* by reminding us that it is a "logic of passion," and entitled to considerable latitude accordingly. If "practical reason" is understood as a special access to "reality," open to those with proper qualifications of moral uprightness and spiritual profundity, and capable of disclosing that what earnest men believe very earnestly must be so, since they could not be as earnest as they feel they should be if they did not believe it, then practical reason is a dubious blessing, and we can hardly blame those who have been inclined to view its revelations with a certain reserve.

Evidently what is needed is some reliable way of distinguishing, among claims pertinent to responsible moral judgment, those that are reasonably credible from those that are not. What is wanted, in other words, is a discipline of practical reason that will function in this field as the methods of science do in theirs. Kant thought he had the basis for such a discipline in a principle of formal consistency, and Hegel sought it in a dialectic that could correct all partial interests and demands from the standpoint of inclusive rationality. Neither method proved adequate to its task, though we owe much in moral wisdom to the use their authors made of them. The problem they recognized is the one with which we shall in this section be dealing. It remains, for practical purposes, the crucial philosophical problem with which modern thought is confronted. How are we to be reasonable about values in an age when "reason" is the property of specialists for whom the refusal to deal with questions of good and bad is a matter of professional policy, while "values" are officially in the keeping of those more concerned for the most part to justify vested "spiritual" interests than to submit them to any sort of independent examination? Each side finds in the limitations of the other the excuse for its own imperfections. If "reason" can tell us so little about the issues of life as the positivists say, who would not see the wisdom of being unreasonable? And if the custodians of spiritual values are as loose in their thinking and as arbitrary in their premises as they can often be shown to be, who could question the prudence of those who restrict the use of reason to fields in which the difference between sense and nonsense can at least be sensibly made out? So runs the argument, and there seems to be no end to it.

And yet all the while men of good will are trying to be both just and intelligent about their desires and their duties, and to make some sort of sense of their conduct in terms of the goods toward which it might reasonably be directed. Perhaps we should be able to make greater progress in this field if we left the partisans of a scientifically pure reason and the partisans of transcendent values to their interminable task of pointing out each other's mistakes and looked instead for the meaning of practical reason in the use that can be made of reliable information, sound judgment, and enlightened good will in the reasonable direction of conduct. If it should prove to be the case that men can be rational about their conduct in this more specific sense, and that the good thus defined makes sense of activities that without it would be narrow, frustrated and incomplete, we shall not be much disturbed by the refusal of the purists to *call* such rationality a use of "reason" or of the defenders of the "deeper" values to submit their claims to its tests. We, at least, shall know what we are talking about. Whether as much can be said for them is a further question on which we may later be able to shed some light.

When I speak hereafter of "practical reason," I shall mean by it the use of reason in the organization of desires and the adjustment of claims in the pursuit of goods judged to be desirable by methods held to be just and proper to that end. Since we are here concerned to discover not merely what does exist but which would be good if it did exist, and is therefore worth accepting as a goal for action, and what is right, fair or just in the sacrifices those associated in a common action are asked to make for it and the rewards they are to receive on its attainment, it is not surprising that considerations will here be pertinent of which neither a physicist, an astronomer, nor an observer of the behavior of rats (a psychologist) would find it necessary to take account in his own somewhat different investigation. If it is stipulated that nothing is within the sphere of reason which their methods do not recognize as relevant or their instruments record, we shall, in this process, have transcended "reason." But we shall not, for all that, have taken leave of our powers of rational discrimination and sound judgment in so doing. On the contrary, we shall find uses for them, which even the most careful observation of rodent behavior could hardly have elicited. Nor shall we be unduly shocked or upset by the discovery that the good thus discerned is one that is relative to the human interests it organizes and articulates, that, in short, it is their good, and that its rational authority lies not in its supposed disclosure of a "reality" outside this context, but in its capacity to bring the desires that operate within it to a level of just and harmonious satisfaction which, by themselves, they could not have discerned. For, while the good it discloses is *their* good, it is not a good which they can set independently of the light which reason thus employed supplies, and reason is not, in consequence, nor should it be, the slave of the passions, though it is, and ought to be, the spokesman for a good in which the passions find their reasonable satisfaction. In trying to see how reason works here and what the differences are between action that, in a moral sense, is right and reasonable and that which is arbitrary and unjust, we shall (fortunately) need no special powers of insight or appreciation vouchsafed only to the elect. Nothing more is needed than reliable knowledge and good will in the understanding and evaluation of matters of public knowledge and issues of common concern. Nothing less, however, will suffice.

Interest and Judgments of Value. How can we be rational about values, when the attitude of reason is one of disinterested, unbiased judgment, and the attitude of valuation is one of interest, preference, bias—a way of being *for* some things and *against* others? If to be disinterested, in the sense in which practical reason requires disinterested judgment, was to be unconcerned, while to have a preference for anything rather than anything else was to be biased in its favor, hence *not* disinterested, there would indeed be a fatal incompatibility between reason and the passions, and to talk of practical reason, as we have done, would be a contradiction in terms. Fortunately for us, and for human nature, no such incompatibility exists. But loose and inaccurate thinking has sometimes led men to suppose its existence, and to maintain in consequence that we can only be rational about things we care nothing or very little about, since in these cases only can a "disinterested" and thus a genuinely rational attitude be expected to prevail. We can reach "objective" judgments about the velocity of light, since no very strong emotions are committed in advance to one conclusion rather than another about it; but to be similarly "objective" in instances about which we care greatly is quite out of the question. This conclusion ministers to a number of interests which have more to lose than to gain by the application of reason to human affairs, and it is not surprising that it has enjoyed a certain popularity. Our first task, therefore, will be to clear up the confusion from which it gains its intellectual respectability and, in the process, to locate more precisely the standpoint from which moral judgments are made and the sense in which they can be, and ought to be, disinterested.

We have agreed that all the goods we can identify in experience possess their goodness in their capacity to satisfy interests, wants, desires. None of these interests is antecedently rational, as conforming to the demands of a reality, discerned by reason, which possesses an inherent excellence of its own and to which it is the business of our desires, so far as they are reasonable, to conform. There may be such a reality, but its inherent excellence, whatever it may consist in, from cosmic immensity to plenitude of Being, becomes a value for us only in so far as we can discern in it a good in which our wills, and minds, and hearts are satisfied. And it is with the good that we can discern that practical reason is reasonably concerned.

But while no interest is antecedently rational, and while reason has no criterion for the good outside that which the satisfaction of human wants itself determines, the satisfaction of our wants can come to be a rational process in so far as we judge the claims of each particular interest from the standpoint of an attainable harmony to which each contributes but in which none has exclusive or unqualified authority. If we wanted only one thing, and wanted it unconditionally, there would be no place for the use of reason in the discovery of the good toward which all our efforts should be directed. Reason would then, and rightly, be the slave, not of the passions, but of that one passion to whose unconditional satisfaction our nature was directed. Nothing is more apparent, however, than that we want many things, and that some of these wants conflict. Moreover, there are things we want if we can have them under some conditions that we should rightly reject under others. Until, therefore, we know on what terms our several interests can be jointly satisfied and to what the satisfaction of any one among them would commit us, in relation to the others and the conditions of their satisfaction, we simply do not know what we want. Nor can we find out simply by listing our "fundamental drives" and inviting them to fight it out among themselves for mastery. Men want power, they have a "will to power," and they struggle for power. But unless they are maniacs or Nietzschean supermen, and therefore less or more than human, they want power of certain sorts, under specific conditions, and there are other things they want as well as power, concern for which will qualify the kind of power they go after and the way in which they use it when they get it. And short of special revelation of some sort or other, the only way in which they can reliably find out what sort of power they want and what they want to do with it, is by considering the urge for power in its relation to other urges and the possibility of their joint attainment under the conditions in which action can effectively be carried on. This possibility of satisfaction will stand, relatively to competing present urges, as an ideal, something not now actual but attainable and worth attaining; and it will reasonably have authority over them simply in so far as it expresses what is wanted not blindly or at random but with knowledge of the conditions under which a secure and comprehensive satisfaction can actually be achieved. For this we require not only knowledge of the external world but self-knowledge as well, the kind that Socrates invited his fellow Athenians to seek. The reason that judges, in the light of such knowledge, what is worth seeking, or what is good, is the practical reason we have been looking for. Plato summed up the case for the authority of reason in conduct by saying that the good for man is a mixture, and only reason can reliably judge how, and in what measure, the ingredients in this mixture can rightly be combined. The claim of practical reason could hardly be put more simply or more conclusively.

In what sense is a judgment "disinterested" when it is made from the standpoint of this desirable and possible, hence, relatively to present action, ideal goal? Certainly not in the sense that the good it defines is one about which we are or ought to be unconcerned. What we want such an ideal to provide for us is a *ground* for preference, a way of being for or against competing demands for action *reasonably*, not at all a way of being indifferent or merely neutral concerning them. The notion that only in refusing to commit himself is a man "objective," and hence judicious in matters of conduct, is a current inanity that has done much harm. A practically reasonable man is not one without convictions but one who makes up his mind with a just regard for the merits of the case before him. This presupposes that the case has merits (or demerits), and that these can be found out and fairly assessed. What is required for reasonable judgment is the kind of impartiality which consists in freedom for such *antecedent* commitment to one interest or another as would blind a man to the issues involved, or close his mind to relevant information concerning them, or impede a fair estimate of conflicting claims. There is no doubt that it is in some cases very difficult to be thus impartial. But it is no less evident that we frequently do expect men to manifest such impartiality, and regard it as a prerequisite for responsible fair dealing in social relations.

A selection board is not expected to show its impartiality by refusing to prefer any of the applicants among whom it has to choose to any other, that is, by refusing to make a choice. Nor is it supposed to be lacking in concern for (hence "partiality" to) the good to which an "impartial" selection is supposed to contribute. Quite the contrary. What is expected is that it will not prefer one candidate to another save in so far as that preference can be justified by the merits of the applicants, that is, by their reasonably judged capacity to perform the services required of them for the sake of which judgment is pronounced. There is really no mystery about this, nor is the ability to act thus reasonably in a practical situation ordinarily regarded as something too great to demand of frail human nature. If such a board favored one candidate to another because of his wealth, or family connections, it would be deciding arbitrarily, not because its decision was the expression of an interest, but because the interest in question was not one which could stand inspection in the light of its professed intentions and the end for which it was set up.

In such an instance, the difference between a decision that is just or reasonable and one that is arbitrary, or unreasonable, is not that the one is the expression of an interest and the other not, but that the one contributes to and can be justified by a more comprehensive good, in reference to which it is judged, while the other is in conflict with this good. Those interests which can contribute to such a good are said to be reasonable with respect to it, those that oppose it, irrational. The good itself has no cogency apart from the satisfaction it promises for genuine human wants. If there was no use in selecting candidates on their merits, there would be no sense in condemning those who failed to do so. But it is not to be identified with any of these wants apart from the meaning it takes on as one factor in a more inclusive good. And what it can properly claim, as a member of that order, is not to be settled by its initial urgency or allegedly primitive status, but only by its eventual contribution to that way of living which we prefer when we know what we are doing and what, on the whole, we want. In articulating the structure of this way of living reason is not the slave of the passions, nor their rival in a struggle for power, but the spokesman for a good which is their good, but which, without its aid, they could not have discerned.

I do not suggest, of course, that such rationality always or even usually prevails in human conduct. We do not always choose the highest when we see it, and we often have neither the good sense to see it nor the will to look where it is to be found. Hence conduct is very frequently arbitrary and irrational in ways in which it ought not to be—that is, it falls short of a range and level of satisfaction which was possible to it, if it had had the wit to understand and the will to make the most of its opportunities. What is here important is to make out the kind of difference that reason makes where it does operate, and the good to which it is rightly addressed. This good is not beyond the powers of human nature to achieve; if it were it would not define a relevant ideal. But it is one that is reliably attainable only when human nature develops in a particular way, when the interests that move men are judged from the standpoint of their eventual collaboration in a comprehensive good, and the knowledge of the good thus identified becomes a factor in the organization of present conduct toward its effective actualization. Apart from this distinctive aspect of human behavior and the rational use of ideas in the context of activity its defines, there is no way of making sense of the claims of practical reason. It is not surprising, therefore, that those who refuse seriously to consider human behavior under this aspect, preferring to reduce it for scientific or other purposes to a congeries of "drives" or reflexes or "frustrations and aggressions," have been unable to make sense of these claims. Perhaps it was not their business to do so. But it is our business, and we intend to pursue it. If those whose understanding of human nature is restricted, perhaps advisedly, to what can be understood in terms of categories derived from pathology, physiology and animal behavior will proceed with their own affairs, there need be no disagreement between us. If, however, they go on to claim that what they have discovered is "ultimately" all there is in the human animal and that, in consequence, we are merely fooling ourselves when we demand "disinterested" behavior of such an organism, we shall have to reply, with less politeness than pertinence, that on this point they quite literally do not know what they are talking about.

Moral Order and Moral Freedom. We have spoken so far of a comprehensive good in which competing interests can attain their reasonable satisfaction, finding in it the measure of fulfilment of which, as elements in an ordered life, they are capable, and of the role of reason in discovering the nature of this good and making it available, as an ideal, in the organization of present conduct. The picture thus presented is true as far as it goes. But there is more to practical reason than that. It is not sufficient to talk of a harmony of interests and a resulting satisfaction. We must go on to ask whose interests are to be harmonized and from what standpoint, and on what level the satisfaction is to be achieved. These are old questions, and they are not easy to answer. Must each man, so far at least as he is reasonable, prefer his own interests to all others, and regard the good of others simply as a means to the end of his own satisfaction? And of what sort are these satisfactions to be? Is it better, as John Stuart Mill declared, to be Socrates dissatisfied than a fool satisfied? And, if it is, how is this betterness to be made out in terms of the satisfaction of interests, which we have so far taken as the goal of reasonable conduct? If we are to understand the use of practical reason, in its application to moral issues, we must answer these questions; for the ordering of satisfactions in the good we accept as our ideal will depend upon our answer, and the reasonable ordering of conduct on the structure of this good.

It is true, indeed it is a truism, that the only interests a man can reasonably be concerned about are his own. But it is no less true, and just as important, to add that he can reasonably be concerned about the interests of others and the claim they make upon him, and can prefer such claims to interests which, if he had had only himself to consider, he would have preferred to satisfy. What the truism says is that he cannot be concerned about the interests of others unless he *is* concerned about them, and unless, in that sense, they are objects of his own interest, in the satisfaction of which he will find at least the satisfaction that comes from getting what one wants, even when what one wants, under the circumstances, is the satisfaction of other interests than one's own. This may sound paradoxical, and a paradox has frequently been made of it. But the puzzle arises from a failure to specify the context in which moral judgments are actually made, and the manner in which the preferences that follow such judgment and are guided by it are determined. What a man would want if he had only his own satisfaction to consider is one thing. The interests which, under those circumstances, would reasonably determine his conduct, and the kind of good in which it would eventuate can, with a certain effort of abstractive imagination, be ascertained. If we label such interests *his own* interests and contrast them with the similarly determined interests of others, of which he may have for practical purposes to take account, but only in so far as they serve as instruments or impediments to the satisfaction of "his own" interests as antecedently identified, we shall have a picture of rational conduct in which the end pursued is ego-centric satisfaction and nothing is accounted reasonable in practice that does not serve as a means to this end. It is not a very edifying picture, and it can be used either to justify selfishness as peculiarly rational or to condemn rational action as peculiarly selfish. It has often been used for both purposes. Its plausibility rests on the dictum that the only good a man can reasonably pursue is that which "his own" concerns or interests dictate, and its fallacious import is seen as soon as it is observed that "his own" has here been defined in terms of a situation which excludes from the start the conditions in which moral problems arise and can significantly be solved.

For it is a manifest fact, though a frequently neglected one, that specifically moral problems arise in just those cases in which a man *is* concerned with the interests and the happiness of others beside himself, either because he values their satisfaction directly as an end worth working for, or because he acknowledges an obligation to respect it. These obligations and values are in this situation *his* concern; they are the objects of his interest; and the good for which he can reasonably work is one in which they must have an appropriate place. To picture them as mere means to a "satisfaction," in which "his own" interests, defined independently of just these concerns, have the dominant place and in respect to which all else functions merely as means, is radically to misrepresent the situation. It is not surprising that the terms of this misrepresentation, masquerading as "rational self-interest," have failed to provide the basis for a sound moral theory.

The object of this concern will, as a rule, be defined by certain approved ways of acting, acknowledged as "right," "fair," or "proper," and felt by the individual to stand as obligations which he is bound to respect in his relations to other people. The keeping of promises, support for aged parents and young children, loyalty to the state and readiness to defend it at grave personal risk in time of war are familiar instances, and there is no society with which we are acquainted, from the most primitive culture to the most developed, in which respect for some such obligations is not a considerable factor in social behavior. To define the good in which men could be satisfied independently of the right ordering of interests in respect to just such obligations would be to define a good which was not their good and in which they could not in fact find satisfaction. It is, therefore, a highly unreasonable procedure, though it is in the name of reason that it is sometimes defended. These rules and obligations are not themselves the product of human reason, save to a minor and limited degree. They include tabus we now regard as cruel and stupid, as well as practices of a more praiseworthy sort. But whether good or bad, from the standpoint of a more reflective morality, they are an essential part of the situation in which men work for the satisfaction of their desires, and they help to determine the structure of any good in which these desires can in fact find satisfaction.

The adjustment of interests that will reasonably satisfy the actual concerns of men must, therefore, have at least the semblance of a moral order—that is, it must be one in which rights and duties are acknowledged and in which decisions, on matters of mutual concern, are regarded as sufficiently warranted only when they can be shown to conform to accredited rules of right action. They may not actually so conform: there is room in such matters for endless hypocrisy and self-deception. And the rules themselves may be blind and arbitrary enough. But so long as they are acknowledged, not merely as threats or commands, conformity to which may or may not be expedient in the furtherance of other interests, but as standards that *ought to be* respected, so that conformity constitutes an obligation which individuals are genuinely concerned to respect, they function as moral rules within the society in question, and men who respect them, in making up their minds, will ask not merely what, on reflection, they want to do, but also, in some instances, what they ought to do. What ought to be done is not necessarily something different from what they antecedently wanted to do. The point is rather that until they have found out what they ought to do, they will not *know* what, on the whole, they want to do. For they want to do what they ought to do, and this is something to be found out, not dictated in advance by the *de facto* urgency of competing interests. There is no doubt, I think, that there are instances in which most men find themselves in this sort of situation. It is no answer to their problem to tell them that they ought to do whatever they want to do, or to "satisfy themselves." That is true enough, so far as it goes, but it will not meet the issue. What they want to do is whatever, under the circumstances, is right and reasonable, and their satisfaction is not to be found short of an adjustment in which other interests than their own demand consideration, not merely as means, but on terms which rules of equity and fair dealing dictate. Practical reason will not have done its work until it has shown us how to meet these situations as reasonably as we can. When Kant insisted that "What ought I to do?" is the basic question for practical reason he was, as usual, keeping his eye on the salient features of the moral situation.

We have, then, the answer to one of the questions asked some pages back. The interests to be harmonized by practical reason are those with which the individual is himself concerned—they could from the nature of the case be no others. But they are those with which he is concerned not merely as a competitive animal or ego-centric calculator of eventual personal rewards, but as a responsible moral agent. As such he can rightly prefer "his own" interests to others only when and in so far as they are entitled to such preference under rules held to be valid not merely for him, but for all those concerned in the moral community. This reasonable preference is by no means the sole or dominant factor in human conduct—nothing could be plainer than that. But it is one factor in it, and a uniquely valuable one. To leave it out when we are estimating the capacities of human nature as a whole is to turn an abstraction, perhaps legitimate for scientific purposes, into an excuse for moral cynicism. And to leave it out when it is moral behavior itself that is under consideration is a kind of blindness of which, in Bradley's phrase, only "a fool or an advanced thinker" could be guilty

This goes a long way toward answering our second question as well. On what level, it was asked, is the satisfaction which practical reason recommends as a worthy goal for action to be achieved? The satisfactions of the fool are not those of Socrates, but so long as each is satisfied in his own fashion, who is to judge between them? And if one is satisfied and the other not, was not the first the wiser man, at least from a practical point of view? The answer depends, of course, on the value to be placed on the man who is having the satisfaction—the value, that is, of being the kind of man who can be satisfied in that kind of way. For we are concerned not merely with the satisfaction of interests, but of persons, and it is only when we have taken account of what persons are, and what worth they are capable of possessing, that we can rightly estimate their value.

The word "person" has all sorts of meanings in a variety of contexts, and the use here assigned it will not agree with all of these. Nor is it intended to do so. In the context of moral behavior, however, a "person" is an individual with rights and duties, one who can properly be held responsible for what he does because he is capable of assuming or bearing responsibility, of acting in the name and for the sake of interests that are his, not merely as a biological organism, but as a member of a moral order. He is capable, in G. H. Mead's phrase, of "taking the role of the other," that is, of the other members of the social group in which he functions, and judging his own conduct in terms held to be valid alike for all. If this meant only the passive reflection of group pressures in individual conduct, it would fall considerably short of what I mean by personality. It achieves this level, however, when the "other" is generalized to represent the verdict of justice and right reason, and the acceptance of its obligations is an active commitment to a good which the individual acknowledges as his own.

It was in Kant's moral philosophy that the notion of moral personality, and its central place in rational conduct, received classical statement. What he saw clearly was that when men cooperate freely, through their reasonable acknowledgment of mutual responsibilities, as members of "a kingdom of ends," a level of conduct is achieved which is of peculiar value, a moral order which makes sense of much in human nature that without it would remain frustrated and unfulfilled. We may not agree with him that nothing in this world or out of it is good without qualifications but a good will, but when we understand ourselves and our purposes we shall find it hard, I think, to deny that good will, as he understood it, is a great good, and that without it many other goods, which men have mistakenly regarded as more important, would lose their worth as well. A "good will," in this usage, is a will freely, and responsibly, directed to the good attainable in such a community, claiming nothing for itself that this common good does not warrant and acknowledging the equal rights of others who are co-workers for its attainment. In Kant's writings this doctrine is hedged around by crabbed distinctions and scholastic complications, but there are sentences in which it comes to splendid expression, as in the great commandment to which every theory of democracy that makes sense must return for its ultimate moral sanction: "So act as to treat humanity, whether in thine own person or that of another, always as an end, never merely as a means."

This dictum is, of course, the categorical, or unconditional moral imperative which Kant regarded as the fundamental principle of all right conduct. It has often been misunderstood by critics, and there are some among the most modern of them who make their inability to understand it an occasion for self-congratulation. Thus Pareto refers to this principle as "a metaphysical entity," which is "still admired by many good souls," and adds that those who "pretend to know what it is . . . can never make it clear to anyone who insists on remaining in touch with reality." [1] If "remaining in touch with reality" means rejecting all ideals which deal with conduct as it ought to be, then this failure is not very difficult to understand. It is, however, remarkably, and even willfully, simple-minded. For Kant was not ignorant of, and had no intention of denying, the fact that "in reality" we constantly use the services of others as means to our own ends, and that it is quite sensible to do so. What he saw was that there is a level of human relationships on which it is possible not *merely* to use men for our own ends but to share with them in purposes that are mutually understood and honored, and that nothing that comes out of such cooperative action is as much worth attaining as the good will and integrity of the men who freely share in it. Humanity—or human nature—at this level of conduct has a dignity or personal worth that accrues to it not just as a means to some further good, but as an end or fulfilment, the actualization of the excellence of which that nature is capable. The injunction to treat humanity, in respect of this capacity in one's own person and that of others, as an end, not merely as a means, does not seem to me incomprehensible or even obscure. Nor do I find it impossible to understand its obvious implication: that those who reduce a humanity capable of such dignity and freedom to a mere instrument for their own ulterior ends are behaving wrongly. For the integrity of free men is beyond price—its

[1] V. Pareto, *The Mind and Society*, Vol. III, pp. 964-965.

worth is not that of an instrument but of an end. And that, I take it, is what the categorical imperative has to tell us. It will be a bad day for our country, and ourselves, if we really cease to understand it.

The notion that social action on such a level is possible and desirable stands, for those who accept it, as an ideal or norm for present action. It does not describe the way in which men always or even usually behave. It represents a good rarely now achieved and perhaps never fully attainable. But without it, and without the possibility it presents of a life lived at some times and in some measure at the height of its human capacities, we should not know what sense to make of other goods to which we are committed and for which we feel very genuine concern. If it is to maintain itself under reasonable examination as a valid ideal for conduct, the possibility it pictures must be a real one—not the "categorical imperative crying in the wilderness" of Santayana's ironic portrayal. It must, that is to say, be reasonably probable that if we acknowledge its claims and act upon them within the limits set by the specific conditions under which action takes place, we can in fact make actual in some measure the goods it promises. No community humanly attainable may in this sense ever be as good as it ideally ought to be; but if concern for what it ought to be is a considerable factor in the direction of policy, it may be considerably better—nearer to what it ought to be—than it would have been if no such ideal had been acknowledged. That is the way in which norms or ideals work in human conduct, when they work at all, and it is the business of practical reason to judge them in their capacity to fulfil this function.

The good thus realized—and we part company with Kant at this point—will still be the good for which our *de facto* concerns and interests provide the material, and the satisfaction it promises will have to be one in which they are satisfied. What is claimed here is that when these concerns are judged as those of a responsible self or person nothing short of such a moral order will satisfy them. It is better to be Socrates dissatisfied than a fool satisfied only if one would rather be a Socrates than a fool, and share in the never finished quest for an excellence that fools would hardly feel the lack of. Socrates, too, might have been satisfied with the pleasures of the fool, but he would have had to be a fool to be thus satisfied. "And suppose a man actually is thus satisfied," the objector queries, "how are you going to prove that he is wrong?" For my own part, I should not attempt to do so. If there is nothing in him that rejects that alternative, if he really can be satisfied in it, then for him it is the best available. A fool's paradise may be a paradise indeed, for a fool. But a man in full possession of his faculties could not live well in it. The principle of moral freedom, like any other moral maxim, is addressed, in the last analysis, to whom it may concern. What I do contend, however, and my confidence in the worth of political freedom rests upon it, is that most men under decently human conditions are by no means such fools as social scientists and cynics frequently take them to be, and that, in consequence, the ideal proposed by practical reason for a just ordering of satisfactions in a community in which each man is respected as a person and no one among them serves merely as a tool or instrument to the satisfactions of others is, for them, a relevant and reasonable ideal. The function of reason here is not to report to fallen human nature a good of which it would otherwise have no inkling, but to bring clarity, comprehensiveness and order to concerns already at work and to enable those who follow it to know themselves and what they are trying to do. It cries not, as Santayana suggests, in the wilderness, but in the hearts and minds of men, and there sometimes and to some extent it finds an answer.

The Good of Freedom.   Among the ideas which the ideal of practical reason helps to clarify, none is more important, or more frequently misunderstood, than that of "freedom." A concern for "freedom" for ourselves and, where possible, for others, is an often expressed motive in American governmental policy, foreign and domestic. Only a cynic, and a rather stupid one, would deny that this concern is often genuine and urgent; but only an optimist who was not very bright would be bold enough to assert that we usually know clearly what we mean by it or why it should assume the central place it does in our scheme of political value. Hence the appeal to "freedom" can be used to exploit our confusions as well as to inspire a reasonable loyalty, and it is more regrettable than surprising that we tend to grow suspicious of its indiscriminate use.

It is beyond my purpose, as it is beyond my powers, to catalogue the various meanings of the term "freedom," each of which may, in its own context, be legitimate and even enlightening. There is one use of it, however, which is directly relevant to our present interest. A man is said to be morally free when his decision on issues that confront him is his own decision and action consequent upon it the expression of his own will, and when he is prepared to accept the responsibility for both decision and action as his own. That does not mean that his choice is arbitrary, capricious or uncaused. On the contrary, he will normally want to show that he had good ground for deciding as he did, and will adduce his concern to act rightly or fairly and his understanding of what, under the circumstances *was* right and fair, as the determining factors in his decision. If, on the other hand, he was shown that his action had resulted from motives fighting it out for supremacy in his consciousness, the most urgent finally winning out and thereby proving its dominance, he would be inclined to say that, on that showing, it was not *he* who had decided at all, but that the decision was something that happened to him, like a toothache or a broken leg. It is no wonder that psychologists who describe human choices in this fashion can make little sense of the notion of moral freedom. The ideas of moral freedom and moral personality are inextricably bound together. A man is acting freely, in this sense, when he decides and acts for himself, makes up his own mind and acts in his own person. A free decision need not be uncaused or self-caused, as has mistakenly been supposed, but it must be caused by the self and therefore not fully determined apart from the specific contribution which the man *as a self* or person makes to its determination.

In the context of moral action, an individual is or becomes a person in so far as he is capable of giving laws to himself, as Rousseau expressed it. That does not mean that he always acts rightly, or is free only when he so acts. What it means is that he acts in such cases as a self or person, and it is to him in this capacity that the action is properly imputed, not to his body, or his fright in early childhood, or the economic system of which he is a part. All these, no doubt, have helped to make him what he is, but what they have helped to bring into being is not just a healthy or twisted body, or a grown-up but still frightened child, or a human by-product of machine industry, but a person capable of reaching his own decisions and demanding for himself and others the right so to decide. The growth of a self, the achievement of human freedom, is one of the most remarkable things that happen in the world, and it is no wonder that much mystery has been made of it. For those who can "rationalize" a process only by reducing it to its causal antecedents, growth is always a mystery, and there will always, I suppose, be those who insist it does not happen because they cannot find the means to understand it. But it does happen, none the less, and is a mystery only for those who insist on interpreting it in other categories than its own. And when it happens men are free, not because they are uninfluenced by anything outside themselves, or insulated causally from their environment, but because what these causes converge upon is a self that acts in its own person, and for ends that it judges to be, under the conditions which the environment sets, the best attainable.

This is a quite special way in which human beings act, and under special conditions. Of a freedom that should function independently of such a way of acting in such conditions we know so little that metaphysicians are at liberty to speculate about it in almost any manner that they please, and skeptics to deny its existence with impunity. But of the freedom which manifests itself in responsible choice we know a good deal, and it is by no means a matter of indifference what we think or say about it. For when we ask what the good of democracy is, or what the reason for preferring a government that preserves the legal right of its citizens to think and to worship as they will, to its totalitarian rival, we shall hardly get an answer that will stand inspection until we reach the point of saying that it is a good thing to foster the conditions in which men are encouraged to make up their own minds on essential issues, because the kind of people who can and will make up their own minds and take the responsibility for their own actions are the kind of people we want and are determined to be. Nothing that a government can offer its citizens—or subjects—is in the long run worth as much as the character and capacities of men who are men enough to judge it, and themselves, by the best they know and to act as their judgment dictates. No political agency can by legal action create that kind of men. But it can maintain the political conditions under which its citizens have a chance to grow to that stature, and it ought to do so. If any one assures us that he has found out from science, or philosophy, or any other respectable source, that *this* kind of freedom is impossible, or "unreal" or unimportant, we shall want to scrutinize his statements very carefully indeed. We must respect "the facts," wherever we find them, in so far as they *are* facts as they claim to be, and are relevant to the issues we are discussing. We shall later have a chance to examine some such alleged facts and come to a conclusion concerning them. Meanwhile we shall know, at least, what *we* mean by the freedom we value, and why we value it. It is bound up with the capacity for cooperative action on that level of understanding and good will which we rightly regard as of preeminent human value. We cannot give it up without surrendering with it, not only our right to be respected as persons, but our self-respect as well. There is no denying that many have made this surrender. What can be questioned is whether, if they still had the capacity to act as free men, they chose well or wisely in so doing. This is a question not of psychology, or of political science, or of logical analysis, but of morals; it concerns the comparative worth of things and persons, and it is only from a standpoint for which the worth of persons has a meaning and men are valued for what they are, or can become, rather than for what can be got out of them, that an unequivocal answer can be given. Those for whom this standpoint has no cogency and no "reality" will not know what we are talking about when we say that freedom as we understand it is more than a political convenience, that it is in fact a spiritual necessity, one of the things men live by on the only level on which they can with human dignity consent to live, and that its willful surrender is not just a bargain, good or bad under varying conditions, but a betrayal. We cannot argue with them about that, if they have been honest in what they say. But if they go on to claim that, without understanding this, they are competent to say what democracy is and what it is worth to those who honor it, they will be mistaken, nor can the wealth of their factual information compensate here for the poverty of their moral understanding.

The good, then, with which practical reason is concerned, cannot adequately be understood merely as the satisfaction of assorted interests and drives or, when these conflict, of the most primitive or dominant among them. The good that is reasonably sought by free men cannot be less than an *order* of satisfactions, which is also a moral order. You cannot here judge the worth of the satisfaction apart from the worth of the self that is satisfied. Nor is the standard that judges the worth of individuals in terms of their capacity for selfhood in a moral community—a kingdom of ends—an external and transcendent one, imposed from without upon a human nature directed to a different good. It is a standard meaningful for those who can find in it an adequate expression of concerns and aspirations already strongly felt but incapable, apart from the articulation it provides, of understanding themselves and the conditions of their comprehensive satisfaction. These concerns count as basic, not through their primitive urgency or pervasiveness throughout the animal kingdom, but through their centrality in the organization of the kind of life in which men can will and act freely, or as persons. The good they define corresponds, in consequence, not to what the human animal always and everywhere is, nor to anything that could be found out about him by psychological tests of backward children, but to what he can become, and wills to become, when he understands himself and his purposes and can be satisfied with nothing less than the best of which he is capable. It is, in other words, an ideal, and it is in the capacity of human nature, sometimes and under fortunate conditions, to respond to ideals and to act wisely in terms of them, that its cogency is to be sought. It is, once more, not surprising that those who have looked for it elsewhere have failed to find it.

The Natural Basis of Morality. But all ideals, as Aristotle and Santayana have warned us, have a natural basis. The moral beings to whom our exhortations have so far been addressed are also, and inescapably, our fellow men, and ourselves; and while at times, and within limits, we hunger and thirst after righteousness, we also have other appetites, and can be hungry, or jealous, or bored, as well as inspired to good deeds, and perhaps, on the whole, more frequently. We want, in our better moments, to love our neighbors, but in a society in which they are constantly getting in our way, the obstacles in the way of this sort of affection are very great. And if we cannot love our neighbors, how are we to develop that measure of good will toward our remoter Allies in the present conflict—to say nothing of those who are now our enemies—which will make it possible for us to live together in some sort of amity in the post-war world? Good will, as Kant so rightly told us, has a preeminent moral value. But it equally, as he unfortunately failed to make clear, has natural and social conditions. The limits of moral agreement are those within which a community of interest and understanding can so far be established as to bring men effectively to care more for the things they have in common than for those that divide them, and to work together for the secure attainment of those things. Mere proximity does not cause men to respect each other, nor does the need for common action by itself create the will to achieve it. A common concern will do it, when that concern is enlightened by understanding, organized in a way that is felt on each side to be substantially fair, and carried through in shared activity and established habits of effective working together. There are such common concerns among us and there are resources in human nature for their cooperative satisfaction. The good they define has for its primary content the creaturely happiness of men who want security and a measure of comfort for themselves and their families, who want to be left alone in some things and like to get together for others, who, with any sort of a decent opportunity, can do well something or other that is socially useful and admired, and who get solid satisfaction from doing it. Given the conditions under which they can do well the things they are fitted to do, without that pressure of fear and suspicion which eats into the very roots of decent living, they are capable of exercising the kind of good will and good judgment in which a reasonable morality finds its effective expression. Even without such conditions, and in a world which seems to make nonsense of all talk of a common good, they will sometimes behave with a heroism and generosity that must astonish and confound the cynic. But the heroic virtues are not enough. They have so far inspired men to die nobly, but they have not developed in them the sustained good will and substantial good sense to live well together. For this longer and harder task something much more pedestrian is wanted—the steadiness of intelligence and purpose that can remove irritating frictions, work patiently and step-by-step in matters of policy, and meet the annoyances incident to the affairs of opinionated men with firmness and a sense of humor. There is also wanted the kind of working honesty that can be known by its fruits and justified by them. These are qualities that the accredited spokesmen for "ideal values" do not invariably possess, and whose relevance to moral issues has not always been seen. But it is essential that they be properly valued, and faithfully exemplified, if moral values are to be made human values as well.

There is a moral in this for moralists which is of primary importance. The moral good is that of a community of persons—a moral order. But a moral community is also a natural and social community, or a community of men who must live and work together under the conditions set by their needs and appetites and by the environment in which these wants must be satisfied. What a community of disembodied wills or pure spirits would be like we do not know, but in no case would it be a safe model to follow in judging of the proper relations of men in this world. The good will such men manifest as persons will be the good will that has been built up and can maintain itself in their lives as parents and husbands, working men or employers, as citizens, as readers of newspapers and seers of motion pictures, in all the activities that determine the manner and conditions of their lives. Any "freedom" or responsible selfhood that for them is worth having will be a freedom that can show itself in their actions on the issues that confront them here. *This* community, whether it have its locus in Chungking or Geneva or Chicago, is the moral community in which those who share in it can actualize their capacities as persons, and it is a moral community not by a theological or philosophical fiat which assures us that men are godlike in their origins or transcendentally free in their metaphysical substance, but by grace of the intelligence, decency and resolute action of those who make it so, more or less, and within the limit of their capacities. Whatever helps to sustain that kind of action and, through it, the community of shared purpose in which the moral good is made actual, contributes to morality. Whatever works to narrow the limits of such a community, to undermine it by self-seeking or arbitrary pretensions, to debase the currency of common understanding within it, is an enemy of the moral order, and of the possibility of good it represents.

An explicit recognition of the non-moral basis and conditions of morality is particularly needed at the present time to correct a misleading sort of moralizing which has gained wide currency under war conditions and is likely to grow in influence when the war is over. In his valuable discussion of the conditions of peace, for example, E. H. Carr has a good deal to say about the need for the development of a new moral purpose to inspire and justify the sacrifices which the building of a new international order will require.[2] He claims that we are in the midst of a "revolution" against the "liberal democracy" of the nineteenth century, with its emphasis on self-interest as the determining principle in social action, and its goal in a harmony of interests. The dissatisfied nations—Russia, Germany and Italy—have been the advance agents of this revolution, and while Carr by no means condones the political conduct of the latter two, he makes it clear that,

[2] E. H. Carr, *Conditions of Peace*, especially Chap. V, "The Moral Crisis."

n his judgment, it is only by a further and more enlightened movement in the direction which this revolution is taking—and away from the errors of "liberal democracy"—that the olution for our problems is to be found. What we need especially for this development is a moral purpose that will "reanimate our political and economic system," by substituting self-sacrifice for the community for self-interest as the approved ideal for conduct. This new faith "will perhaps need o correct the one-sided nineteenth century emphasis on iberty" [3] and to bring the concepts of liberty and authority o a new synthesis in which we shall no longer err by our emphasis on the former.

This view has further implications, directly pertinent to our present inquiry. Carr tells us that the "liberal" doctrine was correlated with an "exaggerated belief in the supremacy of the intellect," [4] and adds that "it is not knowledge that has failed us, but will, not experts, but leaders." [5] The "reanimated" moral purpose will, presumably, be free of such "intellectualistic" errors. The "will" which this new "leadership" expresses will, it is assumed, be the will of "the community," and it is for the good of "the community" that it will demand the self-sacrifice that only a revived moral idealism can inspire.

All this has a plausible and persuasive sound, and Carr's suggestions for postwar reconstruction are sensible and enlightening. It is also based, in part, on a valid moral insight. The ideal of self-interest is, as we have seen, a quite inadequate basis for a moral community, and nothing short of the good of such a community can justify the demands that governments make upon the loyalty and good will of free men. It is disturbing, however, that the offending doctrine is identified by Carr with that of "liberal democracy," and

[3] *Ibid.*, p. 127.
[4] *Ibid.*, p. 114.
[5] *Ibid.*, p. 114.

that he finds his examples of the "revolution" which ushers in the new day in the procedures of the totalitarian states. I should have supposed that John Stuart Mill—that "old" nineteenth century liberal—had a sounder and juster idea of the need and nature of moral purpose in a community than Carr's "revolutionaries" have so far manifest, and that the rise of Methodism in England, with the social consequences which Halévy has so clearly outlined,[6] was a better instance of the operation of moral purpose in social conduct than the rise of the Nazi Party in Germany. If this is the case, then Carr's insistence on the lack of moral purpose in the liberalism we must abandon and its presence in the "revolutionary" new order that is before us is seriously misleading. If it is not the case, then I suspect that what he means by a "moral purpose" is not at all what many of us would understand by it. It is time we came to a clearer understanding on this important point.

What makes a social purpose moral, and what justifies the claims of those who demand the "self-sacrifice" of others for its attainment? There is nothing particularly novel about the view that it would be a good idea if most people did what their leaders told them and were properly prepared to subordinate their own rights or "interests" to the higher demands of a "community" for which such leaders were peculiarly qualified to speak. Nor is there anything particularly moral about many of the "faiths"—the faith in Aryan racial superiority, for example—by which such claims are fostered and made socially persuasive. Self-sacrifice can be the expression of some of the noblest qualities of human nature, and of some of the ugliest as well. Evidently we need a criterion in terms of which what is genuine in such claims can be distinguished from what is fraudulent and demoralizing. And in spite of Carr's strictures on "the exaggerated belief in the supremacy of the intellect," we shall need all the help

[6] É. Halévy, *A History of the English People in 1815*, Bk. III, Chap. I

that practical intelligence can give us if we are not to be deceived.

It is apparent, at least, that a legitimate demand for self-sacrifice must be made in the name of "the good of the community," for which the moral or political prophet is in some manner entitled to speak. But what constitutes a "community" whose good can rightly claim the allegiance of individuals as worth the sacrifice of their other and more immediate interests? Such a community is not constituted by the fact that people occupy a common territory and that some give orders to others. It is a moral achievement and it exists just where, when, and in so far as men's shared interests can be made the basis for cooperative action in which the good sought is, in fact, and not merely in rhetoric, a common good in which all who sacrifice for its attainment can justly and fully share. The purpose involved in work for such a good is "moral," not because of what it asks individuals to give up on the "authority" of others but because of what it asks them to achieve, and of the level of responsible fair dealing required for the achievement. If the moral purpose that Carr desires is to be grounded in a clearer understanding of what *this* good can be and a fuller commitment to the effort needed to attain it, then indeed it merits his eulogy. If it is anything other or less than this, then it just as emphatically does not.

But if this is actually what he meant by moral purpose, then there are some important corrections to be made in what he has said of it. The contrast between self-interest (non-moral) and self-sacrifice (moral) is radically misleading. For, as we have seen, a moral community is also a natural community, and the *content* of its purpose will be precisely the satisfaction of identifiable human interests, at the level at which such interests are capable of joint satisfaction on terms of mutual understanding and good will. A morality of self-sacrifice that cannot be justified by reference to such a

harmony of interests is not something nobler than the ideals
of liberal democracy. It is either a superstitious and anti-
human reverence for needless and wasteful suffering, or a
fraudulent false front for special groups which seek to advance their own interests at the expense of those who are
gullible enough to be imposed on by their claims. I do not
suggest that Carr is the spokesman for any such interests, but
I do believe that what he has written can, and may, be used
for such purposes by those who are. And I think it is important that we should not allow the noble phrases such men will
employ to blind us to the meaning of what they propose.

It is also to be expected that those who moralize in this
sense, and for this purpose, will welcome the suggestion that
the belief of traditional "liberals" in the "supremacy of the
intellect" has been exaggerated. Perhaps in some ways it has.
But there was one use that political liberals assigned to the
"intellect" in its practical functioning, whose value it would
be difficult to exaggerate. That was the use of practical reason,
as we have understood it, to scrutinize the claims and the
performance of those in authority, and to discriminate purposes that were moral in fact, as the expression of a genuine
public interest, from those that claimed to be so but were
not. I cannot think that the procedures of "revolutionary"
governments which are supposed to have superseded "liberal
democracy" give any ground for the assumption that there
will be less need for this sort of scrutiny in the future than
there has been in the past. So long as there is need for it, the
free use of practical reason will remain essential to the validation of any moral purpose that is worthy of the name.

The Meaning of Rational Morality.   The right use of reason
in moral matters, therefore, while it has reference to the ideals
that justify conduct, is by no means confined to the enuncia-
tion of general principles or the celebration of eternal values.
The nature of the good for which men can profitably work
together is not something given in advance in intuitions of

intrinsic value, or uniquely enshrined in the deliverances of a high-powered conscience. It is something to be found out, on the basis of the best information available, about the way in which men can live well together and develop those capacities of which the moral virtues are at once the natural fruition and the spiritual reward. To say "the good is pleasure" or "the good is virtue" or "the good is self-realization" is of very little use for this purpose. Of course pleasure is good, and so is virtue, and nothing matters more, as we have seen, than the kind of self that is realized in the moral process. But a man who made his own moral improvement his chief practical aim would not be in a good position to attain it. He achieves what is best in himself in the process of working for something else. And the answer to the question, "What ought I to do?" is never merely, "be good and do what you should." The claim of the ought is a moral claim and it is to men of good will that it is addressed. But the content of the ought is as wide as all outdoors, in so far as all outdoors is a place that men can live in, and the conditions of their living well in it are an object of their common concern. There is, in consequence, no peculiar area of "moral problems," as if these were some different sort of problems than those a man regularly faces when he wants to make the best of his life and himself. And there are, in this context at least, no other spiritual values presupposed than those that justify themselves to the human spirit at the level of free cooperation in the pursuit and enjoyment of attainable goods. The attainment of such a good is a theme for moral aspiration, but it is also a problem for effective action. Good judgment as to what, under specific conditions, is possible and wise, and good will in carrying it into effect, will here be more reliable instruments of practical reason than proof of the eternal preservation, at the heart of reality, of a perfection whose bearing on the goodness of human action remains, at best, obscure.

This does not mean that we should narrow our moral aims to easily attainable and obviously "practical" ends. Quite the contrary. Nothing short of the best possible is good enough, and the difficulties in the way of its attainment are so great that it seems at times chimerical to speak of a moral community at all; we shall need all the "idealism" we can muster even to keep it in sight as a goal for conduct. An irresponsible idealism, however, which refused to square its spiritual claims with the probable consequences of action and the bearing of these consequences on the needs and capacities of human life under the conditions of human living, is not something too good for this world. It is simply not good enough. Good will is indeed a virtue, but sheer willfulness, no matter how high-minded, is not. The natural basis of morality provides not only the limitations to which our spiritual zeal must submit but also the opportunities for its effective expression. It is our business, as responsible moral agents, to understand those limits and, not less, to take advantage of those opportunities.

We have been trying in this chapter to specify the context in which and the considerations with respect to which a distinction between good and bad conduct can reasonably be made out. To make this distinction as justly as possible is precisely the task of practical reason, and conduct is reasonable to the extent to which it follows the guidance which in this matter, a right judgment of the issues of conduct and the worth of the way of living to which they commit us, can supply. To judge wisely of the worth of conduct, we have said, we need to know what we want when we *do* know what we want, when, that is, we adequately understand our own purposes and the conditions of their joint satisfaction. Among these conditions none are more central than those imposed by our concern that rules of fair dealing and equity be observed and that men enjoy not merely what they want, but what they are entitled to. When this concern operates at a distinctively moral level it finds expression in qualities of character which are valued, not only as means to further satisfactions, but as in their own right a fulfilment of the good of which human nature at its best is capable. It is in terms of the worth of persons, thus specified, that the good of freedom can be understood and the centrality of the values bound up with it established. This good, however, is a good of and for individuals who work together in a natural world; it is expressed not in moral self-admiration but in responsible action, and the worth of action is to be determined not only by the excellence of its intention but by the chances that it actually can contribute, more reliably than available alternatives, to the good it professes to seek. No man is as good as he ought to be unless, within the limits of his capacity and condition, he is doing his best, and no man is doing his best unless he has used such intelligence as he has, as well as his "conscience," to guide him in making his action appropriate to and effective in the circumstances of its performance. Bungling is not a moral virtue, and neither is fanaticism. Action that combines good judgment and good will in responsibly shared work for a sharable good comes near enough, for our purposes, to a definition of what we mean by conduct that meets the requirements of rational morality. It is not offered here as a new identification of "the good," for which moral philosophers have traditionally been searching. There are other goods besides the good of moral conduct; and if moral conduct did not aid in the attainment of these other goods, its own excellence would be without root or basis in the world. It is offered simply as an indication of what we are to look for in conduct whose claim to moral excellence can stand rational examination, and what, therefore, we are doing when we apply reason significantly in the field of morals. That there is some practical use, in these matters, in knowing what we are doing, the following chapter is designed to show.

CHAPTER II

ABSOLUTISM, RELATIVISM AND PRACTICAL REASON

The Use of "Ethical Abstractions." The question with which the "practical" reader is likely to confront the sort of theory developed in the preceding chapter is simply and bluntly, "What of it?" Even if it were granted that the argument seemed cogent on the somewhat lofty level on which it appeared to proceed, what difference would the acceptance or rejection of it make in the more concrete areas of experience in which our thinking habitually, and more comfortably, moves? I think the question is a fair one, and in this chapter I propose to answer it.

The first step toward such an answer, however, is to ask another question. How should we expect a moral theory to make a difference in practical thinking and thus in practical affairs? The answer to this question was given in the previous section. The business of theories and abstractions, as we there discovered, is not to reproduce our direct experiences or to provide a ghostly duplicate of the experienced world in some allegedly super-sensible realm beyond. Their function is to extend and deepen the range of significant experience by showing us what to look for and what is significant in situations where mere gaping and pointing would quite certainly have missed the point, and where action without a grasp of relevant and salient factors is bound to be shortsighted and confused. The alternative to an adequately articulated theory in such cases is not the hard-headed rejection of "mere theory," which simple-minded "realists" like to think they have achieved. It is the uncritical use of theories whose preconceptions are so familiar and habitually accepted that they can be assumed without the painful mental effort which, for many, is required for a first-hand examination of principles. Where such acceptance works well and suffices for the purpose at hand, no further practical question need arise. But preconceptions which make adequate sense for one purpose, under limited conditions, or in a restricted area of experience, may prove altogether inept and confusing where a different or more extended application is called for. Those who persist in employing them under such circumstances are simply not able to make essential identifications and discriminations within the field in which they are trying to work. They cannot even report fairly what they find, for their unacknowledged preconceptions commit them in advance to its systematic misdescription. They literally do not know what they are talking about, for they lack that intellectual mastery of their subject-matter which only a just, discriminating and pertinent articulation of its structure—that is, a good theory—could provide.

Popular and practical discussions of the issues of conduct have suffered much in recent years for lack of a commonly understood theory capable of performing this enlightening function. There is a great tradition of moral teaching to which appeal is made from time to time for edifying and ceremonial purposes. And there are vested interests in "spiritual" values eager to claim for this tradition, and for themselves as its spokesmen, an absolute and unassailable authority in thought and conduct. In times of stress and uncertainty, and in moments of nostalgic reminiscence, we are inspired by the affirmation that the eternal values stand unshaken and heartened to see that there is still a group of men who can speak with such righteous assurance as to their nature. For the rest such transcendent values enter but little into our effective thinking on more mundane issues. Indeed, the nature of their incidence upon such issues is a subject for endless and not very profitable dispute. But we still like to think that they are there, and we are made uncomfortable and resentful by any overt denial of their unconditional validity. Hence the "plain man" is, as a rule, an absolutist on moral issues or, at least, is likely to become one as soon as he hears that familiarly accredited maxims of conduct are being openly questioned. A full-blown moral theory emerges when this incipient absolutism is made the basis for an ethical doctrine, its primary assurances—in a purged and rarefied form, to be sure—accorded the status of self-evident truths, and its conclusions bulwarked by reference to a "reality" which is held "in the end" to guarantee the deliverances of rightly instructed moral judgment.

Such ethical absolutism has its merits, and it has done good service in preserving for our generation—though sometimes in a mummified form—the great insights of the past on which any adequate moral theory must build. But it does not operate in an atmosphere, or on a level, which has proved conducive to the intellectual mastery of our current problems. What it provides is not so much a means of thinking accurately and adequately about these problems as an assurance that, when our thinking fails, we can still confidently claim that what we antecedently wished to affirm is "somehow" true. And if the ground for this assurance is questioned, the absolutist is all too likely to interpret a criticism of his ethical theory as an attack on the foundations of public morals. The ensuing controversies have their uses, but the rational organization of experience is not among them.

In recent years the chief alternative to this sort of absolutism has been the brand of popular enlightenment which goes by the general name of "relativism." It is an odd but, for many, a persuasive amalgam of methodological positivism masquerading as intellectual honesty, of a sharp and still surprised awareness of the diversity of moral codes and customs, and of a brand of "liberalism" or "tolerance" which sums up its somewhat attenuated moral insight in the judgment that no moral judgments are morally legitimate or scientifically respectable. The excellent motives and often plausible theoretical considerations which lead good men and competent thinkers to adopt this theory will become apparent as we proceed. It will be equally apparent, however, that the attempt to apply it in the analysis and evaluation of moral behavior can only end in failure. It can be eloquently defended as a program for the generalization of scientific enlightenment and social benevolence, but it cannot be put to use without incoherence and confusion, for the categories which constitute its intellectual equipment are radically inappropriate to the subject-matter to which they are applied. We are harvesting today, in quite "practical" affairs, the fruits of that confusion.

I propose in this chapter to discuss the nature and consequences of these two ways of dealing with moral problems, as examples of the way in which an "ethical abstraction" does make a difference in the way we think and act. It is not a matter of indifference to such thought and action that those who chiefly function in our society as the spokesmen for the "higher" values have been able to express their moral enthusiasms—and ours—chiefly in the form of vaguely edifying generalities and/or angry attacks on those who differ from them with respect to the dogmatic foundations, theological or metaphysical, on which these generalizations have traditionally been based. Nor is it an inconsiderable factor in our present confusions that those earnest souls who turn to science for intellectual nourishment have so often received the stony negations of moral positivism as the best that critical thinking in this field has to offer. That we have failed so often to estimate rightly the nature of our moral responsibilities and resources in the contemporary world is a consequence, at least in part, of our failure to know where to look for pertinent enlightenment, or how to interpret what we found.

This is an intellectual failure with moral implications and practical effects. It is an illustration of how "ethical abstractions" operate when they are inadequate to their task.

The only cure for an inadequate theory is a better and more adequate one. It is, indeed, only in terms of such a theory that the inadequacies of current views and the possibilities for improvement can fruitfully be exhibited. I believe that, in the theory outlined in the preceding chapter, we have the means for making this sort of correction, not through a polemical destruction of rival doctrines, but by a use of discriminations there developed to set the relevant factors involved in the issues of conduct in such order and relationship that their factual basis and ideal or moral significance can be justly and reliably determined. The true—to repeat our quotation from Spinoza—is the norm or standard for itself, and for the false as well. If we can see, in the terms this theory provides, how and where the mistakes were made which have in the past contributed to our confusion, and what corrections are required to clarify and organize our moral purposes, then its use as an ethical abstraction will have been exhibited. This is what we should expect an adequate moral theory to do for us. The task is an ambitious one, and the reader will see for himself how incompletely its goal has here been reached. But it is, none the less, the sort of task which we must undertake if we are to justify our moral ideals in the only way in which they are capable of effective justification. We must, therefore, accept its responsibilities and do the best that we can to meet them.

The Negations of Moral Positivism. The type of ethical theory that goes by the name of "relativism" is frequently not admitted by its advocates to be an ethical theory at all. Its defenders are in many cases aggressively "plain" men who profess with pride their incapacity to understand what "philosophers" are talking about when they deal with moral issues. As men of "facts," with a proper scorn for "abstractions," and a recently acquired technique of "semantic" criticism with which to dispose of them, the relativists seem to themselves to be in a far sounder position than the philosophers. Yet they do make statements, supposed to be true and well-substantiated, about the nature and validity of moral judgments, and they do use the conclusions which these statements seem to them to justify as the basis of a distinctive type of moralizing in which they frequently and fervently indulge. Thus they employ their supposed discovery that no moral judgment is *really* anything more than the expression of the bias of the person who utters it as a basis for the claim that no moralist has a "right" to impose his own biases on others, and vigorously condemn those who violate this maxim of their moral doctrine. We are therefore entitled, I think, to conclude that they have at least a theory about the nature of moral conduct and the validity of moral judgment which has (or is supposed to have) an important bearing on the further direction of such conduct in so far as it is enlightened and instructed by the acceptance of the theory. This, for our purposes, is what it means to have an ethical theory. We do not ask them to accept the term, but we can fairly ask them to understand the implications of what, as both analysts and lay preachers, they are doing, and to justify its commitments.

An ethical relativist is, in general, a theorist who holds that so-called "moral judgments" are nothing more than verbal expressions of the attitude, preference or bias of those who utter them. Any claim they make—or appear to make—to any further cogency or warrant than that which they possess as such expressions is incapable of any sort of "objective" substantiation, and ought to be rejected. The preference expressed may be that of the individual merely, or of "the group." In the latter case it acquires an added social sanction but no added moral validity—unless moral validity is "positivistically" identified with social sanction, and thus deprived of any independent significance. *For* the individual or the group in question such a preference possesses the urgency which inheres in any *de facto* drive or interest. *For* the objective observer the occurrence of such preferences is a fact to be observed and, where possible, correlated with other observable phenomena. *For* individuals or groups with opposing preferences, it is a factor to be taken account of in cases of actual or potential conflict. So much is sheer, positive matter of fact. From that point on the relativist is likely to become somewhat incoherent, though by no means inarticulate, and to moralize in a manner not easy to reconcile with the primary negations on which his theory is based. It is these negations, however, which are distinctive of his theory. What are the grounds for them, and to what, if consistently accepted, would they commit us?

The two chief considerations which underlie and are supposed to justify the theory of ethical relativism are those derived from "positivism" as a theory of scientific method and from the observation of the diversity and incompatibility of existing moral codes. Since the chief evidence on this latter point is borrowed from the broad area now marked out as the province of sociology, it will be convenient to speak of "sociological relativism" here, as a source of the ethical relativism we are to examine. We shall examine these two sorts of consideration in some detail.

The term "positivism" has a two-fold significance. It stands in the first place, for a theory of scientific method which proclaims the emancipation of the sciences from metaphysics and their right to develop such categories of explanation and description as their own subject-matter and methods of inquiry demand, without regard for the requirements of the "ultimate reality" of the metaphysicians. Whatever may be true of such reality in its absolute or final nature, the facts which a physicist or a biologist will properly take account of are those which can be tested by his own well-authenti-

ated methods of inquiry, and whatever is not thus testable
outside the province of his scientific concern. In this phase
f its development, positivism, as we saw in Part I, is a posi-
ve contribution to a right understanding of the nature and
alidity of scientific inquiry. Its anti-metaphysical emphasis is
quite natural protest against the confusion (still persisting
a some quarters), which ensues when independent inquiry
ato the structure of the physical world is hampered by pre-
onceptions about what "the real" must be and what, in con-
:quence, the physical world must "really" be, even though
cannot, by scientific investigation, be found out to be any-
aing of the sort. The elimination of this sort of consideration
:om the evaluation of scientific truth has, on the whole, con-
ributed to the progress of the sciences.

There is, however, another side to the positivist doctrine
·hich it is less easy to accept. The methods of inquiry which
ave proved their worth in physics and biology tend to take
a, in the minds of their more devoted users, a canonical
uthority comparable to that which metaphysics possessed in
a earlier age. Just as nothing was once "intelligible" which
id not conform to the canons of a teleological metaphysics,
) today nothing is held to make sense in advanced circles
·hich violates a rule of verifiability which "the scientist"
·llows in his experimental research. Applied to the study of
aoral behavior, this means that nothing is to be accredited
s "objective" which cannot be identified by criteria guaran-
:ed as "scientific" through their use in the sciences which
ave become in our time, as were the doctrines of Aristotle
a the thirteenth century, the model for intellectually respect-
ble thinking about the world.

It must be apparent, I think, that positivism in this latter
se bears about the same relationship to the liberating insights
f its scientific ancestors, as do the Daughters of the American
Revolution to their revolutionary progenitors. Each has in-
eed an honorable lineage and a great inheritance, but each

seems at times to suffer from spiritual pride and intellec
tual inflexibility. One good custom can indeed corrupt a
world, and one set of ideas, however excellent and liberating
in its original use, can become a barrier to further inquiry
when it is set up as the measure to which all further truth
however different the context in which it is acquired, must
approximate. It might have been the case that moral inquiry
could proceed successfully with categories borrowed from
physics or biology. It was certainly an experiment worth trying, and all honor is due to the experimenters of the eighteenth century who tried it. And if there are experimenters
prepared to try it again, they are entitled to a respectful
hearing. What is not legitimate, however, is the attempt of
the positivists to settle the question *in advance*, by stipulating
that only what would be pertinent to physics or biology can
count as "objective" in morals. It is as easy to prove in this
way that what is not verifiable by "positive" methods has no
"objective" status, as it was to prove that what did not satisfy metaphysical criteria for Real Being or Existence was,
on the terms set by such criteria, infected with non-Being.
The method is essentially the same in each case. In neither
is the result achieved by its use a contribution to our understanding of the specific subject-matter of moral inquiry.

The transition from methodological positivism to ethical
relativism is easily made. Men judge that some actions are
"right," others "wrong"; that some proposed ends are "good,"
and others "bad." If such judgments are to claim "objective"
validity, the positivist argues, a method must be specified for
determining which are true and which false. Apart from such
specification, judgments of this kind will have to be denied
any theoretical sense, though they can be understood as
expressing the attitudes or emotions of those who utter them.
Not just *any* method, however, will do. The sciences have
their own methods of testing statements that purport to supply information concerning matters of fact. The operations

hat are performed in verifying such statements are *real*, not merely verbal, operations, and the experiences in which they eventuate are objective, authentic, real. If the statements which express moral judgments are to stand critical inspection, it should be possible to verify them in a similar way. If no such verification is available we must—if we properly value "intellectual honesty"—refuse to accept such statements, or "pseudo-statements," as more than emotively expressive but intellectually groundless utterances of "ultimately" arbitrary preferences.

In fact, it is alleged, no such verification *is* available. Scientific method reports what is, not what ought to be; it can discover social pressures, but not moral obligations; it verifies statements about the desired, and the most efficient means for securing it, not about the desirable in any further sense. Hence, if we accept with intellectual honesty the results of critical analysis, we shall be obliged to admit that, as far as reputable examination can determine, so-called obligations are just social pressures, and ostensible value judgments the verbal front for arbitrary bias and demands. Thus the positivist reaches the conclusions of relativism by the route of scientific method, and with much analytic hand-washing to demonstrate the intellectual purity of his procedure. They are not, as we shall see, satisfactory or usable conclusions from the standpoint of practical reason, but if they are, as P. W. Bridgman, for example, asserts, the conclusions forced upon us when, "clear-eyed and self-conscious," we commit ourselves to the "unrestricted use of the brain," what right-thinking man could deny them?

Since we want to be clear-eyed and self-conscious, and to use our brains, if not without restriction, at least to the best intellectual advantage, we shall have to inquire quite carefully whether intellectual honesty and accurate thinking do in fact commit us to anything of the sort. Fortunately, Bridgman has himself provided us with a most instructive instance of the application of just such a method to the analysis of our social and moral problems.[1] The method recommended is "operational." We are to understand the meaning of a concept by analyzing what we do in the situation in which the concept is to be applied. So far so good. But an important distinction must be made between verbal and non-verbal operations. Those of the physicist are proper and scientifically reputable, because they make connection with objective experience and thus eventuate in a non-verbal world. Those of the moralist on the other hand, according to Bridgman, are verbal throughout, not merely in the sense that words and other symbols are employed, but in the derogatory sense that nothing non-verbal, nothing objective and empirical, can be discovered to which they correspond.

The allegedly self-evident truths of the Declaration of Independence, for instance, can be substantiated only by operations of the latter kind. They presuppose a philosophy, and this philosophy "deals with reactions of human beings to their own or others' verbalizing, and therefore is a philosophy which contains no guarantee of objective significance, but is applicable only to those human beings who know how to accept the unanalyzables of the philosophy."[2]

Bridgman does not deny the legitimacy of verbal operations in their place, but he holds, with the "ordinary person," that "he should discard a verbalism once he has been shown that it has no ultimate connection with something non-verbal,"[3] and this carries him a long way. He finds that the whole structure of traditional philosophy and religion is permeated by the "intellectual cancer" of verbalism and is inclined to scrap them both and start again from the beginning. The traditional categories of morals fare but little better. He

[1] P. W. Bridgman, *The Intelligent Individual and Society, passim.*
[2] *Ibid.,* p. 126.
[3] *Ibid.,* p. 88.
[4] *Ibid.,* p. 90.

decides that the notion of duty involves the feeling that we are under some sort of "compulsion." But what, operationally, can this compulsion be? What does it mean (operationally) to say that there are purposes of God or Society that we must serve? "Are the operations that give meaning to 'purpose' any more than verbal? What do I do when deciding that there is this compulsion in any concrete situation? If it is my own purposes that I am considering, then I know that the structure of the world is such that I am compelled to act in certain ways in order to attain my end. But, apart from this, what possible sort of *compulsion* can there be, other than the sort of compulsion that forces me to keep my head above water if I do not wish to drown, etc.? The universe does not blow up if I do not do my duty." [5] And much more in the same vein. It is not surprising to find him concluding, "I think that the vividness of one's apprehension of duty is dimmed by analysis," [6] and adding, "As far as the individual goes I do not see how any one who has thought the thing through can ever again accept the idea of 'duty' with its conventional implications as having pertinence to his own conduct, or as being anything more than a tool for understanding the actions of his fellows." [7] No more do I, if the individual has thought the matter through in Professor Bridgman's fashion and made use of his peculiar method of analysis. It is similarly concluded that "the concept of 'freedom' corresponds to nothing 'objective.'" [8] And so on.

All this, if true, is so important that we ought to scrutinize carefully the method by which it is established. How do we decide which operations are "ultimately" non-verbal and which have an "objective" operational basis? It will not do, as we saw in a preceding chapter, to dismiss as merely "verbal"

[5] *Ibid.*, pp. 113–114, italics in text.
[6] *Ibid.*, p. 115.
[7] *Ibid.*, p. 115.
[8] *Ibid.*, p. 117.

all operations which involve a use of words to designate objects that cannot be referred to by us by pointing, kicking
and the like. Nor is it sufficient to say that those operations
are merely verbal which refer to nothing objective, for the
point at issue is to decide what in this sense *is* "objective," and
it has been alleged that the idea of freedom, for instance,
corresponds to nothing objective, because the operations
which substantiate statements concerning it are merely verbal. The physicist's "operations" are accredited as properly
non-verbal, but they are of little use for the discovery of a
"compulsion" which is supposed to be non-physical in character. Bridgman thinks we will get light on the meaning of
morality if each of us asks consistently, "What would happen
if I violated this or that moral prescription?" [9] But this evidently is not enough. What will happen or will not happen
cannot settle any question of moral obligation unless we are
able further to determine what bearing such happening has
on what ought to be done and what I, in particular, ought
to do about it. The moral relevance of predictable occurrences is not settled by listing the occurrences and observing,
for example, that the universe does not blow up if I do not do
my duty. If this is all that a non-verbal operational method
can establish, then we may well agree that neither duty nor
freedom can "ultimately" be analyzed into a "non-verbal"
meaning.

Bridgman has, however, a more ultimate method of analysis still, and much of what he has to say about morals is
colored by its findings. The final facts to which "the unrestricted use of the brain" leads us are not those concerning
the behavior of objects in our material environment, but
those of our immediate conscious experience. "The concept
of consciousness is perhaps the ultimate unanalyzable, and
when we attempt to express the possibility of getting away

[9] *Ibid.*, p. 138.

from it we attempt the impossible." [10] Why one should want to get away from it may not at first be obvious, but our author's account soon makes it so. For inside consciousness each individual is alone with his own experiences. "The supreme *social* limitation is perhaps the isolation of the individual. Never have I escaped by a hair's breadth the fate that has decreed that I shall lead my life alone in my own 'consciousness.'" [11] You cannot get into my consciousness, for what gets in, if I am aware of you at all, will not be you but only my awareness of you, and I shall be as lonely as before. The artificial pathos which surrounds this last result of an inept epistemological theory is not in itself particularly moving. But it combines with ethical egoism in a curious way. From the standpoint now reached we can go on to say that "only things in consciousness matter," and this means, for each of us, that only the things in *his* consciousness matter or can meaningfully be objects of his concern. And the only things thus *in* his consciousness are himself and his own experiences. For it is, Bridgman tells us, "almost tautological" to say that "my own conscious experience is all that I am ever aware of." [12] It seems to follow that no individual is ever reasonably concerned "ultimately" about anything but himself and his own experiences. What will happen after I am dead, for example, cannot matter to me, and what happens while I am alive can matter only in so far as it affects my own states of consciousness which are the only final objects of my concern. Thus "it is only present states of mind that can count," [13] and for each of us the only present states of mind are his own. The ego-centric position of the individual is thus made the basis for a decision as to what is im-

---

[10] *Ibid.*, p. 142.
[11] *Ibid.*, p. 142. Italics in text.
[12] *Ibid.*, p. 152.
[13] *Ibid.*, p. 245.

portant, and we are reduced to an ethics of solipsism which is, not unnaturally, a solipsistic ethics.

We have here gone further than the more usual type of operational analysis would take us, and fared worse. Whatever the requisite categories for the analysis of moral behavior may be, they cannot possibly be those which apply only to a situation in which I am alone in my own consciousness and nothing but my own experiences matter. On the contrary it is only so far as I am not alone, am concerned with the experiences of others as well as with my own, and am trying *not* to adopt an "ego-centric position" in relation to others that I have any moral problems at all or can make sense of moral behavior. It is no wonder that Bridgman, trying to "think through" moral ideas on such a basis, should have made so little of them. The dubious point is rather that he has made so much. In outlining the requirements of the society which appears good to him, he lays great and proper stress on the primary importance of the individual. But the considerations offered in support of this preference are lamentably weak. "Since the central position of the individual has been one of our cardinal points, society will have to be such that each individual in it is accorded his own central position. The primary demand must therefore be that society be so constructed that it serves the individual, not that the individual serve society." [14] This, on the author's premises, is a very curious conclusion. If the central position of the individual is the one Bridgman's analysis accorded him—that of being, by inexorable fate, alone in his own consciousness and concerned with nothing else—then nothing society can possibly do can "accord" it to him or take it away. Indeed, on this level, no "society" exists, except as a construct from private states of consciousness. If the "central" position demanded, however, is that which an individual *as a social being* is accorded by a society of which he is a member, it is very

[14] *Ibid.*, p. 283.

difficult to understand apart from some reference to the "freedom" which was discarded as a mere verbalism some way back in the analysis. As it stands, I think, we must set down Bridgman's liking for it as a benevolent inconsistency which does more credit to his moral sentiments than to his operational procedure.

But why should an eminent scientist and acute critic have supposed that the way to "think through" our moral situation is to reduce its concepts to the performance of operations under conditions in which no moral problem arises, and no sense could be made of it if it did? It seems a curiously arbitrary and unfruitful assumption. Whatever an analysis in which I am alone with, or in, my own consciousness may apply to, it does not apply to the situation in which I am *not* alone at all, and in which it is the fact that I am not alone that gives rise to moral problems. Nor will the operational determination of what will happen if I act in one way or another settle any moral question, until the relevance of such action, with its consequences, to ends judged good and standards acknowledged as just has been determined. How could it? If an inquiry that carries us beyond the prediction of happenings to the estimation of their moral relevance and worth is "verbal," then *of course* the "operations" of moral inquiry are "verbal" and it needed no extended analysis to demonstrate that fact. Whether they are merely verbal, however, or whether the claim they make can be justified in the process —or "operation," if you prefer—of practical reason in the organization of interests for ideal ends and the adjustment of claims in the cooperative work of a moral community, is another matter altogether. That is the justification that would be appropriate to them, and it is in its terms, surely, that their sense and validity should be judged. *Of course* all moral claims are "arbitrary," if that means that they express a human concern, would have no meaning apart from it, and can have no cogency for those who from native or professional incapacity are unable to share in it. But, as we have seen, it is the need to order these concerns themselves that directs us toward a standard or comprehensive good in whose terms some claims are rational, or on the side of reason, as contributing to the attainment of this good while others are arbitrary as in conflict with it. Apart from the acknowledgment of such a good, the moral distinction between what is arbitrary and what is not, simply fails to make sense. In proclaiming this fact once more, the positivists have no doubt performed a service, but in identifying the resulting "nonsense" with the analytically purified content of rational morality they have been mistaken as only intelligent men can be mistaken when they systematically refuse to pay attention to what they are talking about because they are antecedently committed to the doctrine that it *must* be something else.

The basic objection to be brought against such "analysis" is that it is intellectually irresponsible—it sets up criteria of significance and validity without proper regard for the nature of the subject-matter to be analyzed and the aims of the activity whose results it pretends to evaluate. This is a type of "rationalism," as we saw—a kind of petrified rationalism which proclaims its unqualified devotion to canons of rationality—or "empirical procedure," or scientific method—as peculiarly reputable and authoritative for right thinking men, independent of the capacity of such procedures to articulate and make sense of the issues to the analysis of which they are applied. For those whose understanding of numbers was limited to the so-called "rationals," the discovery of numbers not *thus* "rational," we are told, was an upsetting experience. The "irrationality," however, proved to be not in the numbers that failed to fit the predetermined pattern but in the minds of those who were unprepared to see them for what they were. It is not too much to hope that the "mystic" character Bridgman finds in the value men attach to respect for duty will similarly cease to be mystifying when it is seen for what it is, the good of responsible action in a community of men concerned about a common good and working together to achieve it.

Are moral judgments "verifiable," or are they not? This seems to be a plain question, and we can give it a plain, though not a simple, answer. If "verification" means proof or disproof by reference to agreement or disagreement with observed matters of fact, the answer is that they cannot. For such reference, while essential, is simply not sufficient to determine the moral worth of actions. We need also to know the relevance of facts thus ascertained to ideals whose cognitive authority is not that of an *is* but of what ought to be, as this concerns, not scientific curiosity, but a rightly directed will or purpose. If "scientific method" is identified with the procedures by which matters of fact are ascertained, then practical reason is not reducible to scientific method, though it depends at every turn on information which the sciences supply. And if nothing is to be called "objective" which cannot be substantiated by "scientific method" in this sense, then the conclusions of practical reason about, for example, the worth of freedom are not "objective," for they are not thus substantiated. So far we agree with the positivist. We further agree in holding that what you get if you try to measure the correctness of moral judgments by these standards is nonsense.

All this, however, says very little, and says it in a misleading way. For while moral judgments cannot be verified, like the predictions of physics, they can be substantiated, and it is extremely important that they should be. And while the method of their substantiation is not "scientific," it is and ought to be rational, in a sense in which what is reasonably grounded is distinguished from that which is biased, arbitrary and unsound. And while, again, the conclusions thus reached are not "objective" as physically measurable, they are publicly justifiable within a community whose common concerns they bring to reasonable expression and adjudication, and it is essential to their validity that they should be so. Thus understood, they are not nonsense, and neither are they *merely* verbal manipulations of uncriticizable biases. It is precisely their function to criticize such biases reasonably, and in their fulfilment of this function they further the work of reason in conduct by the only methods that would be sensible or appropriate to this purpose. The outcome of this process when stated will, of course, be words, and so "verbal." But it will be words used to express and to produce moral enlightenment on issues of profound human importance. It is hard to see how even a clear-eyed physicist can get on without some measure of such enlightenment.

There is, of course, no possible objection to the experimental physicist abstracting from moral considerations in his own research. They do not seem pertinent to the physical behavior of the objects with which he is professionally concerned. How far he can abstract from them *as a person* is a personal problem which is his own affair. But when he attempts to abstract from them, when it is the sense of moral concepts and the validity of moral judgments that he proposes to analyze, the result is moral positivism—a systematic disparagement of moral ideas for which no plausible translation into "scientific" terminology can be found, plus irresponsible moralizing on the basis of "facts" whose moral relevance has not been ascertained. We shall have to examine a good deal of this kind of moralizing in later sections of this book. It has had its share in the moral confusion of our time, and it is our business, if we can, to dissipate that confusion.

Sociological Relativity and Ethical Relativism.   A second main source of contemporary relativism is the observed relativity of existing moral codes to the habits, interests and conditions of life of the societies in which they are accepted. Since these codes are different and conflicting, and since each *seems* valid to those who adopt it, the conclusion has been drawn that each is "right" from its own standpoint and none "really" right in any further or more absolute sense. It is further held that a recognition of this relativity of standards will make for tolerance, since it makes plain the natural and social basis of all morality and deprives the advocates of any particular doctrine of authority over the preferences and beliefs of others. This view has enjoyed wide popularity in recent years, and will merit critical examination. The problem is precisely one of determining the moral relevance of "facts" whose factual status is not in question, but whose significance for the evaluation of conduct has been variously interpreted. Social scientists of various persuasions have in recent years brought in additional evidence of what, in a general way, we already knew—that the actual standards by which men in different groups and societies distinguish right and wrong are different, that what is considered obligatory in one group may be regarded as indifferent or even be condemned in another, and hence that terms of moral praise and blame, in their actual usage, at least, have no unequivocal meaning apart from the folkways and group-approvals of the societies in which they are employed. Hence it has become fashionable, as a mark of critical caution, to enclose terms like "good" and "bad" in quotation marks, in order to indicate that it is what is *called* good in a particular social group that is under discussion. No commitment is so far made as to whether what is thus *called* good is "really" so or not, in any further or normative sense, and where the purpose is simply to describe the actual diversity of social standards, no such commitment is required. There may be dispute concerning the extent of this diversity and the reality of "underlying" uniformities that show that "human nature" after all is really the same everywhere, and at all times. So far as this is a factual question and not a dispute about the inner "realities" of a common humanity which underlies observable behavior but is only dimly discernible in it, the answer to it is to be sought in anthropological investigation. And while the evidence is still incomplete, there is enough of it at hand to indicate that the diversity in moral standards is so great that no man could act rightly according to any specific moral code that has ever gained wide acceptance without offending against some of the precepts of other codes which are felt to be no less binding for those who accept them. Hence in this sense what is right for one is wrong for the other, and there is no common standard, acknowledged by both, in terms of which this difference can be adjudicated.

Such is the factual situation, what is its moral relevance? How should the knowledge that existing criteria of good conduct are thus relative and variable affect our judgments of what in fact *is* right and wrong, when we are not merely describing and cataloguing such judgments but making them for ourselves? So long as we remain on the descriptive level no such problem arises, and a scientist who is content to leave the matter there has no need to be concerned about it. But when—and if—he goes on to moralize about it, we have a right to demand that he do so responsibly and with some regard for the requirements of practical reason. Suppose our moral standards are thus relative: what of it? The usual answer of the relativist has been that this discovery ought to make us more tolerant of the opinions and actions of those who differ from us. They are "right" by their standards, as we are by ours, and where such standards differ, what right have we to claim that *our* "good" is the right one and theirs simply wrong? Thus E. Westermarck, whose compendious researches into the variety of moral codes have added considerably to our information on this matter, does not hesitate to pass from social variety to ethical relativity, and to claim a considerable moral advantage for the position thus reached. "Could it be brought home to people that there is no absolute standard in morality, they would perhaps be on the one hand more tolerant and on the other hand more critical in their judgments. Emotions depend on cognitions and are apt to vary according as the cognitions vary; hence a theory which leads to an examination of the psychological and historical origin of people's moral opinions should be more useful than a theory which postulates moral truths enunciated by self-evident intuitions that are unchangeable." [15]

This may prove to be a sound observation, but, if so, it is as a judgment about the way in which people *ought* to feel, not as a description of the way in which they uniformly or even usually *do* feel under such conditions. No one has stressed the relativity of moral ideas to particular races and cultures more than have the Nazi prophets of Aryan superiority. The Germans are a peculiar people, and their morality a peculiar morality, which lesser breeds will "naturally" fail to appreciate. There is no absolute standard of morality for all people, but one code for the masters and another for those they are peculiarly fitted to rule. It is by no means the case that stress on this doctrine has led in fact to tolerance of the views of others or to greater self-criticism in Nazi circles. Nor is there any reason in the fact of a diversity of standards why it should. The knowledge of one's moral peculiarity may serve as well to feed national pride as to induce humility and self-criticism. The descriptive scientist can catalogue such differences, but it is not within his province to judge that one response is reasonable, proper and appropriate and the other not, unless this judgment is made by reference to some standard which he accepts as right and proper, not only for himself, but for those who disagree with him as well, since it is here of the rightness of their response that he is judging.

There is, then, no reason whatever for accepting the "fact" of social relativity as a justification for tolerance or a ground for condemning the most intolerant and arbitrary of moral judgments until the moral relevance of this fact has been

[15] E. Westermarck, *Ethical Relativity*, p. 59.

made out by reference to a standard of enlightenment, fairness and benevolence to which such judgment ought to conform, a standard to whose authority the would-be moralist commits himself in judging and which he applies to the conduct of those who differ from him as well. Short of this he would simply be recording the autobiographical observation that the discovery of social relativity did in fact affect him in this particular way. This would be of interest, no doubt, to his friends and associates, but it could have no more bearing on the justification of tolerance than the quite different effect a similar doctrine has had on Hitler's Dr. Rosenberg. Whatever the ground for moral tolerance may be, it cannot possibly be a refusal to take the responsibility for making moral judgments, for it is only in terms of such moral judgment that tolerance—or anything else—can be justified. It would be well if those who claim to make such judgments with the authority of "science," but refuse to take the responsibility for them which only an adequate moral theory could warrant, would understand this.

The Good of Tolerance. Yet there clearly is a moral insight which the relativists have been trying to express through their insistence on the diversity of accepted codes of conduct and the importance of taking account of such diversities when we are tempted to impose our own opinions on those who differ from us in their valuations. The trouble is that they have been prevented by their theory as to the nature and validation of moral judgment from stating this insight clearly and defensibly. The straightforward questions to ask, surely, would be: What *good* is tolerance? What is there in the end sought which justifies the measures recommended to attain it? And how is the existing diversity of moral standards relevant to the attainment of this good? These, however, are questions of practical reason, of the organization of interests and purposes around ideal ends rightly judged to be worth achieving, and of the obligations reasonable men will acknowledge as co-workers for this achievement. But the relativist is committed in advance to a refusal to deal with moral issues on a moral basis. He dare not make moral judgments except by disguising them as statements of existing matters of fact. Since the whole point in adducing the variety of codes and customs as a ground for tolerance is to provide a *reason* for one course of conduct and a basis for the condemnation of its intolerant opposite, the result of this procedure can only be confusion.

The results of this confusion are of practical importance. They reflect upon the very genuine good the relativists are interested in defending the dubiety which attaches to their mistaken ethical theory, and thus weaken a case that should be made as strong as possible. For there are and will continue to be men interested in discrediting the worth of tolerance as a human ideal who will know how to use such weakness and confusion among "liberals" in a very effective way. And indeed, if no better sense is to be made of the good of tolerance than the relativists have made, its opponents have a strong case against it. Thus Professor Pegis, in criticizing "a dangerous and indeed tragic conception of tolerant objectivity" [16] which he believes to be widespread among modern educators, identifies such "tolerance" with the view that, for example, political ideas cannot be rationally defended and are finally nothing more than preferences and pleasing prejudices. This he takes to be a kind of skepticism about the foundations of rational morality, and he quite plausibly maintains that such "tolerance" is not a secure basis for the case for human freedom. "The very thing which we wish to maintain, liberty, is the very thing which intellectual skepticism can be guaranteed to ruin. It is surely a poor liberty to allow men the right to be the victims of their own inability to know true principles with finality and to act in their light with deliber-

[16] Anton C. Pegis, "In Search of Man," in *Science, Philsophy and Religion*, Vol. I, p. 352.

ateness; and it is a poor democracy which must build upon such an inability." [17]

In fact, of course, the case for tolerance, and for secular freedom in education, has a very different foundation than this. The good of tolerance is a spiritual good. We respect the right of others to make up their own minds and their right to express freely convictions thus arrived at, not because we think these opinions are as likely to be right as our own, or that there is no genuine basis for discriminating right from wrong with respect to them, but because we think it important that the convictions should be their own, and freely arrived at, and that they should accept the responsibility for them. The freedom of the mind that is worth having is not an indefinite suspension of judgment, on the ground that there is so much disagreement on these matters that no opinion can really claim any rational cogency. It is a freedom for each man to make up his own mind, in the light of the best he knows, and with a decent respect for the right of others to come to a similar decision for themselves. It is grounded not on what we cannot make up our minds about but on what we can—the preeminent worth of human personality and of the freedom of inquiry and of speech which are its essential preconditions.

The liberty which, in this country, guarantees to every man the right to make up his mind on basic issues, the issues of religion among them, is not at all a poor sort of liberty, nor the democracy that for one hundred and fifty years has maintained it a poor sort of democracy. Yet both liberty and democracy are constantly open to attack, both from avowed enemies and professed friends, who burn with self-righteous indignation at the political toleration of beliefs which contravene their own, and seek to substitute indoctrination for inquiry and responsible judgment as the ideal to which our educational system should approximate. It is not indifference or skepticism but reasonably grounded conviction of the

[17] *Ibid.*, p. 355.

worth of freedom of thought and of conscience which leads us to reject such claims. It is to be hoped that those who have recently been so active in denouncing the false ideal of tolerance which they view with alarm, will be equally zealous in defending the true ideal of tolerance, with its political and educational implications, against the attacks, both secular and ecclesiastical, which are being and will be made upon it.[18]

There is another difficulty which impedes an adequate understanding of the worth of tolerance, and here, too, the doctrines of ethical relativism have played their part in the ensuing confusion. The problem here is not as to the worth of tolerance, but about its application. Each man may properly judge for himself, it is said, but what "right" has he to claim that what seems right to him is right for others as well? After all, they are right from their point of view, as he is from his own, and to claim that his opinion has any validity as against theirs, or is more than an expression of his own bias, preference or point of view is to be "intolerant," and hence unjust. Thus we seem to return to the position of ethical relativism, and this time in the name of equity and fair dealing. For to assume that one's own moral judgment was better than that of others, or had a prior right to general acceptance, would be to claim a special privilege for oneself and to violate the principle of equality to which all sound morality is committed.

This sort of view had a considerable vogue among college students a few years ago. To all questions about right and wrong they would pose the counter question, "Who's to judge?" with the conviction that for any one party to a dispute to claim that privilege, so long as there were others who disagreed with him, was so obviously dogmatic, arbitrary and unfair as to merit no further consideration. *By what right* does any man set himself up in the privileged role

---

[18] I have discussed this issue more fully in an article, "Sectarian Absolutes and Faith in Democracy," in *The Humanist*, October, 1941.

of judge of the actions of others? Here again "tolerance" emerges as a refusal to make moral judgments on the high moral ground that those who do so are committing the morally blameworthy sin of intolerance, or of dogmatism, in a situation in which their *right* to judge cannot be defended.

It is obvious, I think, that those who assume this position are not themselves refusing to make moral judgments, but are making them in a peculiarly confused and whimsical way. For, once more, it is only by reference to a standard of what is right, just and appropriate that a distinction can sensibly be made between moral judgments *rightly* condemned as "arbitrary," and "dogmatic," and those which are just and reasonable. If all are condemned alike by the very fact of being moral judgments there is no sense left in the condemnation nor, for that matter, in the good of tolerance to which this disintegrating liberalism remains incongruously addicted. The reasonable answer to the query, "Who's to judge?" is surely this: in a community of free men each must judge for himself, but he must judge responsibly, that is to say, *not* arbitrarily or merely in his own behalf, but with respect for principles which hold for all alike. It is only for and in respect to such judgment that the distinction between what is arbitrary and what is just and reasonable makes sense, or has any sort of moral significance. The individual who judges thus—and only so is he a moral agent—is not claiming a privilege which he refuses to accord to others as well. He is accepting a responsibility and exercising a moral function that he cannot honestly avoid, though he may through carelessness, confusion, or mere indifference disavow it. This disavowal, however, where and in so far as it occurs, is not to be dignified as scientific objectivity or moral enlightenment. It is an evidence of failure to see in what the nature of tolerance consists, or to make sense of its claims and commitments.

The failure to see this point is, of course, the outcome of

the prior failure to distinguish the standpoint of practical reason from that of mere bias, preference or special interest. It would indeed be arbitrary and unjust to claim that one's own "point of view," considered simply as a personal bias or idiosyncrasy, was entitled to greater public credence or authority than that of anyone else. But the only standpoint from which this verdict of "injustice" makes sense is that of a rational moral judgment which itself purports to be more than a bias, preference or idiosyncrasy, and to be valid not only for the individual who makes it, but for all men who can rightly understand and estimate the merits of the case. In making such a judgment a responsible moral agent *ought* to take full account of existing diversities of code, custom and point of view, and to respect the *right* of others to follow their own bent and genius on all cases in which such diversity is compatible with the essential conditions under which a community of shared purpose and mutual respect can actually exist. To impose any narrower conditions and thus *arbitrarily* to exclude from the moral community those who in fact have the capacity and the will to share in it is illiberal, intolerant and morally wrong. Nor should any of us be over-eager in condemning the motives of others when he is not in a position to understand them. The commandment "judge not" is, in its context, one of the most excellent of moral judgments. But once more, the decision that such liberality is morally excellent makes sense only with respect to a standard which the judger acknowledges as valid not only for himself, but for all who share in the community whose moral structure that standard defines. To try to moralize in the name of such a standard—to speak of "rights," and "justice" and a "tolerance" which right and justice enjoin—without accepting its commitments is not to be peculiarly mentally and morally enlightened. It is to be mentally and morally confused and irresponsible on fundamental issues.

There is, then, no honest way for the moralist, however

"relativistic" his preconceptions, to escape the responsibility which moral judgment entails. We can raise the dictates of conscience to the level of the best we know. We can use the fact of sociological relativity as a valid reminder that our own initial moral preferences are likely to be parochial and one-sided and that they need the closest rational scrutiny we can give them. But when all proper self-examination has been made, we must judge of the right as we see it, and we cannot see it with any other eyes than our own or judge it with any minds but the minds we have. To have a mind of one's own is part of the peculiarity and the dignity of being human, and we shall gain nothing humanly worth having by denying it.

This, too, is a matter of some practical significance. Resolute action depends for most men upon a genuine conviction of the rightness of what is being done. In the years before the war it had come to seem that in sober truth "the best lack all conviction" and that resolute action was, in consequence, to be expected only of men stupid, fanatical or unscrupulous enough to be undisturbed by the ultimate groundlessness of their practical commitments. The confusions of ethical relativism were by no means exclusively responsible for this situation, but they played their part in it. For, being committed in advance to the view that moral discriminations are arbitrary or illegitimate or meaningless, those who accept this view tend to avoid them as long as possible and to make them furtively or apologetically when they can no longer be avoided. Those who denied the authority of moral judgment naturally suffered from the pangs of conscience when they were called upon to act with moral resolution. They hesitated to pronounce an adverse judgment even on the enemies of human freedom lest they seem "intolerant" in making up their minds on a moral issue, though it was the issue of protecting the freedom they honored against the forces that sought explicitly to destroy it. The moral debility of much recent "liberalism" is traceable, in part at least, to this sort of uneasy conscience, and we have seen enough of its fruits to know it for what it is.

The reasonable alternative to this sort of relativism is not the dogmatism and fanaticism which practicing liberals have always, and rightly, opposed. It is the standpoint of practical reason on which the great liberals of the past took their stand, and its basic tenet is that of the dignity of man as a "rational creature" and of his capacity and his right to judge reasonably and to act with resolution on the primary issues of conduct. Its essential elements were never better conjoined than in the words of Lincoln's second inaugural address: "With malice toward none, with charity for all, with firmness in the right as God gives us to see the right." We shall have need of that firmness in the future if we are to preserve and broaden the tradition of tolerance which is our liberal heritage.

The Limits and Conditions of Tolerance. To readers familiar with the traditional "isms" of ethical theory—and forgetful of some of the conclusions of the preceding chapter—the position we have now reached may seem indistinguishable from the "ethical absolutism" which was criticized at the outset. We have agreed with the critics of relativism in their insistence on the rational cogency of enlightened moral judgment. And we have argued, further, that the recognition of such cogency involves the acknowledgment of moral or spiritual values of a distinctive sort. This latter conclusion is sometimes expressed by saying that freedom, justice and good will have an absolute value which "transcends" the biases, interests and desires of the individuals who acknowledge them. Now it is by no means always easy to determine what the term "absolute" in this usage is intended to mean. If it means only the denial of the sort of relativism we have discussed and the affirmation of the human and rational validity of properly validated moral judgments, then we must, of course, agree that in *this* sense there are absolute moral values.

To do so is only to reaffirm the moral theory already developed and we shall be more than ready to make common cause with those, whether they call themselves "absolutists" or not, who subscribe to it. Unfortunately, however, the theory that moral values are absolute and "transcendent," and that they require an absolute "foundation," usually means something quite different from this, and something in its own way quite as misleading as the "relativism" it attacks. And since this theory, too, has consequences that illustrate the impact of "ethical abstractions" on practical judgment, it will be worth our while to consider it further and to state our own position with respect to it.

There are, if our previous theory is a valid one, at least two important senses in which moral values are not absolute and transcendent, and in which the judgments that affirms them do not require substantiation by reference to a transcendent or "absolute" reality. First, the good of tolerance, for example, is a good that is realized under social conditions in a natural world. And what is good is not "tolerance" as an ideal merely, but its realization under the conditions which make its attainment possible. These conditions alter with time and circumstance, and what is a valid ideal for the achievement of tolerance at one time and place may be quite invalid and misleading at another. Apart from the possibility and conditions of its attainment we simply do not know what, in any specific instance, the realizable good of tolerance *means*, or to what its acceptance would commit us. To will the end independently of the means and context is to will an incompletely specified end; it is a peculiarly lofty and pretentious way of not knowing what one is doing, and of enjoying the emotional satisfactions of an "idealistic" attitude without accepting its intellectual and moral responsibilities. For a good that is "absolute" in the sense of being worthy of our acceptance independent of the conditions of its realization, practical reason, as we have understood it, gives no warrant.

Second, the spiritual good which is realized in a moral community is an immanent and not a transcendent good. The dignity of man as a moral agent belongs to him in virtue of what, in such a community, he is or is capable of becoming, not in virtue of some ulterior guarantee that moral values correspond to or are supported by some metaphysically or theologically guaranteed "reality." Such a further guarantee may be forthcoming, and it will inspire the faith and hope of many. But to maintain that it is required to justify the value we acknowledge in human nature at the level of responsible personality is to deny that this value, where it can be realized under natural and social conditions, is of worth enough *on its own account* to justify the measures required for its preservation. And to seek to exclude from the moral community those who are unable to accept such metaphysical or theological commitments as the basis for their moral conduct is to narrow arbitrarily the limits within which tolerance, good will and human freedom are effectively attainable. It is thus an offense against both the theory and the practice of practical reason.

Each of these points as stated is in the nature of an "ethical abstraction." But they have a bearing on current political and educational controversy which is unmistakable.

Consider, first, the practical meaning of the recognition that tolerance, as a moral achievement, has natural limits and social conditions. How and under what conditions is a moral community actually developed and maintained? It rests, inescapably, on a basis of common interest and shared concern in a society in which men are so related that they can, on the whole, respect their fellow citizens and have some confidence that they are worth respecting. Men who are agreed on the essential needs and purposes of their society can afford to differ on issues which, with respect to the public interest thus constituted, can safely be regarded as private. They cannot, however, afford to extend their tolerance to those activities which undermine the essentials of common under-standing and cooperative action. Moral tolerance is a spiritual good, but it is not a disembodied one. Those who claim its perquisites without accepting its responsibilities, and the responsibilities of the community in which it must be actual-ized if it is to be actual at all, are no friends of freedom or of tolerance, however loudly and frequently they may invoke their names. A newspaper that uses its immunity from govern-ment control to spread irresponsible gossip and political dis-sension, or an individual who claims the right to his own opinion without acknowledging the duty to make that opin-ion as just and informed as is humanly possible is as morally irresponsible as any other social parasite and by no means the least harmful among them. To condone this sort of irre-sponsibility, or, what is worse, the active hostility to free institutions which, in recent years, has demanded its "right" to operate freely in our midst for the destruction of free-dom, is to exhibit not supernormal liberality and virtue but subnormal social intelligence. It is another instance of that empty-headed "idealism" which combines devotion to the "highest" spiritual goods with ignorance of or hostility to the means of their realization. When and in so far as men are members of a moral community and act as its members, they have a right to share in the goods of that community. Except as actual or potential sharers in its goods and responsibilities, they have and can have no "rights" at all, and there is no sense, though among the gullible there may be some ad-vantage, in claiming them.

This point has some relevance, I think, to the familiar query as to whether or not we have a "right" to be "intoler-ant" of intolerance. The question is supposed to imply that there is something paradoxical, if not contradictory, in the position of those who believe in the good of tolerance and yet refuse to "tolerate" those who work for its overthrow. And it is further supposed that those who extend their "tolerance" indiscriminately to the enemies of human freedom are somehow on a higher level spiritually—though they are perhaps less "practical"—than those who do not. Nothing could illustrate more clearly the moral confusion of our time. To glorify "tolerance" independently of the conditions under which it is effectively attainable is not to be exceptionally benevolent but peculiarly irresponsible. Those who condone, and therefore "tolerate" the interests which, if successful, will destroy the conditions under which a free community can exist, are not the friends of the good they profess to honor. It is, of course, of great importance that we inform ourselves properly as to the nature of these hostile interests and do not mistakenly interpret as an attack on the foundations of society what is only an honest and perhaps enlightening proposal for its reconstruction. And it is above all important that we try to include in this community all who are capable of sharing in its responsibilities. Which is only to say that here, as elsewhere, reliable information and good sense are essential adjuncts to sound moral judgment. But where it is plain that the intent *is* hostile, and that interests which enjoy the protection of our tolerance propose if they are successful to deny others the "rights" they now claim for themselves, there is no question as to the moral or practical issue involved. Rights imply duties, and those who are not prepared to act as members of a moral community have no just claim to enjoy its privileges. To take, under such conditions, the measures needed for our protection is not to be "intolerant" in a situation in which the exercise of tolerance would be appropriate, but to be resolute in the preservation of the conditions within which tolerance can be effectively achieved.

The conditions for a moral community must not, of course, be restricted to the limits of any particular state, class or race. Ideally this community should include all men everywhere, in so far as they are capable of sharing in common interests and working together for a common good. Actually, it comes, for most purposes, considerably short of that. We do not know each other well enough, or care enough for the things we have in common, to find in the community of all mankind more than a very tenuous basis for cooperative action. As the relativists point out, there are many matters on which we differ at present, without any reliable basis for a common understanding in sight. Where such differences exist, the part of wisdom is, on non-essential issues, to get in each other's way as little as possible, to remove sources of friction where we can, and to develop such common interests as are discoverable to the point where a better understanding may, in their terms, become a practicable achievement. Those who work for the development of such a community of understanding and action are the friends, also, of human freedom, for they are bringing into existence the state of affairs in which men can be free. But there is little use in talking and acting as though such a community existed independently of the actualization of such conditions, and there may be great harm in it, if it leads us to neglect our responsibility for *making* actual the good we profess to seek.

This, too, would seem to have its point in relation to our current problems. Mr. Henry Luce, in *The American Century*, has written vigorously of the "international moral order" we must build if our own democracy is to work successfully. The ideal he offers is an inspiring one. But what it ought to inspire is some very careful and patient thinking about the necessary foundations of mutual respect and good will for such an order, which, even in an American century, must include a number of other nations on something like equal terms. And what it emphatically ought not to inspire is the sort of moralizing, too common in this country in the past, which manifests its idealism by lecturing other nations on their failure to act as if such an order were already in existence. In a world in which some securer basis for international order had been established, the break-up of the British Empire might reasonably be demanded as a contribution to ideals of freedom which could then receive a more comprehensive actualization. In a world in which no such order exists, and in which America's contribution to it consists chiefly in self-righteous isolation broken at intervals by a belated intervention in wars which, with our help, might well have been prevented, such a demand is ill-timed and unwarranted. If and when we are prepared to accept the responsibilities which the maintenance of an international order would entail, we shall be in a position to ask a comparable contribution of others. Until that time, our international moralizing is likely to be an unhappy combination of sentimentality and cynicism, as we alternately exhort the rest of the world to achieve a righteousness which, without our help, cannot be made a basis for political action and are outraged to find that our admonitions are unheeded and the world, for all our urgings, remains as wicked as before. This is idealism of a sort, but it is the idealism of adolescence which has yet to achieve the stature, and the stamina, of moral responsibility.

The recognition of the natural and social conditions under which our moral judgments have a legitimate application is, therefore, not an alien intrusion upon an "ideal" morality which would be essentially complete without it. It is an essential element in the determination of the ideals that have moral validity because they represent an attainable good and direct our efforts reasonably toward its attainment. A devotion to ideals which fails to acknowledge this responsibility or lacks the intelligence to meet it is not something too good for this world. It is, from the standpoint of practical reason, simply not good enough. And the same, precisely, is to be said for the ethical absolutism in which such "idealism" finds

The Foundations of Democracy. The second type of absolutism previously mentioned—that which insists that our its theoretical justification.

moral values require some theologically or metaphysically guaranteed foundation in an underlying reality—has also found expression in recent political discussion. In recent years we have reflected much, and rightly, on the spiritual foundations of our democracy. It has been widely felt that the defense of political democracy is incomplete unless it finds its completion in a recognition and authentication of the spiritual values that make it, as a form of government, worth defending. To reaffirm the "reality" of these spiritual values, and to defend it against skeptics and unbelievers would seem, therefore, to be an essential part of the larger patriotic task in which we are now engaged, and there are many able and well-intentioned men prepared to undertake it. This reaffirmation, however, is associated in many minds with the acceptance of theological doctrines that not all honest and earnest defenders of democracy share. And there is a very real danger that in this instance a welcome support for our political loyalty will be confused with the imposition of beliefs about which, in a democracy, men have a right to differ and that insistence on these doctrines as essential to the defense of democracy will impede instead of furthering our common cause. We need, in consequence, to see quite clearly what the spiritual goods are that make democracy worth defending and what sort of guarantee or substantiation of their validity is required or would be appropriate.

I take it that when we speak of our form of government as democratic we mean at least the following: (1) Responsibility of government officials and agents to the popular will as expressed at free and regular elections, and their removability by legal methods when the electorate so determines. This is a matter of degree, of course, and does not apply in the same way to all government officials, but it does express the primary reference of governmental responsibility and the efficacy of popular control, when the people wish to exercise it. (2) Definite restrictions on state interference with

those things which it is generally felt that a man ought to decide and act on for himself. These will not be the same at all
times. Freedom of business enterprise may rank at one period
among the sanctities, and later be limited with impunity.
Freedom of thought and of religion are at present held to be
such essentials, and rightly so. But where the essentials are,
there will political liberty be also, if the conditions of democratic government are to prevail. (3) Political equality before
the law and at the ballot box is a minimum requirement. How
far such equality can exist and be effective without a considerable measure of social and economic equality as well is
a further question, into which we need not here enter. Professor Tawney has said, it seems to me, what is of primary
importance concerning it.[19] This summary statement is not
intended as a definition but rather as an approximate identification of the subject-matter of our present discussion. This
is the sort of government we value as democratic. To what
extent does it possess or require a moral foundation?

It possesses, at least, a moral justification, in so far as the
goods the enjoyment of which it makes possible are moral
goods and are actually worth having under the conditions it
establishes. Political liberty, or guaranteed immunity from
governmental interference, is not the same thing as the personal freedom which is morally of primary value. Neither
is the legal right of sharing in the direction of political affairs
a guarantee that those who have this right will exercise it
responsibly and with due regard for the common good. Nor,
finally, is equality before the law a sufficient basis for the
community of interest and understanding in which a common
good can genuinely and effectively exist. But while none of
these political conditions is *sufficient* for the good of freedom
in a moral community they all contribute to it in their fashion
and without them it cannot securely exist. Thus we rightly
place a high value upon them as the political framework for

[19] R. H. Tawney, *Equality*, *passim*.

a moral order and we link democracy with freedom in the sense in which, as we have seen, freedom is not a political convenience but a spiritual necessity. Democracy can be justified on other grounds, of course, those of economic self-interest, political caution and the like, and there is on these grounds something to be said for it. But those who insist on the moral implications of democracy are right, I think, in feeling that such accounts are not adequate to the good we look for in democracy and would sacrifice both economic self-interest and political caution to secure. For no account is adequate that leaves out the moral good of freedom and the fact that what men are and can become is as much our concern as what can be got out of them. It is its capacity to make secure the conditions in which this freedom can develop that political democracy makes sense and it is in this context that we can best make sense of our allegiance to it.

Is *this* "the spiritual basis of democracy," which our spiritual leaders have in mind when they tell us, for example, that "The spread of totalitarianism can be checked only by a democracy which has recovered that living belief in the objective moral and spiritual order which is its deepest source of strength"? [20] It is so only in part. The "objective moral and spiritual order" which we have been talking about is one that exists in the world of space-and-time events whenever and in so far as the political organization of democratic government achieves the level of fair dealing, tolerance and common understanding which makes it, to that extent, a moral community. This order is objective just in so far as it is actualized in the behavior of men whose conduct at this point lives up to their professions, and it is guaranteed or sustained by the conditions which make such cooperation effectively possible. It is the spiritual fulfilment under natural conditions of an order in nature and human nature which good will and good judgment, working with the materials of social cooperation, can sometimes, and under fortunate conditions, make actual. To believe in it is to believe that it is both possible of attainment and worth attaining and to commit oneself to a course of action required to bring it into being or to preserve it when it already exists.

The order recently demanded by the seven Princeton professors, however, is of a somewhat different sort. It is an order transcending history in which a "cosmic spiritual power," "the source of meaning and life" is recognized as personal. It is, in other words, a supernatural order and the doctrines enunciated concerning it are those of an attenuated but still vigorous theology. If the acceptance of doctrines about the personal character of the cosmic spiritual power which is the ultimate source of meaning and life are required for the checking of totalitarianism, there will be many opponents of totalitarianism, notably among our Russian and Chinese Allies, who must be held unqualified for their work. And there will also be many genuinely religious men and some theologians who, not believing that cosmic power is personal in character, will fail to meet the requirement. It seems a pity, at a time when their help was so much needed, and has so far proved so useful.

What, in fact, has the belief in a supernatural cosmic order to do with our reasonable commitment to political democracy? There is no doubt that such a belief has often helped men to think more highly of others, and of themselves, as sharers in a more than human origin and destiny and has thus inspired a worthy devotion to the ideal of human freedom. The correlation is by no means one-one, for many believers in supernatural religion have shown no sort of friendship to political democracy, while among the heroes of democracy there are those whose acceptance of a supernatural spiritual order is notoriously difficult to trace. Where the connection does exist, however, it is a very valuable one, and we can join wholeheartedly with the Princeton professors in hoping that its contribution to the defense of democracy will be a large one.

Two reservations must, however, be made explicit. The linkage of respect for the spiritual values which are to be found in the moral community which political liberty helps to create, with belief in a supernatural cosmic order that transcends history, may reasonably be held to be desirable if, on other grounds, this belief can maintain itself in the light of the best knowledge we have. But such a linkage cannot properly be held to be essential to respect for and loyalty to these values. It is the worth of free men in themselves, or in their own persons, not in their genealogy, whether natural or supernatural, that we are asked on the moral level to acknowledge. The man who cannot find the freedom and happiness of his fellow citizens, as well as his own, worth defending without a supernatural validation of their claim to respect must take a very low view of human nature. And if he cannot love his neighbor whom he has seen, without such extrinsic sanction for it, how shall he love a cosmic spiritual power which he has not seen? Since the supernatural guarantee is in any case so variously interpreted, and since it remains inaccessible to many good and generous men, it is indeed fortunate that adherence to the theology of neither Princeton, Moscow nor Rome is required for effective action in defense of democracy, nor for loyalty to the goods of the human spirit in which it is justified and made complete.

The second reservation has to do with the relation between the theological content of the beliefs recommended and the natural and social conditions under which the beliefs are propagated. It is not difficult to maintain, in theological or metaphysical debate, that a belief in a supernatural foundation for the highest human values is better nourishment for the democratic virtues than are mere secularism and agnosticism. Since Spain under Franco encourages and insists upon the inculcation of such beliefs, while Republican Spain did not, it might be concluded by the unwary that the Spain of Franco provides a better environment for freedom, enlightenment, and human brotherhood than did the Spain which made the first and bravest stand against Fascism in the war we so tardily entered. I shall not, I think, be guilty of overstatement in saying that this conclusion would be a mistake. Men do not gather grapes from thorns, figs from thistles, or spiritual freedom from "values" whose "sanction" is anything less or other than the good that proves itself in their work together, freely, generously and in the open. When such freedom is not to be found, the authoritarian indoctrination of approved theological principles will not serve to take its place. Where it does exist, democracy has a soil in which to grow and it is in its growth under natural conditions rather than in its supernatural affiliations that the proximate substantiation for our faith in it is to be sought.

The Finality of Moral Judgment. The argument of this chapter has to a considerable extent been negative in form but it is constructive in intent. We have found two opposing half-truths competing for supremacy in the field of moral theory. And we have further found that two half-truths, thus projected into competing philosophical "isms" do not add up to a whole truth, but to a distracted and divided state of mind—the state of mind in which the "practical man" so often finds himself when he tries to think clearly about moral problems. He goes to the absolutist for inspiration and to the relativist for facts. He finds the facts stated in such a way that their pertinence to the inspiration is obscured or denied. And he finds the inspiration so sentimentalized or so hedged about by ulterior and controversial doctrinal commitments that its application to existing problems cannot be securely established. In neither case is he able to discriminate what is valid and constructive from what, as the opposing theory rightly claims, is one-sided and indefensible. This is the outcome, not at all of a lack of moral theory, but of the acceptance of theories too broad at some points and too narrow at others to delineate accurately the structure of the practical situations with which he has to deal.

We have sought to maintain against these theories the standpoint of practical reason and to show what, in its terms, can be made of the issues with which they deal. At some points our theory will seem dangerously relativistic to the defenders of the absolute, at others dubiously, or even "mystically," idealistic to the positivists. It was not developed, however, to satisfy either sect, or to achieve a higher unity in which the best features of both are somehow synthetically preserved. Its aim is rather to make clear certain salient features of a situation about which each, in its own fashion, has been confused, and to indicate their relevance to problems which today demand the most enlightened judgment we can bring to them. That judgment must be clear, adequate and philosophically responsible if it is to meet our present needs. It is the purpose of the moral theory here presented to help to make it so.

We have argued, in substance, for the autonomy and finality, in their proper context, of the judgments of practical reason against both those who would deny them any autonomous significance and those who hold them insufficient for their purpose apart from some ulterior or "absolute" support. And since the argument has been long and devious, a reaffirmation, in summary form, of the position maintained may be in order.

The judgments of practical reason are fallible. We may err through ignorance or prejudice or confusion. But the only way in which we can reliably find out whether or not we have been mistaken is by the further use of practical reason itself. There is no right substitute for a wrong moral judgment except a better one, even if this be the judgment that, in the circumstances, no conclusion on the subject-matter of a previous judgment can properly be made. If we appeal to *facts* to correct our prejudices, we confront the fact that no fact is conclusive in moral issues until its moral relevance— its bearing on what ought to be and what we ought to do about it—has been ascertained. If theological doctrines and supernatural sanctions are invoked to humble our pride in mere human reason, we can accept their verdict only when they have made out their claim to the credence and respect which distinguishes proper humility toward that which rightly claims our allegiance from the fear and superstition which are its unworthy substitutes. It is true, of course, that men are often biased and irrational but if they had not some capacity to understand and criticize themselves they would not know that this was so, and unless they were at times concerned to correct their biases and be fair to each other they would not count the fact of bias as an impediment to the good they seek. It is on this knowledge and this concern that we base the work of practical reason. No one is asked to be more reasonable than he can be, but if he is as reasonable as he can be he will be more reasonable than, without this concern and criticism, he often is, and while his judgment may be wrong at its best, it is much less likely to be wrong at its best than at the confused and careless level at which it more usually functions.

Nor does the work of practical reason ask anything of men which runs counter to what, on other grounds, we know them to be capable of achieving. A mystery has been made of moral freedom, but there is nothing mysterious about it, when it is understood, as it should be, not as the capacity of a self to be unaffected by his natural and social environment, but as the capacity to act and produce effects in it, on the level at which what a man does is the expression and fulfilment of his moral capacities. Human nature, apart from the concern which makes for righteousness and its development into enlightened moral good will, shows no reliable tendency toward virtue and may be considered merely as a battleground for frustrations and aggressions, or for fixations and sublimations, according to the interest and perceptive powers of the observer. But human nature apart from this concern and its development is not all that human beings are and have been, and far less than they are capable of becoming. And it is on human beings and their capacities for good rather than on the dicta of specialists in pathology or animal behavior that we base our hopes. The good that is to be attained in human development is a social achievement in a natural world, and is subject to all the ills and vicissitudes to which both nature and society subject us. There is no guarantee of its success on which we can depend, apart from the opportunities that this world provides and our own ability to make the most of them. What will happen if we do make the most of them is yet to be seen. But we shall not see unless we make the experiment and there is more to be gained from life when we are doing our best in it than on any poorer level of effort and understanding.

There is, in sum, no other or better way of doing the work that practical reason attempts to do than through its own more effective exercise. And we cannot get on without it. Hence its claims are final, not as infallible, or metaphysically sanctioned, but as humanly essential to the attainment of the good that men seek before they understand the world or themselves but seek more wisely and generously when they know what they want to do, and what they are capable of becoming. This is the only ultimacy or finality we should wish to claim for it.

CHAPTER I

CRITERIA FOR INTELLIGENT SOCIAL ACTION

We have heard so frequently in recent times, and on such good authority, that the "rational man" is a myth, at least so far as observable and predictable social behavior is concerned, that it is not surprising that we have come to believe it. The result is that we tend to look with scorn or suspicion on analyses of current social problems in which considerations of "justice" and "right reason" are treated as having any genuine relevance to the "realities" of economic and political affairs. It is this sort of suspicion, the grounds for it, and the consequences that it has had and is likely to have in social action, with which we shall, in this section, be proximately concerned.

That men as members of groups and subject to group pressures and imperatives do not regularly behave in harmony with that rationality which was once supposed to be their defining character as human is, of course, no news. The reformers and planners of a better world have long recognized the traits in human nature, in both its social and unsocial aspects, which impede cooperative effort for the attainment of ends judged to be desirable and, with an appropriate expenditure of good sense and good will, attainable, and have condemned these traits. What is relatively novel, at least in our own history, is the claim that the condemnation, and the programs for a more reasonable social order which accompanied it, are themselves based on a misconception. Assuming that men are reasonable by nature, if not in actual performance, the reformers looked in the direction of enlightened good will and a freer use of cooperative intelligence for the righting of existing wrongs and the building of a better world. It is this assumption that has now been challenged, and in the name of the social sciences which owe their own free and socially supported development to the fairly widespread belief in its validity. From the appeal to "reason" and to "nature" by men who were prepared and even eager to submit the principles of their action to the judgment of mankind, to the control of "the masses" by the manipulation of ideologies which it would be nonsense to regard as true or rationally grounded and in the interest of ends recognized as arbitrary though, for political purposes, not avowed as such, is a considerable transition, and a disturbing one. It can, of course, be considerably exaggerated. The eighteenth century reformers were hardly as impersonally "rational" as they thought they were, as twentieth century historians have been pleased to point out. And our contemporary realists are less drastic in their divorce of power politics from moral principle than some of their more trenchant utterances have led their followers to believe. A fortunate deviation into practical good sense at some points mitigates the cynicism of their official position. The fact remains, however, that while in the eighteenth century the climate of enlightened opinion was one in which it seemed natural and appropriate for men to look for good reasons for what they proposed to do and to manifest a decent respect for the opinions of mankind in doing it, today, the learned terminology into which their descendants translate their social purposes and plans is one which renders the appeal to reason anomalous and suspect, and puts a premium instead on a lack of scruple about "principles" which, always common enough among "practical" men, has now become a mark of intellectual emancipation as well. And, as the one set of preconceptions tends to make those who respect it try to seem better than they are but also, in fortunate cases, to live up to their professions and assume the responsibility for their ideals, so the other, in its praiseworthy zeal to be done with sham and hypocrisy, has at times developed in its users a trained incapacity to see moral issues and acknowledge the "reality" of moral claims that are of primary importance. How this change has come about, and where it places us today, when we try to the best of our ability to decide what we, and our country, ought to do in the situations that now confront us, we must now attempt to understand.

First of all, however, and in pursuance of a policy now sufficiently established, we shall try to determine what we are looking for when we talk about reason in social action, how reason works, and could reasonably be expected to work, when applied to the task of developing sound policies, organizing means for their efficient execution, and meeting the responsibilities which a shared concern for a common good can reasonably lay upon us. This is a very special sort of activity, and the demands it makes on human intelligence and good will are very great. To meet those demands rationally is not, of course, simply to apply to our problems methods of inquiry and preconceptions as to what is real and relevant carried over from other contexts and activities in the assurance that, having served the purposes of reason there, they must here be accepted as canons of rational procedure. Human affairs may easily be shown to be as irrational as you please, if one insists on treating them in this fashion, but the result is evidence less of the incurable irrationality of the subject-matter dealt with than of that of the analyst who insists upon so arbitrary a procedure. Rationality, as we have seen, is not a property of selected ideas in their own nature, but of the manner of their use in the organization of experience in the light of the best knowledge and widest understanding relevant to the specific purposes with respect to which enlightenment is sought. What this use will prove to be when the activity in question is that of the determination of social

policy is a matter for contextual investigation, not for pronouncements based on a use of "reason" the applicability of
which to this context has by no means been made out.

This conclusion is a dividend from our previous inquiry,
and might here be used without further comment, were it
not for the unhappy confusion which the failure to recognize
it has imported into the social sciences—a confusion which
threatens to block the path of our inquiry at the very outset.
We shall have enough to do to make out the measure of
reason that can be discerned in the management of human
affairs. It is, therefore, important that we do not waste our
time in looking for a kind of "reason" which should not
have been supposed to be there but the non-appearance of
which is none the less the source of current claims that the
hope of rendering morals reasonable is a chimerical one.

Thus in the essay on "Morals" in the *Encyclopaedia of the
Social Sciences*, Horace Kallen has a very short way of
dealing with systems of ethics and their protagonists. These
systems consist, he tells us, of "logical elaborations of special
items selected from the aggregate of morals. This aggregate
has no unity and no structure. It is a jungle of secondary and
tertiary growths of habits, most of which an engineering comprehension of the dynamics of human and cultural survival
would strip away and all of which it would rearrange. Unhappily moralists are persons who take an engineering view of
other men's ways of life. To a man his ways are his life: he
clings to and endeavors to preserve them regardless of cost.
A 'scientific, rationalistic morality' is thus a contradiction in
terms. Morals in their roots, their growth and their sanctions
are as irrational as the lives they inform; they are to be
rationalized but hardly rendered reasonable." [1] Consider what
this appears to say. An engineering comprehension would
strip away most of the beliefs and customs from which systems of ethics derive their initial content. But would an

[1] *Encyclopaedia of the Social Sciences*, Vol. X, p. 649.

engineering comprehension be at all wise or judicious in so doing? Apparently not, for Mr. Kallen assures us that men cling to their ways of life and refuse to be denuded in this fashion. And who could blame them? The "moralists" (who are supposed to be the proponents of reason here) are alleged to take an engineering view of other men's lives. If so, they are, it seems to me, not only being quite unintelligent but immoral as well, since an engineering view, if that means anything specific, is the kind of view men properly take when they are planning the manipulation of material forces for ulterior purposes. To take a merely "engineering view" *of men*, when it is their moral purposes and claims that are under consideration, is a plain violation of the categorical imperative. No more mistaken idea has in recent years been fathered by spokesmen for the social sciences—who have fathered many—than this notion that the "engineering view" is the "scientific," hence "rational" way of understanding the relations of men to each other. It does Mr. Kallen credit to see that a "scientific rational morality" thus defined would be a contradiction in terms, but it is not, as he supposes, because men are unreasonable that this is the case, but because the proposed analysis is flagrantly so.

But while men properly cling to their ways of life in defiance of any such "reason" as this, they also sometimes change them, and one of the factors in bringing about this change, sometimes and under some conditions, is an alteration in their beliefs as to what, under the circumstances in which they act, is possible, or desirable, or just. They have been known to cease the practice of hanging women accused of witchcraft because they came to regard such charges as incredible. They have become more humane in their treatment of the insane through their knowledge of the nature of this malady. And they have at times shown a generous concern for the welfare of men in remote countries because the area of their sympathetic understanding had been widened and they had grown to appreciate the needs and aspirations of such men as they had not appreciated them before. On the other hand, they have sometimes been led into destructive and self-defeating action through their acceptance of beliefs which in fact were false and which could not have won wide and continued acceptance if open and honest inquiry concerning them had been possible. Moreover, they have themselves been the authors of the situation in which inquiry could no longer function, partly through carelessness and stupidity, partly, also, through their fear that knowledge, publicly disseminated, would set a limit to arbitrary and imperative desires they no longer had the will to criticize or control. There is a clearly recognizable difference, I think, between the first sort of instance here and the second. In the one case social purpose is enlightened by knowledge and sustained by the good will that can turn its relevant disclosures into guides for cooperative action. In the other, the willful narrowing of the area within which men can know what they are doing is the means by which interests which could not stand inspection maintain themselves in power. I propose to describe the first sort of procedure as that of reason in operation in the context of social action. There is no doubt that it does sometimes operate and that it could function more widely and reliably if we better understood its use and its value. The "rational man" in whose behavior it is manifest is not a myth, though he is, both in and out of academic circles, more of a rarity than he need or ought to be. And, similarly, when I speak of conduct, with respect to social action, as "irrational," I shall mean not that it resists the misguided zeal of social engineers to rob it of its moral content, but that it resists the efforts of good sense and good will to raise it to the level of practical and moral enlightenment. There is, again, no doubt that such conduct occurs and that its results are socially important.

Those who ask us to resign ourselves to the inevitable "irrationality" of human behavior—so far at least as the "masses" are concerned—have usually not meant to act as apologists for this latter kind of conduct or to discourage constructive effort for its correction. Their contribution to the cult of unreason has been of a more devious sort. For, by identifying as "rational" a way of thinking and acting that would be inappropriate to intelligent human behavior, and as "irrational" all that fails to satisfy the terms of this identification, they have left their disciples, and themselves, without the means of discriminating, within the area of the "irrational" thus determined, those modes of thought and behavior which are effectively reasonable from those that are not. It is this failure of discrimination, which is a failure of philosophical intelligence, that in its turn opens the way for every sort of obscurantism in the actual conduct of affairs. For how, except by the best use of reason available, are we to judge between the competing "irrationals" that clamor for support and offer their own arbitrariness and internal incoherence as evidence that they are in tune with the deeper "realities" of a world which, as the wise men have told us, is profoundly "irrational" as well? Reason in its socially effective operation has enough to contend with from its avowed and genuine enemies. It is well, therefore, that it should not be subject to attack from its would-be friends, the intellectuals, who are so misguided by their preconceptions as to what "reason" in practice must be that they do not know it when they see it.

What, then, are the requirements for the right use of reason in the context of social action, and how, in terms of them, can we discriminate sound policies from their opposites? I suggest that the following are the chief characteristics of the socially effective use of reason.

(1) The primary and indispensable basis for reason in any field of operation, and not least in this one, is reliable information concerning relevant matters of fact. Such information is harder to get when human hopes and preferences are

at issue than in the more "objective" fields of physical science, but it is by no means less important. We shall not know what we are doing or what we want in the conduct of affairs until we know what materials we have to work with and what will probably happen if one course of action or another is pursued. With respect to any proposal for action, therefore, the first question to ask is what assertions it makes concerning matters of fact and what reason there is to suppose that these assertions are true. And since the kind of information required is, for the most part, not to be picked up haphazard, or revealed to the uninstructed mind without inquiry, it is imperative, for the social operation of reason, that organized, responsible inquiry be accorded every opportunity for effective investigation and for the free dissemination of its findings. Those forces, whatever they be and under whatever name they function, which seek to circumscribe the gathering and dissemination of reliable information obtained by methods of tested inquiry and pertinent to issues of public concern are the enemies of human reason in its social operation. This is true whether the issue be birth control, or the management of public affairs, or the probable future of the capitalist system. There may be "deeper" needs in human nature than the need for "abstract" or "cold" or "merely theoretical" truth but, hot or cold, reliable information is an indispensable requirement for action that is not to be frustrated and blind, and the organizations through which it is acquired and disseminated are the organs of human reason in its social operation.

(2) I have spoken of *relevant* information, however, and it is clear enough that what the information is relevant *to* is decision with respect to a plan of action with a future reference. We need, therefore, to know not only what is happening or has happened but what probably will happen or would happen if proposed alterations of one sort or another were initiated. This reference to the desirable and to the possible

is inescapable, and those who would limit reason to the report of what was in the beginning, is now, and, unless we intervene to alter conditions, ever shall be, have simply condemned themselves—and us, if we follow them—to ineffectiveness in the field of social action. For reason in this context is planning intelligence. Even those who prefer to see the future as much like the present as possible devise ways and means of impeding the activities of the "social planners" who—misguidedly in their opinion—seek to alter the "natural" course of events. They assume that such action to impede changes that would otherwise occur is possible and desirable and will accomplish a result which, apart from this intervention, would not have been brought about. They are thus, in their own fashion, social planners also, though they would not like the name, nor is it greatly honored by the association.

While, therefore, we shall expect reason, in this usage, to have the utmost respect for relevant facts—for reliable information about the conditions, possibilities and probable results of action—we shall not expect it to have any comparable respect for "realities," when "realities" are simply selected present conditions canonized as the "natural" order of events and projected into the indefinite future as the norm to which all proposals for action must—if they are "realistic"—conform. For one of the facts which we shall find to be of great relevance to enlightened conduct is the fact that men, by taking thought, have sometimes altered the "realities" which were supposed to set an inflexible limit to their aspirations in ways rightly judged to be feasible and desirable. Reliable information about what exists can lead as reasonably to action to alter what exists as to pious veneration of things as they now happen to be. A factually oriented reason can be, and in this usage ought to be, a planning and reconstructive reason. The actual is here judged in the light of the possible, though it is on the basis of a rational interpretation of the actual that we must judge what is possible and what is not.

(3) Reason in social action is *practical* reason, that is, reason addressed to the attainment of ends accepted as good, by means considered proper for their realization. In consequence, to eliminate considerations of better and worse, with respect to ends as well as means, from the sphere of social inquiry is to exclude from rational consideration the very factors in the situation that most urgently require it. And since an end accepted as good and used as a guide in the selection of means and control of conduct designed to secure its attainment is an ideal, it follows that all "practical" men, in so far as they are intelligently practical, are "idealists." There is nothing esoteric about this. To be practical—if it means anything that makes sense—means to direct one's conduct toward an attainable good. Unless the end is good and attainable by the means proposed, the man who seeks that end by that means is, in that situation, a very impractical man. But to act in the light and for the sake of an as yet unactualized good is to act for the sake of an ideal. An impractical ideal is simply not a good enough ideal, not one that can function rationally in the situation to which it is applied. And a "practical" man who scorns "ideals," who does not understand what he is trying to get, or what it is worth is, as Socrates remarked, a man who does not know what he is doing. It is an unhappy factor in our present confusion that the term "ideal" should have come to be applied so frequently only to unattainable or irrelevant and therefore unintelligent ideals, and "practical" only to shortsighted and therefore unintelligent conduct. It is another instance of the pass to which our failure to come to terms with the nature and use of practical reason has brought us.

(4) Practical reason, in its social application, is cooperative reason. The ends proposed for action are to be attained through the work of many men who must work together and who, over long periods, and especially in times of crisis, will work well and reliably only if they believe in the worth

and meaning of what they are called on to do. A plan of action that will enlist their effort and sustain their loyalty is more than a blue print for action by self-selected planners—though it should be that also, as has been seen. It is a common cause and it tends under pressure to provide the material for a crusade. And it is important that men believe in it. Mr. Spykman has perhaps overstated the case in the following passage, but his testimony, since it comes from one of the more "realistic" analysts of social behavior, is impressive. "For the preservation of the national morale, it is absolutely imperative that the nation maintain an unshaken faith in the justice of its cause. In man's idealism lies both his strength and weakness as a fighter. He can be made to fight for his personal and social survival, but it is easier to inspire him with a call to service for abstract values than with a promise of material gain. In terms of interests men divide; only in terms of the defense of a moral order can they unite." [2] We shall later find that this statement has a disquieting context in Mr. Spykman's own thinking, but as it stands it seems clear enough. Its pertinence to our present interest is also clear. Men act rationally in practice when they act effectively for the attainment of ends rightly judged to be good. And they will so act, reliably and on the whole, only when the ends proposed for action are those that they *can* believe in and care greatly about. The sort of ideal that can thus unite them in a shared social purpose is not just a scientific hypothesis, and is quite certainly not a merely factual report of an existing state of affairs. Those, therefore, who limit the work of reason to fact-finding, or social "engineering" will naturally conclude that such ideals—or "ideologies," to use the currently accepted term—are irrational in their content, "social myths" which move the masses but are quite beyond the limits of rational substantiation. Our conclusion so far, however, has been that ideas qualify as rational—in the sense

[2] N. Spykman, *America's Strategy in World Politics*, pp. 37-38.

in which rationality is ascertainable and humanly valuable—not in their origin or conformity to conventional standards of intelligibility, but in their capacity to inform, clarify and direct to a reasonable conclusion the activities in which they function. An ideology—or widely accepted social ideal—so functions when the goals toward which it directs men's efforts are goods which will adequately satisfy the interests in whose behalf they are pursued, and when the pursuit of them is enlightened by, and can stand the light of, the best knowledge relevant to both ends and means that is available. In their defense of ideals of human freedom and equality, liberals have frequently appealed to values nowhere adequately or unequivocally manifest in the existing state of affairs. They have sometimes been carried away by their enthusiasms and deceived by false hopes. But in believing that the ideal—or "ideology," or "social myth"—of political democracy is an ideal worth defending, because the community in which its principles could adequately be actualized stands as a real possibility for the cooperative social action of men who value freedom and will make sacrifices to maintain it, they were not deceived. Their ideal corresponded—and corresponds—to a good that is attainable—not melodramatically and all at once to be sure, but in good measure and under specific conditions —in the course of the activity in which men who can assume responsibility and place public interest ahead of private advantage work together in a political community. And when we are being reasonable about the determination of social policy, it is hard to see what other or better correspondence was to be expected or would be in point.

(5) Cooperative social action requires morale and morale requires at least the semblance of public or political morality. It is a truism, which Pareto and his satellites have recently rediscovered, that in any organized society there will be rulers, or managers, or an élite, on the one hand and those who take orders and perform the more ordinary work of

the community on the other. The rulers will always rule, for if they didn't someone else would, and then they would be the rulers. And the subordination of the subordinates is an inescapable, even a tautological consequence, so long as anyone gives orders and anyone else obeys them. And since the rulers have "power"—the power to give orders and enforce them—which the underlings lack, and use that power to accomplish their purposes and satisfy their desires, it might appear that we are faced with the "realities" of a political situation to which ideals of shared purpose and cooperative action are hardly appropriate.

There is, however, a further discrimination to be made. Men often submit willingly, even cheerfully, to authority when they believe it to be exercised well and responsibly in the pursuit of ends of which they approve and in whose benefits they will justly share. The rulers have "power," no doubt, but there is at least a "myth" to the effect that this power is exercised in the public interest and that the purpose which the "powerful" satisfy in their capacity as public servants is not one that sets them in competition with their "weaker" brethren, but one which can be shared and in the name of which men can reasonably work together. Even the realists observe that the semblance of such disinterested devotion to a common cause must be preserved if morale is to be maintained. Hence the recently debased term "social justice" has a perennial significance in the field of social planning. For it is only in the terms that it provides—the exercise of power as a social function responsibly directed to the attainment of a common good—that "the masses" at least are persuaded to make the sacrifices and submission required for their share in the social enterprise.

Mr. Tawney has said this well and clearly in a memorable passage: "Efficiency rests ultimately on psychological foundations. It depends, not merely on mechanical adjustments, but on the intelligent collaboration of contentious human beings, whom hunger can make work, but mutual confidence alone can make cooperate. If such confidence is to be commanded by those vested with the direction of economic affairs, their authority must rest, not on the ownership of property, but on a social title, and be employed for ends that are not personal, but public." [3]

The effectiveness of a social ideal is in this way bound up with the belief that those who speak in its name are disinterested, not in the absurd sense that they have no interests to satisfy but in the specific sense that their concern for the public interest, for which they are responsible, has the controlling place in their decisions on matters of public concern. The definition of this public interest, and of the rules of justice according to which it ought to be pursued, will vary from one community to another. Much depends here on custom, on special conditions, on historical accident. But there is no community in which reciprocal obligations felt to be right and reasonable in the relations between rulers and ruled are not acknowledged and in which at least ostensible conformity to these obligations is not a factor in effective social action.

And since the *semblance* of such public morality is important, the actuality of it is so as well. For men will not go on indefinitely believing what they have good reason to know is false or accept as just procedures which violate principles of fair dealing they have learned to respect. If a social policy cannot stand inspection on the level of public morality and justice, it can be maintained, in the long run, only through sustained coercion and fraud, and while these are not unfamiliar instruments of national policy, they do not provide the cement for a stable and enlightened order. When we judge of the reasonableness of a social policy, we cannot, therefore, leave out the question of the justice of the ends it proposes and the extent to which they will effectively be honored by the agencies as-

[3] Tawney, *op. cit.*, pp. 262-263.

signed to carry them out. The struggle for power, on a human level, operates in the name of a righteousness it frequently—but fortunately not always—fails to achieve. Until such power has been validly characterized as responsible, reasonable and, in the circumstances, just—or the reverse—we simply do not know its social meaning and are not in a position to estimate its relevance to reasonable action. Those who profess, in the interest of scientific objectivity, to ignore this moral factor in their interpretation of history and analysis of events, deprive themselves of an essential instrument of rational discrimination in the context of social action. That they sometimes do it with methodological hand washings and professions of intellectual purity adds something to the humor, but nothing at all to the sense of their procedure.

(6) A reasonable social policy is a liberal social policy. The content of social ideas will in the first instance be derived from the traditions and preconceptions of the communities in which they are developed. The "equality" that an Englishman demands is by no means that which has traditionally suited an American and both are very far indeed from what the classless society, of which the Marxists used to tell us, would ostensibly provide. What is righteously accepted as just and reasonable at one time and in one community is condemned elsewhere with as great sincerity. To attempt to "rationalize" these customary commitments and tabus, either by idealizing them as the dictates of universal and timeless reason, or by stripping from them all that a universal and timeless reason could not of its own nature dictate, is a very simple-minded performance though not, alas, an unfamiliar one. The social aspirations of men grow out of the conditions of their lives and must apply back to them. If would-be absolutists in morals are still viewing any frank avowal of this circumstance with surprised indignation it is by this time their surprise rather than the situation which elicits it that should be reck-

oned as surprising. For most of us, at least, the relativity of the content of moral ideas is no longer news, and we can compose ourselves to understand and work with it.

But it is, once more, the use of ideas, not their origin or *a priori* plausibility, which qualifies them to do the work of reason. What we must ask, therefore, is how the local and all-too-human ideas which proximately define our knowledge of good and evil can be used to render that knowledge clearer, broader and more secure. What happens to an idea when it becomes an ideal for conduct and makes pretension to a rational authority it did not initially possess? It may be used narrowly, stupidly, fanatically, to exclude from the area of moral approval everything not definable in its initially limited terms. We know enough of that kind of morality, and its consequences. It may, however, be used as the greatest of the Hebrew prophets used the Scriptures, to generalize obligations first discerned only in a special instance and to awaken sympathies that, once aroused, can extend to Jew and Gentile, bond and free. It may be guarded resentfully against the kind of matter-of-fact knowledge which would require a reconstruction of its too-literal doctrines, or it may be vital enough to absorb in its own development the best knowledge of its time and raise it to the level of an inclusive human wisdom. There is a difference between these two sorts of use, and it is in terms of this difference that the discrimination between the rational and the irrational in social action must finally be made. It is something of this sort, I think, that Bergson meant by his distinction between a "closed" and an "open" morality. He did little service to clear thinking, however, in his use of it. In his philosophy, reason is always on the side of "static" ideas, fixed distinctions, and the like, while the dynamic, creative urge which breaks through such barriers and rises to new heights of spiritual insight is depicted as something essentially superrational. It is, in consequence, quite impossible for him to give an account of the mundane expressions of this dynamic morality in responsible and discriminating terms. The "dynamism" of the life force he celebrates is an unhappy mixture of secular mysticism, emotionally ill-defined humanitarianism and romanticized biology.

The "dynamism" of enlightened social action is of a different sort. It is bound up with what Whitehead calls adventures of ideas, the extension of theories and standards to areas where their pertinence was not previously seen, and with the widening of the area of shared experience and possible cooperative action which accompanies a better understanding of men's common nature and needs and an awakened concern for their secure satisfaction. It operates only within limits and under favorable conditions. It is useless to talk of common good and understanding where the material basis for securing them does not exist. Apart from the effective control of such conditions appeals to universal reason and justice become as empty and sentimental as they often appear to be. But it is an essential part of the merit of reason as a guide for social action that it can sometimes understand these conditions and show us how to achieve them. It can also, in the process of its development, correct its own initial limitations and widen the area of its effective operation. It is thus that reason works, not independently of the varied and relative moral ideals of common men, but through their continued reconstruction and adjustment to situations more accurately delineated and purposes more adequately understood.

And since it is the continued work of understanding that is important here, the most important question we can ask of any social policy, from the standpoint of its adequacy to the demands of reason, is whether or not it is compatible with, and lends effective support to, the activity through which this work of reconstruction goes on. Does it require for its operation special sanctions and peculiar sanctities which can survive only so long as they are protected from inquiry and removed from the area of common understanding and concern? If it does, no matter what its professions of "dynamism" or its claim to move forward on the "wave of the future," it will shut itself, and those who serve it, off from the resources for growth in human experience by which men, and ideas, continue to live. There is no virtue in any fragment of experience, in any uniquely "rational" principle, or in any social élite, that can maintain itself in independence of or opposition to the wider sources of humanly sharable experience. It is because reason, in its appropriate social use, is the spokesman for those wider sources and the means of access to them, that it justifies itself in operation, and confirms our faith in it.

The term "liberalism" has had many meanings, and it may be that many who today condemn "liberalism" as a social policy mean only to reject those elements in the liberal faith that have pretty obviously outlived their usefulness. If so, we shall not be disagreeing with them in what follows. But one thing that "liberalism" has often meant, and still means to many people, is "the attitude which tests the validity of behavior and of institutions in terms of the rational consent of men" [4] and, as I should want to add, that insists on the maintenance of political institutions in which such consent can be freely given and made effective in the determination of policy. And in this meaning, liberalism is not a doctrine that has been outmoded, or is likely to be. The demand it makes is not primarily for free trade, or free labor or free competition, though these at times may serve its purpose, but for such freedom of the minds of men—quite common men among others—that they may explore the possibilities of cooperative social action and act responsibly as their judgment dictates. That kind of liberalism is an essential precondition for the effective use of reason in social action, and if we surrender it, through misunderstanding, or inertia, or sheer failure of moral stamina, we shall not find either a "new" or an "old" order fit to take its place.

[4] H. Laski, "The Rise of Liberalism," *Encyclopaedia of the Social Sciences*, Vol. I, p. 103.

What takes its place is tyranny—the arbitrary exercise of irresponsible power—and the slavery, political or spiritual, which is its complement when men surrender the responsibility for making for themselves the decisions in terms of which their lives are to be determined. The freedom to make such decisions is not a peripheral accessory of a bourgeoise culture, to be weighed against the competing charms of security, national aggrandizement or "charismatic" submission to a presumably inspired leader, when the comparative convenience of various forms of government is being discussed. It guarantees the conditions under which and the area within which we act as morally responsible persons, and those who think they have found a more humanly excellent way of living and acting will do well to think again. For what shall it profit a man if he gain the whole world and lose his own soul?

Such, then, are the primary requisites for the effective use of reason in the context of social action, and such the criteria in terms of which the reasonableness of specific proposals can properly be judged. Ideals are "rational" in so far as they meet the requirements and further the aims of reasonable action under these conditions. That not all ideals proposed are thus rational, that few indeed are even nearly as reasonable as they ought to be, is sufficiently obvious. If they were, the distinction between the rational and its opposite would be of little use in practical affairs. The use of this distinction is to tell us what to look for when we are trying to decide which among competing ideals will serve as reasonable guides for action. It is thus that I propose now to use it in a survey of the contemporary status of social ideas.

CHAPTER II

THE CURRENT ILL-REPUTE OF
RATIONAL IDEALS

In the preceding chapter I quoted an emphatic passage from Mr. Spykman on the importance for national morale of a widespread belief in the righteousness of any cause for which united support is wanted. "In terms of interests men divide; only in terms of the defense of a moral order can they unite." The way in which he continues this passage is of particular interest. "Because man loves peace, it is always the opponent who is the aggressor, and because he prefers decency, it is always the enemy who fights unfairly and with cruel and dastardly means. National struggles invariably become conflicts between good and evil, crusades against sin and the devil. Modern wars can be fought successfully only in an atmosphere of unreality and makebelieve." [1]

What this appears to say is that the actual use of the "idealism" which concerted national effort generates is to enable men to deceive themselves enthusiastically about what they are doing and to exacerbate their conflicts. An ideology which functions in this fashion is mythical in its content, but is by no means "unreal" in its influence and effect. Those who know how to use it as an instrument of mass manipulation can enhance their power position accordingly and we have recently heard much of their techniques and of the extent of their success. No one can seriously question the accuracy of Mr. Spykman's characterization as applied to some, at least, of the contemporary manifestations of "idealism." The

[1] *Op. cit.*, p. 38.

remarkable fact, however, is that he regards this mode of functioning as bound up not with a misguided or dishonest idealism, but with any judgment of economic and political issues in moral terms. If this were true, any serious attempt to discriminate morally between right and wrong, just and unjust, in such conflicts would be an instance of this kind of self-deception, since it would be merely the expression of one's own "ideology." "Just" and "unjust" must then be enclosed in quotation marks as "true" and "false," "good" and "bad" have previously been, and the man who respects the "realities" of the situation will not permit himself to be taken in by them. But what are the "realities" of the situation which are to be discerned only when we have freed ourselves from the atmosphere of unreality and make-believe in which disputes about political "good" and "evil" go on? There remain as securely "factual" only the struggle for power, stripped of all moral (or "ideological") implications and the interest of the side one happens to be on in that struggle in gaining control of all necessary means to its successful prosecution. The enlightened manipulator of such means will thus have great regard for ideologies as instruments but no respect for them as ideals, or rules of right action to which he is in any realistic sense obligated to conform. This lack of scruple, in turn, will further enhance his efficiency in the struggle for power and make him a figure worthy of emulation by those, similarly emancipated, who are concerned to get what they can by the most effective means. It will not, of course, be advisable to announce this attitude too frankly to those who are to be manipulated, for they, at least, must go on believing in the ideologies they follow. Thurman Arnold observed, in *The Folklore of Capitalism*, that "polar words" like "just" and "unjust" are highly misleading to the social diagnostician. "Our enthusiasms are aroused by these words and therefore they are excellent tools with which to push people around. Both the Rebels and the Loyalists in Spain are fighting for justice. That is what enables them to kill so many people in such a consecrated way." [2] Nevertheless, he goes on to say, "We are not attacking the use of polar words on the public stage for purposes of creating morale or enthusiasm, because we cannot conceive what the human race would be like if it did not react to them. However, we are pointing out that from the point of view of the diagnostician these words contain traps which ruin his judgment. *They should be used in public but he should not believe in them.*" [3]

The state of mind in which as able and public-spirited a man as Thurman Arnold is led to this sort of conclusion about the proper relations between the enlightened diagnostician and those—in political matters, the electorate—who are to be manipulated by the "polar" words he uses but does not believe in, is worthy of further examination. Pareto has brought into currency a distinction between "the élite" who, in any society, are the effective rulers, whatever the form of government may be, and "the masses" who are the instruments of their purposes. The rejection of ideological commitments combined with the manipulative use of ideological appeals is evidently a doctrine for the élite, not for the masses, and there have undoubtedly been members of the former group, even in our own country, who have heard it gladly. It is a doctrine that carries us a long way indeed from the position outlined in the previous chapter, and it will be necessary, if we are to justify the position there reached against very potent and currently fashionable counter-movements in the social sciences, to see how it is arrived at, and how far it can be defended.

The first thing to be observed is that both Spykman and Arnold are writing not primarily about social science but about *social policy* and the attitude in the making of social policy which an enlightened man, who understands the na-

[2] Thurman Arnold, *The Folklore of Capitalism*, p. 168.
[3] *Ibid.*, p. 174, my italics.

ture and function of ideologies (or "polar words" and their kindred) will reasonably take. In refusing to be imposed on by such ideologies he will take the position, if he follows Spykman, that the "underlying realities" to be dealt with are those of power politics. "If the foreign policy of a state is to be practical, it should be designed not in terms of some dream world but in terms of the realities of international relations, in terms of power politics." [4] How "realities," as the basic elements to which in the last analysis we must accommodate ourselves, are ascertained is a further question about which there will be more to be said later. But there is at least no doubt that they are the factors chiefly to be taken account of in social action and that the "realist" who builds his plans upon them will have a different sort of recommendation to make for, say, post-war reconstruction than will his "day-dreaming" competitor in world planning. So, too, an emancipation from polar words can hardly fail to carry with it a characteristic attitude toward proposals in which our support is asked for one cause or another on the ground that it is "just" and as such "merits" our aid since we, too, have expressed a concern for "justice," "democracy" and the like. The tone in which Mr. Arnold describes the Spanish Civil War is particularly noteworthy. The attitude it reflects was not without influence on the further course of public opinion concerning American foreign policy. Whether the influence was "good" or "bad" is a question which the diagnostician, who eschews "polar words" in his thinking, would hardly be in a position to judge.

But while the attitude recommended is concerned with the determination of social policies, the ground for it is held to be scientific or factual. It is something that has been found out about the ideals to which we appeal and the reasons we give for our actions that now leads those whose business it is to understand these matters to write of them as Arnold,

[4] *Op. cit.,* p. 446.

Spykman and many others have done. We may not like such conclusions, we are told, but facts are facts and a mind trained by the methods of modern science to distinguish between things as they are and will be whether we like them or not, and our own hopes and fears concerning them, will face the "realities" and make the best of them. Since we value so highly the attitude of clearheaded objectivity thus invoked, and its contributions to the life of reason, we are likely to be impressed, or even intimidated, by these pronouncements. Surely we must face the facts, whatever they are found to be. But what are the facts and what bearing do they have on the conclusions reached? These questions deserve a more critical analysis than they have so far received. We shall do our best to supply it, deferring a noble resolution to proclaim the disagreeable truth, whatever it may be, until we are somewhat clearer as to what, on these precise issues, the truth *is*, and in what respects it is or should be disagreeable.

We shall find, I think, that we are faced not with facts of unequivocal import, nor with a well-articulated and verifiable scientific hypothesis, but with a peculiar state of mind generated by the attempt to assimilate facts to a point of view quite inadequate to their reasonable interpretation. The realists of the era just now ending and the "debunking" popularizers of their views have found out that human reason, applied to the determination of social policy, did not work in the way in which they thought it ought to work to be accredited as properly rational. They have announced this observed discrepancy as a disclosure of the "deceptive" and/ or "mythical" character of the social ideals by means of which men normally try to justify their conduct and have concluded that those who would understand the issues of social policy objectively and face realistically the requirements for effective action must free themselves from these deceptions, though they may well be prepared to use the ideals of others for their own more realistic purposes. There are discriminable stages in the development of this point of view, and in the thoroughness with which its apparent implications are accepted and applied, and not all those who sometimes make use of its assumptions would wish to be committed to all the doctrines that have been propounded in its name. It will be worth our while to outline these stages and to notice particularly the manner in which the transition from fact to interpretation and then to the determination of the realities by respect for which social policy ought to be guided is achieved.

(1) The term "ideology" as a substitute for "ideal" came into general currency through its use by the Marxists to designate the status of a particular sort of ideal—that which serves as a rationalization or idealistic false front for class interests and bias. It is the combination of the pretension to disinterestedness (in the moral rather than the scientific sense) with the fact of a determining bias whose special claims the ideology portrays as universal values, that gives an ideology its peculiar status. The Marxists held, of course, that in a class society the ruling ideas will necessarily be the ideals of the ruling class and will justify as right and reasonable whatever that class finds to be useful and expedient. In the classless society such ideological bias will presumably wither away since the classes whose struggle it projected on the plane of ideals will disappear. Since the time for that happy eventuation, however, seems still remote, we are likely for some time to come to have to deal with a world in which the exposure of ideals as "ideologies" will be a favorite form of social criticism in advanced Leftist circles.

The notion of ideology can be generalized, however, and such generalization has been found of use for other purposes than those of Marxist controversy. It is not only the economic interest that leads men to present their less reputable wants under the guise of universal rules of reason or to discover just those particular rules of reason that will suit their controversial purposes. "Rationalization," with the help of the Freudians, has become a term of reproach among us, and everybody knows that the motives men profess for their actions are by no means always those that in fact guide their conduct. To point out this now familiar but always entertaining aspect of human behavior has been the task of the debunking biographer and historian. The devotees of "propaganda analysis" have learned to view with alarm, and enclose in warning quotation marks, any appeal for public action which used "loaded" words or "glittering generalities"—every appeal, in other words, that makes use of the distinction between right and wrong as a motive for action. The theologians have not lost the opportunity to sound a warning note. Thus Reinhold Niebuhr, long on the lookout for sin, has found in "the ideological taint, the dishonest pretension of universality, which accompanies every partial perspective in history," [5] the palmary example of human pride and self-assertion at its sinful height. Nor have the literary critics been idle. Oscar Cargill, hailing the recognition of the role of ideologies in the history of thought as a discovery comparable to the smashing of the atom in physics, goes on to say: "Ideologies are comparable to cosmic storms of force; sweeping the universe of thought, they determine much of human action, particularly on the grand scale, for few men act outside the influence of some ideology. A study of their impact on any past or present culture, a description of their tendencies and strength, is a new study—it is not criticism properly, nor history, nor philosophy, though it may make use of all these. Such a study deserves a new name, and for it I propose a new word—IDEODYNAMICS: *the descriptive study of ideologies and of the results of the forces which they exert.*" [6]

In Mr. Cargill's hands ideodynamics proves still to be some-

---

[5] Reinhold Niebuhr, *Christianity and Power Politics*, p. 113.
[6] O. Cargill, *Intellectual America*, p. vii. My italics.

hing remarkably like literary criticism, or "literary loose alk," as Max Eastman once called it. But there can be little loubt that whether or not ideologies are much like cosmic torms of force the furor over ideology is at least a tempest n the teapot of the intelligentsia, and a movement therefore which no consistent reader of the best non-fiction can afford o neglect.

It is, however, something more than that, and if we are to inderstand it at its best we must see the way in which the notion is used by a critical historian who is also, though he would perhaps not admit it, a philosopher. Few men now iving have contributed more to our understanding of the history of ideas than has Carl Becker. His book *The Declaration of Independence* is a model of scholarship and a delight o the mind. Yet it is apparent throughout that the standpoint from which he interprets the philosophy of the Declaration colors considerably some of the most important things he has to say about it. The document, he tells us, was presented as a moral and legal justification of the action of the American colonies in severing political relations with England. It is on grounds of principle that this justification is offered and if it is valid it is, presumably, because the principles to which it appeals are sound and the application just. So, evidently, the framers of the Declaration viewed the matter. "In the Declaration the foundation of the United States is indissolubly associated with a theory of politics, a philosophy of human rights which is valid, if at all, not for Americans only but for all men." [7] And it was to the verdict of reasonable men everywhere that its framers submitted their case.

In following Mr. Becker's account, however, it soon becomes apparent that while the appeal was to universal reason, the persuasiveness of the reasoning to the minds of those who accepted it was a much more local affair. The principles of

[7] Carl Becker, *The Declaration of Independence*, p. 225.

universal reason proved to be the characteristically eighteenth century notions of "nature," "human nature," and "natural rights," all curiously entangled with survivals from medieval theology and borrowings from Newtonian physics, and adjusted in their political application to the rather special needs of American farmers with an urge to manage their own affairs. No wonder they held those "truths" to be self-evident. "How should the colonists not accept a philosophy, however clumsily argued, which assured them that their own governments, with which they were well content, were just the kind that God had designed men by nature to have?" [8] The intellectuals turned back to John Locke for the theory of the revolution. And Locke did not fail them. For "This was Locke's great title to glory, that he made it possible for the eighteenth century to believe with a clear conscience what it wanted to believe, namely, that since man and the mind of man were shaped by that nature which God had created, it was possible for men 'barely by the use of their natural faculties' to bring their ideas and conduct and hence the institutions by which they lived, into harmony with the universal natural order." [9]

This, then, was the function of the ideal superstructure. It "made it possible to believe with a clear conscience" what those who invoked it already wanted to believe. As such it served its purpose, for those times and interests. But they could hardly have gone on believing it with a clear conscience if they had thought that that was its only claim to validity. They spoke not of ideologies congenial to their habits and temperament, but of truths that were self-evident. What can we, in the enlightened twentieth century, make of such "truth"? Mr. Becker is quite definite in his answer. "To ask whether the natural rights philosophy of the Declaration of Independence is true or false is essentially a meaningless

[8] *Ibid.*, p. 73.
[9] Carl Becker, *The Heavenly City of the Eighteenth Century Philosophers*, p. 65.

question." What is true of course is that men *seek* such a philosophy, and *want* it to be rationally defensible. "To them it is 'true' because it brings their actions into harmony with a rightly ordered universe, and enables them to think of themselves as having chosen the nobler part, as having withdrawn from a corrupt world in order to serve God or Humanity or a force that makes for the highest good." [10] Their philosophy was "true," in the sense that it performed a useful function in their mental economy, but it would, he holds, be not false but meaningless to call it true in the sense in which they themselves supposed it to be so. Hence, though Mr. Becker does not specifically draw this conclusion, it seems to follow that those who accepted this ideology were deceived as to the nature of its validity.

This conclusion is not here stressed in order to view with alarm the suggestion that the founding fathers were in some important matters mistaken. It seems to me, on the contrary, fairly clear that in some respects they *were* mistaken. They too readily identified the special conditions of political liberty as of 1776 and in the North American Colonies with the universal rights of all men everywhere. In so doing they overstated their case and paved the way both for the easy refutation that later came from the nineteenth century apologists for political and chattel slavery, and for the more devious reasonings of those other apologists who, in the name of Thomas Jefferson, have in our time sought to limit human freedom to the special forms of it which in his time and for his purposes were important. If the tendency to confuse ideas of limited scope and validity with principles of universal reason and later to sanctify the special interests that profit by this confusion as defenders of eternal truth is evidence of ideological bias, then there are ideological elements in the Declaration, and some of the uses to which it has since been put are as suspect as the critics claim.

[10] *The Declaration of Independence*, pp. 277-278.

That, however, is not the central issue here. If the Declaration could be shown to be mistaken in some respects, it might also be shown to be right in others, and it might even prove that the right ones were of considerable pertinence to the present decisions of reasonable men. To characterize its basic tenets as a philosophy which it is "meaningless" to set down as *either* true or false but which remains "a humane and engaging faith" for those who, like Mr. Becker, have a taste for such things is a very different matter. For there are other tastes and other times and it would surely be absurd for those who happen to favor the old style of thinking about human rights to reject as false the views of those whose taste in doctrine differs from their own. It is a credit to the soundness of Mr. Becker's moral and political convictions that, in a later (1942) preface to a new edition of this volume he records the conviction that " 'liberty, equality and fraternity' and the inalienable rights of men are phrases, glittering or not, that denote realities—the fundamental realities that men will always fight for rather than surrender." [11] Is this conviction supposed to be "true" in any such literal sense as that what it states to be so is so? Or is it simply another expression of the need of men, when they are ready to fight, to give expression to this sort of sentiment? If the latter, we may find it "humane and engaging" in its turn, but hardly more than that. The truth is that Mr. Becker, like many others, has assumed a standpoint in the criticism of ideas from which the sort of claim that he wants to make when he is himself concerned about issues of political right and wrong cannot consistently be made. We may well be glad that he makes it none the less. But we shall want to examine further the logic of the thinking which leads him to this rather awkward position.

The first step here is the discovery, quite sound and historically accurate, that men often are deceived about the

[11] *Ibid.*, p. xvi.

universal validity of the principles on which they rely as "reasons" for their actions. This deception may amount to deliberate fraud on the part of leaders who persuade the gullible masses that the action proposed is for the common good when it actually serves only the interest of a favored group or class. It may be a form of self-deception by which "conscientious" men conceal from themselves the motives for their action. And it may simply be the too sweeping zeal of intelligent men with a good cause to universalize local interests without removing their local limitations. In any case it is likely to lead to errors that impede the rational use of social ideas. To point out these errors, and their source in the combination of a limited outlook with unlimited pretensions is a service to clear thinking and practical reason. So long as the criticism of ideologies remains on this level its values cannot properly be questioned.

(2) It rarely does remain on this level, however. The transition we have already observed in Becker's analysis is an easy one to make. We see that the philosophical ideas of Jefferson were in some respects not true, by which is presumably still meant that they were actually mistaken. But we see at the same time that they filled a socially useful function, and we sympathize with the sentiments they expressed. Is it then of any real importance whether they were true or not? And, further, how could they have been expected to be "true" at all? They were clearly not statements of scientifically verifiable fact—there is no scientific technique yet developed for detecting the existence of natural rights. Moreover, the assertion of such rights is obviously bound up with the expression of very strong emotions. But science has nothing to do with the expression of emotion—its field is the reporting of verifiable facts about which all qualified practitioners can agree. Hence, if we restrict the "truth" to what is ascertainable by the methods of the sciences, statements about rights cannot be "true" at all—or "false" either, for that

matter—since they are neither confirmed nor confuted by sci
entifically objective methods. We are by this time familia
with this kind of thinking and need not now elaborate on it
Suffice it to say that it has proved so generally persuasive in
the social sciences that the claim that an ideology can be
neither true nor false is now commonly regarded as so obvi
ously correct as to need no substantiation—only, perhaps, an
expository comment or two for the layman who has no
previously been instructed in the scientific outlook. Its use
is obvious. It enables the cautious social scientist, who would
rather be caught with an incendiary bomb than a moral pref
erence, to deal with the history and influence of social ideal
without any commitment as to their validity. He can leave
the quest for a "true" ideology, like the search for God, to
"disciplines fitted by long success for such a search." [12] More
over, at least part of what it claims is clearly true. If we
identify "truth" with what is scientifically verifiable, then we
shall have to say that ideologies are not "true" since the tests
which verify a hypothesis in the sciences would be sufficient
neither to confirm nor to confute their claims. Why then
should an insistence upon it be regarded as objectionable or a
step in the direction of social cynicism?

The answer is plain enough. The identification of truth
with what is scientifically verifiable leaves social ideals beyond the pale of truth and in the dubious company of myths.
delusions and fantasies which equally fall short of "truth."
If there were some further way of distinguishing within this
group those ideas which are reasonably grounded and rationally justifiable from those which are, in the more usual
sense, mythical, delusive or fantastic, this would be a matter
of relatively small importance. But this further distinction, if
it exists, is one that the scrupulous investigator who follows
the scientific model is not prepared to make. The ironical
politeness with which he professes to refrain from judgment

[12] Crane Brinton, *The Anatomy of Revolution,* p. 21.

on such issues is in effect the announcement that so far as he, in his professional capacity, is concerned no such distinction can be made out and, in consequence, that within the limits of his investigation, the philosophy of, e.g., natural rights has no rational validity at all. It is to be understood, like any other of the unverifiable myths which move men in more or less mysterious ways, as an expression of sentiment, interest or bias, a means of securing social cohesion, but not as a serious claimant to rationally grounded acceptance or rejection.

Now this, too, is a judgment on the merits of the belief in question, reached, however, by the devious method of refusing to make a judgment. The ideal is treated as mythical not because it can be shown to be false, but because, by the method accredited as appropriate to the objective study of social phenomena, it cannot even come up for a hearing. To be sure, philosophy or ethics may have something to say about it, but the working assumption, among such critics, is that what philosophy and ethics have to say cannot concern the serious investigator and, therefore, in effect, the verdict passed upon it *in absentia* must stand. The system of classification used recognizes only claims to truth (as defined) and expressions of sentiment. Falling in the latter category, the ideals that guide the masses are not true but mythical and while they may correspond to "reality" in a rough way—to be more fully explained later—they do so only as expressions of hope and fear, not as hypotheses about events, and are to be judged accordingly.

The clearest and most explicit development of this method of interpreting and evaluating human actions in their social significance that we have so far had is that provided by Pareto in his massive and very influential work, *The Mind and Society*. It is particularly exemplified in the distinction there made between logical and non-logical conduct and the use that is made of this distinction. Pareto claims to speak as a scientist rigorously committed to the use of the logico-experimental method. "Throughout the course of these volumes, we are in the logico-experimental field. I intend to remain absolutely in that field and refuse to depart from it under any inducement whatsoever." [13] In this field, we are further told, the final appeal is always to "observation" and "experiment" and these terms are to be used "in the meanings they have in the natural sciences such as astronomy, chemistry, physiology and so on." [14] All consideration of what *ought to be* is, of course, rigorously excluded. "Imagine a chemist saying: 'It is a pity that when mercury protochloride is exposed to light it should change spontaneously into mercury bichloride, a virulent poison. I shall therefore look for a chemical theory that will render such a thing impossible.' Yet there you would have a widely cultivated type of moral theory." [15] Pareto leaves no doubt at all that it is the chemist and not the moralist whose example he proposes to follow.

It is particularly interesting, therefore, that he finds it possible to distinguish, from this logico-experimental standpoint, between *conduct* that is logical and that which is not. Here, evidently, we are concerned with judgments of the ends to which actions may reasonably be directed and the means appropriate to secure them. But a prior distinction is needed before Pareto can deal with this issue. "Every social phenomenon may be considered under two aspects: as it is in reality, and as it presents itself to the mind of this or that human being. The first aspect we shall call *objective*, the second *subjective*." [16] Conduct is logical when it "logically conjoins means to ends" not only from the standpoint of the subject performing the action but also objectively—"from the standpoint of other persons who have more extensive knowl-

13 V. Pareto, *op. cit.*, p. 14.
14 *Ibid.*, p. 33.
15 *Ibid.*, p. 313.
16 *Ibid.*, p. 76. Italics in text.

edge" [17] and are thus in a better position to judge of what in reality things are. There is no doubt as to who this person of wider knowledge, competent to speak for "the realities," in so far as human knowledge can achieve them, is to be. It is the scientist, pursuing the logico-experimental method or, in this case, it is Pareto himself. An action is logical if the subjective end to which it is directed is identical with the objective end to which (in the judgment of the objective observer) it will lead. In all other cases it is non-logical.

This classification enables Pareto to group together as non-logical (from the logico-experimental standpoint) two sorts of action which in other respects would seem to differ considerably. One sort, which he is never tired of illustrating, is that in which an actual mistake has been made about the relation of means to end. A devout Greek sacrificed to Poseidon before starting a voyage because he believed that Poseidon existed, had the power to guarantee a safe voyage, and could in this way be influenced to do so. Here the end sought was an empirical occurrence—a safe voyage—but the action did not logically conjoin means to end because it tried to secure the end by means which we have good reason to believe do not operate in the way anticipated. The Greek did not know this, hence his action seemed reasonable enough to him. But from the standpoint of our wider knowledge we can see that the objective end, or probable outcome, has no logical connection with the means used to secure it and the conduct in question must thus be termed non-logical.

The second sort of action is *prima facie* of a different sort. Here it is the end itself that is said to be non-logical and the conduct that aims at securing it is, in consequence, non-logical as well. The objective end cannot coincide with the subjective aim, for here there is no objective end at all, i.e., none that the logico-experimental method can certify as genuine. In logical conduct "the objective end is a real one,

[17] *Ibid.*, p. 77.

located within the field of observation and experience, and not an imaginary end, located outside that field. An imaginary end may, on the other hand, constitute a subjective purpose." [18]

Among such imaginary ends (from the logico-experimental standpoint) conformity to principles of justice, conceived as an ideal which ought to be respected, must evidently be included. Pareto leaves no doubt on this point. "There remains the question as to what *ought* to be done, the *precept*. This is a class of relations that may lie entirely beyond experience, even when the related terms are experimental. What takes it out of the experimental field is the term 'ought,' which does not correspond to any concrete reality." [19] "From the logico-experimental standpoint to say that an 'injustice,' whether done to one person or to many, involves an equal offense against 'justice,' is to say a thing that has no meaning. There is no such person as 'Justice,' and one cannot imagine what 'offenses' could be offered her." [20] And when there is talk of a "higher" justice which nations ought to respect, our author wittily inquires "Just how is the height of this or that justice to be measured in feet or inches?" [21] Nor is this (from the logico-experimental standpoint) a surprising position. For "the terms of experimental science correspond to realities within more or less extensive limits. . . . But as for 'Zeus,' 'justice,' 'the good,' all correspondence with experimental reality fails, and there is no question of limits." [22]

This does not mean, of course, that the man who is concerned about justice need be mistaken about any scientifically ascertainable matters of fact. His action is non-logical simply because the thing he is after cannot be located "in the field of observation and experience" by an "objective" observer em-

[18] *Ibid.*, p. 78.
[19] *Ibid.*, p. 312. Italics in text.
[20] *Ibid.*, p. 731.
[21] *Ibid.*, pp. 1004-1005.
[22] *Ibid.*, p. 1836.

ploying the methods of astronomy or chemistry, or measured in feet and inches by that of Paretan sociology. Why should it be expected to be thus located and measured? Because, if it is not, it falls outside the "reality" which the logico-experimental method is competent to report on and is in consequence merely imaginary or, as Pareto prefers to say "fantastic." And everybody knows that the pursuit of merely imaginary or fantastic ends is, from any objective point of view, non-logical conduct.

It follows that, so far as the "objective" scientist (if he follows Pareto) is concerned, there is no difference in rational credibility between superstitions and moral principles. "People who continue asking whether a thing be 'just' or 'good' and so on, are not aware that to ask such questions differs little if at all from asking whether a given number be 'perfect.' " [23] Nor is this objectivity confined only to pure scientists. It is also the one that Pareto is delighted to discover among farsighted statesmen. Such men have little regard for scruples in their own conduct, but they are shrewd enough to recognize the considerable part that sentiments play in the behavior of the unenlightened masses. "The person who is able to free himself from the blind dominion of his own sentiments is capable of utilizing the sentiments of other people for his own ends. If, instead, a person is prey to his own sentiments, he cannot have the knack of using the sentiments of others, and so shocks them to no purpose and fails to derive any advantage from them. The same may be said, in general, of the relation between ruler and ruled. The statesman of the greatest service to himself and his party is the man who himself has no prejudices but knows how to profit by the prejudices of others." [24] When we recall that the "dominion of sentiment" refers to all "non-logical" conduct and that among the prejudices from which the statesman frees himself are

[23] *Ibid.*, pp. 587-588.
[24] *Ibid.*, pp. 1281-1282.

those of respect for moral principles as binding on his own conduct, we see something of what this means. But if there is any doubt Pareto, who is nothing if not explicit, will remove it. "Nowadays no one believes that lunar or solar eclipses have the slightest influence on the fortunes of war, but many people do believe that they are influenced by the 'justice' or 'injustice' of the cause that is committed to arms. Modern rulers are no longer compelled to worry about eclipses, but it is just as well if they go to some pains to make people believe that the cause for which they are fighting is 'just'; and it is not bad either if they are not too sure of that themselves, if, that is, they follow the example, not of Nicias, who believed in the influence of lunar eclipses, nor of Napoleon III and his minister Ollivier, who placed their reliance in the justice of their cause; but, rather, of Themistocles, Epanimondas, Dio, and Alexander, who knew how to use omens for the furtherance of their plans, or even of Bismarck who listened while other people chatted about justice, but as for himself saw to it that he was the strongest in guns; and when he began tinkering with the Ems dispatch, he did not ask the advice of a moralist, but inquired of Moltke and Roon whether the army was ready and able to win." [25]

We have come a long way, it seems, by the strict use of the logico-experimental method; far enough to decide that politicians who treat moral principles as of no account are more enlightened than those who allow "superstitions" about oracles, either astrological or moral, to limit their freedom of action. There is only one step further to be taken to complete the process. This capacity to use the scruples of others without having any of one's own is not at all widespread. Most people will continue to be guided by their sentiments and will need to believe in the validity of the ideals they profess. "There is a distressing contradiction between having a faith

[25] *Ibid.*, p. 1762. Note.

that is to inspire vigorous action and considering that faith absurd." [26] It is as well, therefore, that the masses are unaware of the non-logical character of their conduct and can go sentimentally on in their concern for what they think is "just" and "right." For "it is advantageous to society that individuals not of the ruling classes should spontaneously accept, observe, respect, revere, love the precepts current in their society, prominent among them the precepts called—roughly, inadequately to be sure—precepts of 'morality' and precepts of 'religion'—or we might better say of 'religions,' including under that term not only the group-persistences commonly so named, but many other groups of similar character." [27]

To whom, precisely, this advantage accrues is a further question. "Utility" or advantage makes sense only when a standard in terms of which it is to be measured has been set up, and what is "useful" by one such standard will be harmful from another. And from a logico-experimental point of view, the choice of a standard must be an arbitrary one. We may suspect, however, that the actual beneficiaries of such manipulable devotion will be the emancipated élite who will know how to make use of such loyalties without feeling any reciprocal obligation with respect to them. Power and gain are the aims of the rulers, and it is to these that the "advantageous" use of moral ideas contributes. "If we look at all these facts from the outside, trying so far as possible to free our minds from the ties of sectarian passion, prejudices of country and party, utopian perfections, ideals and so on, we see that substantially and whatever the form of government, men holding power have, as a rule, a certain inclination to use that power to keep themselves in the saddle, and to abuse it to secure personal gains and advantages, which they sometimes fail to distinguish clearly from party gains and advantages,

[26] *Ibid.*, p. 1693.
[27] *Ibid.*, p. 1345.

and almost always confuse with the gains and advantages of the country." [28] That this is called a "confusion" rather than a deliberate subordination of all other "advantages" to the logico-experimentally identifiable ends of power and gain for the rulers must be taken, I suppose, as evidence that even the élite are to some measure still addicted to moralistic "rationalizations" of non-logical conduct.

In this account every step in the development of the state of mind we are examining is present: the ostentatious refusal to judge of that which lies outside the scope of the scientific, or logico-experimental, method; the subsequent judgment that from the standpoint of this method there are no discoverable "realities" to which the ends of conscientious moral action correspond; the conclusion that, in this respect, which is all that is "logico-experimentally" important, the status of moral principles is the same as that of myths and superstitions which there is good reason to believe are false; the practical judgment that ends which are thus unreal or fantastic are not worth taking seriously, and that statesmen who refuse to take them seriously, save as means for manipulating the sentiments or loyalties of the masses, are facing "realities" while those who respect the claims of "justice" are not; the consequent cleavage between the élite who are capable of using ideals masterfully to advance their own ambitions and the masses who are imposed on by them, and the final explicit approval of those political parties and programs which accept this cleavage and act accordingly. Pareto knew how to pick his men. It was in 1912, long before the world at large had heard of Mussolini, then editor of the *Avanti*, that he wrote: "So it is that the men who write for the *Avanti* show that they have the qualities of virility and frankness, the qualities that insure victory in the end and which, after all, are beneficial to the nation as a whole. The fox may, by his cunning,

[28] *Ibid.*, p. 1608.

escape for a certain length of time, but the day may come when the lion will reach him with a well-aimed cuff and that will be the end of the argument." [29] The metaphor is instructive, though inaccurate. For we have come to see that it takes more than brutality and cynicism—here miscalled "virility and frankness"—to make a lion of Mussolini. It also takes more to make a statesman. But what that "more" is we shall need other methods than those of Pareto to discern.

(3) The reference to Pareto has carried us somewhat ahead of our story. The pervasive character of the second stage in the current analysis of ideologies is simply the assertion that, from the only standpoint which an objective inquiry into social behavior can properly assume—that of scientific verification—social ideals, however reasonable and eternally true they may seem to their adherents, belong in the category of "myth" and "rationalization." Their origin and influence can be traced but their claims to validity cannot be made out, and need not even be seriously examined. It follows, of course, that those who want to distinguish between one such ideal and another, in terms of, e.g., "justice," will get little help from the would-be scientist of social behavior. This has some important consequences. Thus, Mr. James Burnham, in a recent and widely read volume, *The Managerial Revolution*, has identified the Nazi regime in Germany as the "nuclear first stage" [30] in a "managerial" super-state that will develop in Europe, whether we like it or not, and has indicated that so far from being essentially opposed to this type of political and economic organization, "in terms of economic, social, political, ideological changes from traditional capitalism, the New Deal moves in the same *direction* as Stalinism and Naziism." [31] It is consistent with this position, of course, to hold further that "the historic direction of the New Deal

[29] *Ibid.*, pp. 1789-1790. Note.
[30] James Burnham, *The Managerial Revolution*, p. 251.
[31] *Ibid.*, p. 257. Italics in text.

as a whole runs entirely counter to the ideals and aims of liberalism." [32]

That the present policies of the American government move in the same direction as those of Germany and Russia to the extent that to an increasing degree they vest the control of industry in the hands of governmental managers and administrative boards, rather than in those of private capitalists, is obvious enough. And there is some, though by no means conclusive, evidence to show that this tendency will continue when the war is over. If a "totalitarian" government is one that assumes a large share in the control of an economic activity, then the American government is becoming "totalitarian," and the proximate beneficiaries, so far as power in the direction of affairs is concerned, are those who "manage," as governmental agents, the activities concerned. We need only take one step further to complete the picture. Thus Mr. Burnham points out that Hitler and Stalin also are "in reality not unlike modern managers. They direct masses of people in ways analogous to those used by managers in directing production; they have similar habits of thought, similar methods, similar manipulation of the possibilities of advanced technology. Stalin or Hitler prepares for a new political turn more or less as a production manager prepares for getting out a new model on his assembly line." [33] And that, if we are willing to allow for a little leeway in the "more or less," would seem to complete the argument.

The striking fact about this analysis is, however, not what it says but what, with considerable pride in its objectivity, it refuses to say. For many of us the resemblances between Hitler's government and our own have been less striking than the differences. One of these would seem to be that the Hitlerian "management" is accomplished by violence and treachery, whereas the management so far achieved in this country

[32] *Ibid.*, p. 258.
[33] *Ibid.*, p. 156.

has conformed to the will of a majority of the people, expressed through the forms of democratic government, and has served the interests of these same people, on the whole, fairly honestly and responsibly. And when we condemn the German "managerial" new order and question the inevitability of its continuance we use words like "justice" and "freedom" in the discussion. This taxes Mr. Burnham's patience somewhat. His concern, he repeatedly tells us, is not to praise or condemn, but simply to show what is now happening and will probably continue to happen. From this standpoint, the talk of justice is beside the point. "There is no historical law that polite manners and 'justice' shall conquer. In history there is always the question of *whose* manners and *whose* justice. A rising social class and a new order of society have got to break through the old moral codes just as they must break through the old economic and political institutions. Naturally, from the point of view of the old, they are monsters. If they win, they will take care in due time of manners and morals." [34]

This seems to me a remarkable passage. It refuses to take sides as between the rival claims to "justice"—that is not the province of the scientist—but in so doing it conveys the impression that the only thing that matters as between such claims (from an objective standpoint, of course) is which one is strong enough to prevail, which, that is, is on the winning side. And it treats as natural, and even necessary, the violation of moral codes which those who oppose "a rising social class and new order of society" will, of course, just as "naturally" condemn. It is the demands of technology that count in modern society and those who control the basic instruments of production are the managers, not the moralists. We can go further. There is much talk of restoring the freedom of the smaller nations in Europe now controlled by Hitler. But those who face the facts can hardly take it seri-

[34] *Ibid.*, p. 229. Italics in text.

ously. The managerial superstate is on the way (whether
Hitler or some other manager is at the head of it). The
plurality of small sovereign states in Europe strangled the
division of labor, "the flow of trade and raw materials made
possible and demanded by modern technology." [35] Hence
these states are on the way out and no "highly moral fictions"
can restore them. It is technology that makes demands in this
world and men, confused though they may be by "ideological" fictions, who obey. And it is the managers who
understand that this must be so, and act accordingly. That
will not, of course, prevent them from using any convenient
ideological devices to gain their ends. There are, we are told,
among the *real* New Dealers a group of younger men "admin-
istrators, experts, technicians, bureaucrats," who are defi-
nitely on the make in the improvement of their power position. "They are ready to work with anyone and are not so
squeamish as to insist that their words should coincide with
their actions and aims. They believe that they can run things,
and they like to run things." [36] In the managerial society that
is to be, it appears, their future is bright.

I have dealt with Mr. Burnham's "managerial revolution"
not because I am greatly interested in his map of the future
but because I am considerably interested in his state of mind,
and that of the very many of his colleagues and critics, as
well as the would-be managers of the rising order, who have
heard him gladly. What does it mean, for the determination
of a just and reasonable social policy, that responsible men
thus interpret the issues that now confront their country?
I think it means a good deal. It is quite true that "polite manners and justice" do not of their own nature deflect the
tendencies of history from their "natural" course. But men
who were concerned about "justice" as something rather different than "polite manners" have sometimes done so. They

[35] *Ibid.*, p. 173.
[36] *Ibid.*, p. 255.

were, in a manner, "squeamish" about promises that they had made and responsibilities that they had incurred, and "the old moral codes" they honored had some considerable bearing on their behavior. Before we decide that the rising ruling class of the future must be of a different order we shall want, I think, to hear not only the "demands" of technology but the demands of men whose way of life while "more or less" like that of Hitler's Germany is also "more or less" different, and to whom that difference is important.

But, it will be answered, Mr. Burnham is not denying the *value* of "justice" in our sense. He simply, for his purposes, takes no account of it. And that is true. But he is presenting the issues of social policy from a standpoint from which such values cannot get counted, and he is offering the situation thus delineated as the one in terms of which we must make up our minds as to what the future is to be. To see that this is so, it is necessary only to compare his version of the "managerial" economy with that of an older and, I think, a wiser student of our current social problems, Mr. R. H. Tawney. In his book *Equality* Mr. Tawney saw clearly enough what Mr. Burnham now sees, that inequality of power is inevitable in organized society, and that, with the increasingly technical development of modern industry and the increasing scope of government participation in its management, either through public ownership or bureaucratic control, the power of the men whom Burnham calls the managers will probably increase. What does this mean? For Burnham, using his terms in a strictly "neutral" sense, of course, it means that the managers will constitute the new ruling class, the socially dominant group, and will have "the power and privilege and wealth in the society, as against the remainder of society." [37] To maintain this power it will be necessary to curb the masses, and such means, ideological or coercive, as are requisite to this end will be employed. We shall have a government

[37] *Ibid.*, p. 59.

of, by and for the managers and a set of social ideals calculated to convince the masses that this "exploitation"—the privileged position of the managers and their preponderant share in the economy's goods—is necessary for the good of the community. The ideology of "liberalism," now on the wane, made palatable "exploitation" by the capitalists, and the ideology of the future will operate in the interest of the new ruling class. Will this new inequality of power be "good" in any further sense? That, naturally, is a question the objective reporter will hardly ask.

It is characteristic of Mr. Tawney, however, that he does ask it, and has an answer to give of some significance. "It is not difficult to state the principles which cause certain kinds of inequality to win indulgence, however difficult it may be to apply them in practice. Inequality of power is tolerated, when that power is used for a social purpose approved by the community, when it is not more extensive than that purpose requires, when its exercise is not arbitrary, but governed by settled rules, and when the commission can be revoked, if its terms are exceeded. . . . No one complains that captains give orders and that the crews obey them, or that engine-drivers must work to a time-table laid down by railway managers. For, if captains and managers command, they do so by virtue of their office, and it is by virtue of their office that their instructions are obeyed. They are not the masters, but the fellow-servants of those whose work they direct." [38]

The principle to which Mr. Tawney here appeals to discriminate one type of "managerial" society from another is a very old one. When Thrasymachus asserted (*Republic*, Bk. I) that the powerful ruled in their own interest, Socrates replied that if the powerful were the rulers, their interest was determined by their responsible function or office and that in this they were the servants of the people, not competitors with them in a scramble for individual gain. To make

[38] *Op. cit.*, p. 139.

that answer good, Socrates was obliged to offer a definition of justice as an ideal, and such an ideal as has yet to find an adequate actualization. He was not mistaken, however, in thinking both the answer and the idea of justice profoundly relevant to the doctrine of Thrasymachus, as they still are to that of his latter-day disciples. For apart from a standard of justice it is simply not possible to understand that division and coordination of function—to which inequality of power is incident—which constitutes the spiritual well-being of a state. *Of course* the rulers rule and subordinates submit, and the managers manage and, in an advanced stage of technological development, the typists type. And if they didn't, somebody else would and they in their turn would be the rulers, subordinates, managers, and typists of the rising new order. But whether they work together with a measure of freedom, good will and human dignity or are reduced to the level of "managers" and "managed" in Hitler's Europe will depend in part on whether the cause they mutually serve is one that commends itself to them, not as "just" but as just. And where they still have the means of making up their minds on this matter for themselves it will be important that the justice preached and practiced is one that can stand their critical inspection. If they are fools, they can be "manipulated" indefinitely; and if they are cowards, they can be coerced. But it would be premature, I think, for the rising "managers" or their press agents to assume that they are either. And if and in so far as they are not, consideration of "good manners and justice" will have some bearing on the course of history, which still is sometimes the history of free men in control of their own political affairs. In treating this concern for what is right and reasonable only as a factor in the "ideological" curbing of the masses in the interest of the exploiting "managers," Mr. Burnham has excluded from the picture just what was essential to make sense of it from the standpoint of reasonable social action. The inept use of a familiar methodological device has thus resulted in a failure of moral discrimination, and a consequent reduction of the facts of human cooperation to a level on which the principles which mark out the good in such functioning from the bad can no longer even be stated. And on this level, there is indeed not much to distinguish one set of "managers" from another.

This refusal on principle to make distinctions of principle between ideas that are true, or good, or just, and their opposites has had curious consequences at, or near, the level of the popular mind. One of these, which will repay a brief inspection, is that carried on under the title of "propaganda analysis." The discovery that well-meaning people are often misled by unsound argumentative devices and pseudo-logical appeals, and that what masquerades as truth or reason is by no means always what it seems can hardly be regarded as recent. But new currency was given to the notion by a disillusioned post-war analysis of the devices used in the first World War to enlist popular support for a cause which was not, in all respects, what it had been advertised to be. A suspicion of appeals to "reason," "justice," "democracy" and the like was thus aroused; and this suspicion soon merged with more general current doubts about "ideologies" and their illegitimate pretensions and, in collaboration with much praiseworthy zeal for clear and accurate thinking on practical issues, assumed the proportions of a minor crusade. To detect and analyze "propaganda," and thus, presumably, to free oneself from its deceptive sway, was the objective of groups of serious thinkers all over the country. To assist them in this good work an "Institute for Propaganda Analysis" was set up.

The history of this enterprise is instructive. It enlisted able and distinguished support, and its earlier efforts to expose the rabble rousers of the day and to lay down rules for clear thinking on social problems were of genuine value. But from the start there was confusion as to its purpose. For what is "propaganda" and under what circumstances do we wish to be freed from its insidious influence? "Propaganda," said *Propaganda Analysis*, the bulletin of the Institute, is "the expression of opinion or action by individuals or groups deliberately designed to influence opinions or actions of other individuals or groups with reference to predetermined ends." [39] That there is a great deal of the "propaganda" thus defined seems obvious. Men are constantly expressing opinions (or actions) for the purpose of influencing the opinions (or actions) of others for ends they regard as desirable. Such is the manifest nature of social cooperation; and if the Institute had taken seriously its task of "detecting" it in the various areas of social behavior in which it occurs, it would have been very busy indeed. It was busy enough, as it was. But the propaganda efforts it selected for attention were limited for the most part to attempts to influence opinion on political issues by argumentative devices which purported to be valid and logical but were in fact not so. Their "detection" and "analysis" was also, therefore, in the nature of an exposé. And this, too, though a more restricted task, is unquestionably a useful one.

But how can one analyze "propaganda" when it is the accuracy of statements made or the validity of methods of arguing that is in question except by determining whether the statements are in fact true and the reasoning logically sound as they purport to be? The fact that the arguments are advanced by men interested in influencing opinion is in itself hardly a decisive consideration. Men rarely argue with others unless they want to convince them and have an "interest" in so doing. True statements are sometimes made by bad men for evil purposes, and the devil not only quotes scripture for his purposes but—if Milton is a reliable reporter—can argue very cogently on occasion. There is, of course, the further question as to whether the "propaganda" appeals analyzed

[39] *Propaganda Analysis*, Vol. IV, No. 13, p. 4.

are such that, whether true and well reasoned or not, it is socially desirable that they should be widely disseminated and believed. What one would have expected was that an Institute designed to help the rest of us think clearly and effectively on social issues would have been much concerned to discriminate among propaganda appeals those that were true and in their influence good, from those that were not. But it is just here that the enlightenment of the debunking era shines clearest. The Institute in a final statement, "We Say Au Revoir," gave explicit attention to this matter. It observed that some students wanted the word "propaganda" to refer only to a so-called "bad" variety, thus distinguishing it from other activities such as education which are included in the more general definition but serve a good purpose none the less. The rejection of this proposal was firm. "The Institute holds that 'good' and 'bad' are relative terms; that what is good for one man is bad for another, depending on whose interest is served. The important question is whether the propagandist's interest coincides with ours." [40] This has a familiar sound; we have heard its like before. What is here instructive is the effect that this refusal to evaluate had on the actual evaluations of "propaganda" that the analysts were constantly making. There were warnings in the press and alarms in the country about "fifth columnists." Such warnings were intended to influence opinion and action, and frequently did so. The Institute therefore got out a bulletin announcing that this influencing was going on and that if people permitted themselves to believe what they were told popular action against "fifth columnists" was to be expected. [41] Well, in the vernacular of the period, so what? If there were men engaged in the kind of activity thus designated, and if the allegations were true, and relevant to action, what better than that we should be awakened to our danger? The Institute, however, does not deal with propaganda as "good" or "bad"

[40] *Ibid.*, p. 4.
[41] *Ibid.*, Vol. III, p. 93ff.

—that all depends on your point of view. Nor does it deal with facts about fifth columnists, of whom as we now know there were many about whose activities there was good cause to be alarmed. It deals only with "fifth columnists," with allegations made by "interested" parties and likely, if they are believed, to stir men up considerably. There is no doubt that the effect of this sort of analysis is mainly to render men suspicious of any statements made that reflect emotion on the part of those who make them and are likely to incite to action those who believe them. And this is done without providing the means of ascertaining whether or not the statements in question are or are not valid. They are in any case "propaganda," and the Institute was prepared to meet them with a lifted eyebrow, a plentiful supply of cautionary remarks and a fine "objective" refusal to recognize as "good" what, by that very failure of discrimination, was left in the company of Hitler's speeches, and Father Coughlin's, which the Institute also had "detected" as propaganda and analyzed accordingly. So, when British "celebrities" in this country, before our entrance into the war, were "detected" stating Britain's case to us and pointing out "reasons" why we ought to be concerned about it, the Institute was on its guard. For "the lecturers," as it warned its readers "cannot help but carry on propaganda. As Englishmen they naturally want to rally support for the cause of the Allies. Some realize this, as does Mr. Duff Cooper, who, in his talk at Columbia University, said that his propaganda was good propaganda because it was based on 'truth.' " [42] That it might be based not on "truth" but on truth and be not merely "good" but good for the ears of those who only later and against the cautionary warnings of the "analysts" came to realize the peril in which they stood, was a further point, not so easy to deal with. And so throughout. The betrayal of Czechoslovakia might well have been supposed to be an issue of great moment to

[42] *Ibid.*, p. 32.

Americans concerned to think well and effectively, but what they got from the Institute was the "betrayal" of Czechoslovakia,[43] a case of "name-calling" obviously, and thus a piece of "propaganda" as even the least instructed reader might have guessed. Then there were "glittering generalities," against which the analysts have always been suspicious. And there are, as Carl Becker has well observed, "generalities that still glitter," the principles of liberal democracy among them, and a valid appeal to them is perennially pertinent to the conduct of American policy. Such an appeal is none the less "propaganda" and can be "detected" by the familiar methods. As to whether it is "good" or "bad" propaganda, who is to say? Surely not the Institute for Propaganda Analysis.

It may appear that a minor incident in our recent intellectual history is here being taken too seriously. But in its implications it is not without its serious lesson. For here were well-intentioned people, eager to use the best available methods for good thinking on social issues, presented with a method which systematically warned against making the very distinctions most essential to good thinking in this field. They were thus unable to recognize the truth when they saw it because all they could see was "propaganda" and within the ambiguous area thus designated they had not the means for a just and discriminating evaluation. If it is true, as alleged, that a cautious Congresswoman still refused to credit the truth of reports of the Japanese attack on Pearl Harbor two days after the event on the ground that they were just "propaganda," we need hardly be surprised. It seems the fitting climax to this tendency in current thought and it provides a sufficient commentary on its value.

(4) A further stage in the development we have been charting is reached when the analysts, while refusing, in their professional capacity, to judge an ideal in terms of its claim

[43] *Ibid.*, Vol. I, p. 83.

to rational validity, insist on judging it as an ideology in terms of its "correspondence" with the "realities" in the social situation which their more "objective" research has identified. The ideology of liberalism, for instance, has recently had some very hard things said about it by those whose business it is to face the "realities" for us and report the results of their findings. Mr. Burnham identifies it with the ideology of a capitalist society and finds little hope for it in the kind of world we now live in. "At the present time, the ideologies that can have a powerful impact, that can make real headway, are, naturally, the *managerial* ideologies, since it is these that alone correspond with the actual direction of events." [44] What these "managerial" ideologies are, and how they are to function in the curbing of the masses, has already been seen.

But what does it mean to speak of an ideology corresponding to the actual direction of events? How is "the actual direction of events" ascertained, and what kind of conformity to it is to be expected from a "myth" that, as has previously been claimed, cannot properly be called "true" or "false." The answer, in Burnham's terms, is not hard to give. The actual direction of events is the drive of the managers for power, and the basic realities are the technological requirements of modern industry which put them in a position to make good their demands. The only ideology that can succeed, therefore, will be one which serves the purpose of the managers and aids in the consolidation of their position. The "ideology" that is to prevail must "correspond," that is, to the demands of those who will use it. It must also, of course, be one that actually is effective in enlisting the support of the masses, otherwise it would not serve its purpose. But Hitler, Stalin and the New Deal have all been successful in their use of ideological appeals for managerial and anti-liberal purposes and even in America "liberal" ideas, represented for Mr.

[44] *Op. cit.,* p. 190. Italics in text.

Burnham by Roosevelt's Republican opponents, have been helpless against them. Liberalism, then, no longer agrees with the actualities of our political situation.

Now this is an explicit judgment, and an adverse one, on the validity of the ideal in question, though it is reached in a somewhat round-about way. For, as we saw in the preceding chapter, an ideal that fails to represent a genuinely attainable good is, in that situation, not a good ideal. If liberal ideals are incapable of performing the function of uniting those who accept them in a cause that has a sufficient chance of success to make the risks it entails worth taking, then they are simply not good enough for the times in which we live and a continued devotion to them, in other than a sentimental and nostalgic sense, is really as "fantastic" as the critics say. We must indeed face realities, if we are reasonable men, and we should only be deceiving ourselves and others if we held stubbornly to ideals which "the actual direction of events" had ruled out as possibilities for successful action.

Let us then face the "realities" in question, and with a critical eye. We shall find them a curiously shifty lot. The coming triumph of the managers we have already seen to be the equivocal outcome of a somewhat extravagant extrapolation of currently fashionable movements. No doubt our industrial system will have to be managed, those who manage it will be managers, and they will have the power necessary to do their work. But what kind of people they will be, how responsibly and justly they will perform their function, and how far the cooperation of the masses, who are also their fellow-countrymen and co-workers will be secured not by fraud and coercion, but by free and responsible cooperation in a good rightly held to be of common concern, are further questions, and, for liberalism, the all-important ones. For the liberalism that is alive today even, to some degree, in the "New Deal" whose "managerial" tendencies Burnham has discerned, is not a view about the competition for power of capitalists and managers, but a view about the nature, conditions and value of human freedom. In so far as historical liberalism earlier limited the conditions of such freedom to those which furthered the expanding economic interests of the rising middle class and thus confused the rights of man with the interests of businessmen, it was mistaken, and the consequences of that mistake are still with us. But the means for its correction were long since developed.

If that type of "liberalism" is still current it is not in the writings of practicing liberals but in those of the critics who, by identifying liberalism with its past mistakes, can considerably simplify their refutation of it, and thus pave the way for the anti-liberal doctrines they wish to recommend. The thing that needs to be said plainly about Burnham's account, and there are many others like it, is that its author would not know a liberal if he saw one, for he has systematically deprived himself of the means of recognizing either the ends for which a liberal works or the resources in human nature to which he appeals. The "realities" the critic acknowledges are not the forces in nature and human nature which set the limits within which effective action must work and also, in the context of enlightened planning, provide the opportunities for reshaping existing conditions for good ends. They are rather the last dismal results of a reductive analysis in which the factors essential to an intelligible statement of the meaning of human freedom have been eliminated. *Of course* men struggle for power, since "power," on the human level, is the capacity to produce desired results and without it both good and bad causes are helpless. There is no virtue in being ineffectual and no vice in power as such. The thing that matters, on the level of political action, is that it be used responsibly and that those who submit to it be in a position to hold its users responsible for their acts. That, too, is a question of "power" to be sure, but of the just exercise of power by responsible leaders with the effective consent and cooperation of those in whose name they act. It is, in short, a question of justice and freedom, and of whether or not men are sufficiently concerned about them to act resolutely for their preservation. It is not surprising that Mr. Burnham can find nothing that "corresponds" to this in the "realities" with which he is dealing. He left it out at the start.

Mr. Spykman has a much sounder appreciation than Mr. Burnham of the demands on human nature that a genuinely "liberal" program makes. But he, too, has compared the "social myth" of liberal democracy with the realities, and found it wanting. The following passage makes his view explicit. "Liberal democracy as an ideology for a revolutionary campaign in the modern world has certain obvious drawbacks. Because of the responsibilities which it inevitably places on the individual, it runs counter to certain inherent tendencies of human nature. Modern man lives in a society confronted with problems so complex, so difficult to comprehend, so hard to solve, that the average man feels hopeless in the face of them. Asking him to master its difficulties in order that he may vote intelligently on matters of policy is asking the impossible, and it is not surprising that the confused crowd should cry for leadership and dictatorship . . . This contemporary urge for security finds no answer in Anglo-Saxon liberalism with its emphasis on individualism and its stern insistence on personal responsibility." [45]

This sounds formidable and it calls proper attention to the very real difficulties that contemporary attempts to make human freedom a political fact must face. But it shows the same sort of tendency to state the "realities" of the situation in abstraction from the context of effective social planning in which the liberal program alone makes sense. *Of course* liberalism "runs counter to certain inherent tendencies of human nature" if by human nature we mean a nature that functions apart from that organization of purpose which

[45] Spykman, *op. cit.*, pp. 257-258.

makes rational action possible. Every step in the improvement of human behavior that was ever made ran counter to tendencies in human nature as they operated before its development and would probably have continued to operate apart from its intervention.

The human nature to which any reformer must appeal is not a datum antecedently existing but an achievement of that very activity which is still in process of attaining its goal. There is, to be sure, no good, and much harm, in asking the impossible, but what is possible is a function of conditions which are themselves sometimes within the area of rational control. If "the average man" feels hopeless today, it is not merely because inherent tendencies in his nature dictate that feeling but because men who ought to have known better have made an unhappy mess of things. And among those men the analysts who today offer him no better ideal than that of snatch and grab, under the presiding genius of an irresponsible leader, are to be included. The urge for security must indeed be satisfied, but whether men seek security in the will of a dictator or the freedom of democratic action will depend in part on what they judge to be the fruits of dictatorship and on the resolution with which even average men in a democracy will sometimes cooperate to maintain their way of life. The inflated prestige of dictatorship today, a nine years' wonder in a world which moral skepticism as well as political ineptitude had helped demoralize, corresponds less to the inescapable realities of human nature than to blunders that could have been and can still be corrected and to failures that even today are being made good. We cannot ask the average man to grasp all the complexities of modern society, but he might, very far short of that, have wit enough to discern, e.g., the difference between Roosevelt and Hitler. We must not ask the impossible, but if we cease to ask the possible which is not yet actual, when it is also the humanly excellent, we shall have run counter to at least one inherent, and very valuable, tendency in human nature, the tendency to use ideals as guides for action. It is to that tendency which liberalism appeals, and there is no good reason to believe that that appeal cannot and will not be in good measure successful.

Enough has been said, I hope, to show that the "realities" to which the skeptics appeal are by no means the same as the conditions a reasonable man should take account of in deciding on a course of action. Yet it is only when they are so regarded that the negative judgment against a liberal ideal (or "ideology") as a valid basis for effective social action can be made out. Hence the case against liberalism has not been proved, and is in fact unsound. But we cannot leave the matter at that point. We have still to understand why so many able and well-intentioned theorists have supposed it to be valid—the embodiment of a clearheaded "realism" that all sensible men would do well to emulate. The habit of thought they manifest is one of the factors in the present situation of which serious account must be taken. For what is antecedently possible is only of human importance when it comes also to be what men believe is possible and are willing to work to bring about. A realism that persistently narrows the area of the effective possible by discrediting as "day dream" and "fantasy" whatever transcends the boundaries of the only "reality" it is prepared to acknowledge is important in proportion not to its truth but to its influence. In current American thought that influence has been, and promises to be, a potent one. I am not optimistic enough to suppose that it can be seriously undermined by such arguments as I can bring against it. But *one* of the reasons why this sort of theory gains adherents is that it is thought to be true. If we can show that it is not, that discovery may have some bearing on its further career.

The "realistic" analysis, we have said, is both unsound and misleading. But there is some truth in it, as there usually is in a theory which gains the support of intelligent men, and this truth is by no means without pertinence to contemporary problems. Let us take a simple instance. "Man is a beast of prey," said Nietzsche, and Spengler, following the master, announces that he will "say it again and again." [46] There is some truth in this. Men often behave like beasts of prey—or worse—and an idealism which fails to reckon with this aspect of their behavior is not wise. Yet man is also, sometimes and under some conditions, not a beast of prey, in any usual or straightforward sense. Of course, if you use your terms unscrupulously enough any human action can be described as predatory and when Spengler goes on to characterize experimental science as "the interrogation of nature under torture—the stratagem of intellectual beasts of prey" [47] there are those who find such pretentious loose talk significant. Short of that, however, and in the cases where we want to distinguish predatory actions from others, the fact remains that some human actions are *not* predatory in the sense required. This, in fact, is recognized by the theorists, who greet it with shrill and vituperative ejaculations. If man is a beast of prey by nature and yet isn't a beast of prey in his actual behavior, then the behavior in question must be set down as unnatural, unhealthy, perverse, world-denying and vulgar. And so indeed they have set it down. This tells us something about Nietzsche and Spengler, but what does it tell us about human behavior? When is man a beast of prey and when isn't he? And what difference does it make?

The answer, sometimes found impressive, is that he is one really, or naturally, or essentially or ultimately, or—let this phrase be carefully considered—in the last analysis. And what is the last analysis, which alone reveals what man naturally, essentially, really and ultimately is, appearances to the contrary notwithstanding? This question the analysts do not

[46] O. Spengler, *The Hour of Decision*, p. 21.
[47] O. Spengler, *Man and Technics*, pp. 82-83.

coherently answer, but we can see the answer from a study of their procedure. The last analysis is the one which the analyst regards as fundamental or basic for his purposes and which he proposes to use as normative for further judgment on the facts in hand. The determination of "the last analysis" is, in fact, a proposal, or the announcement of a resolution to treat a certain type of consideration as basic in the interpretation of further facts within the area investigated and to estimate the significance of such facts by reference to the "realities" of its preferential interest. But it masquerades as a discovery about the real nature of the objects or processes analyzed and thus, for the unwary, offers a principle of organization or interpretation in the guise of an independent discovery of the nature of the world. It is ironical that those who have given such extensive consideration to the "ideological" factors in the thought of others, should have been so slow to recognize its palpable operation in their own research.

The choice of "ultimates," or of a last analysis, need not and ought not to be an arbitrary one. There are always considerations that motivate such a choice and there should be considerations that justify it, or render it wise and reasonable under the circumstances. It is the province of philosophy to examine such choices and the grounds on which they can reasonably be made. But while the analysts we are now considering, like the rest of us, have philosophical commitments in their choice of ultimates, they have not been critically aware of them or known what they were doing when they made use of them. The confusion that is the consequence of this irresponsible sort of philosophizing is a not inconsiderable factor in the situation which, as Mr. Spykman tells us, the average man finds so perplexing.

To say, with Spengler, that man is a beast of prey, is to say that it is the combative aspects of his behavior that are to be regarded as natural and appropriate. When he behaves in any other way, or tries to escape the "reality" of the "doom" to which the attempt to civilize an essentially predatory animal is condemned, he is set down as a coward, an idealist and a poor specimen generally. Reformers and rationalists, who set up any other goal for conduct than that of fighting and exploiting and, rather queerly for a beast of prey, accepting with fortitude the doom which the "physiognomic tact" of Spengler discerns as the fate of mankind, are the worst of the lot, for they have "the presumptuous intention to control living history by paper systems and ideals." [48] And that is a thing, surely, that no well constituted beast of prey would ever do. To characterize their conduct as unnatural is, therefore, to put it mildly. All this is accompanied in the *Decline of the West,* by much erudition, some rather shrewd observations of the current trend of events in Europe, and a vituperative terminology which begs in advance every important question raised. It is true, no doubt, that the words of the rationalists were mostly inscribed on paper, but even *Man and Technics,* though got out in this country in a very dressy binding, was hardly carved in stone. "Living history," for purposes of the argument, is the kind of history Spengler writes, and it corresponds to the "realities" of the secular course of events only when everything in it that does not correspond has been ruled out, like the "tamed beast of prey," as "mutilated, world-weary, inwardly dead."

It is to be expected, of course, that one man's "last analysis" will be another man's poison. We shall have something to say, in the final section of this volume, about the way in which such claims are reasonably adjudicated. It is enough for our present purposes to see what, in the context of effective social action, the "realities" are of which account must be taken. They will be the things that the analyst regards as of primary importance, the first things that must be put first, as a trite expression has it, and to which all else is to be subordinated. And hence, to tell us we must face "real-

[48] O. Spengler, *The Hour of Decision,* p. 115.

ities" is not very enlightening until we know what the selected realities are and with what intent they were selected. Mr. Spykman has some interesting things to say on this point. He is proposing a "realistic" foreign policy for the United States, one that is "designed not in terms of some dream world but in terms of the realities of international relations, in terms of power politics." And why are we to accept the terms of power politics as defining the "realities" we seek? It is because in the absence of international government "the struggle for power [between states] is identical with the struggle for survival, and the improvement of the relative power position becomes the primary objective of the internal and the external policy of states. All else is secondary, because *in the last instance* only power can achieve the objectives of foreign policy. Power means survival, the ability to impose one's will on others, the capacity to dictate to those who are without power, and the possibility of forcing concessions from those with less power. Where the *ultimate* form of conflict is war, the struggle for power becomes a struggle for war power, a preparation for war." [49] This is not what Americans like to think. Our "social myth" stresses rationalism, "a legalistic approach, and a faith in the compelling power of the reason of the law. This almost instinctive preference for a moral and legal outlook on international affairs tends to obscure for the American people *the underlying realities of power politics*." [50]

Among these underlying realities are the facts of our strategic situation, as political geography reveals them. To maintain our power position, Mr. Spykman holds, we must control this hemisphere as far south as the bulge of Brazil and ally ourselves with powers in Europe and Asia to prevent our "encirclement" from those continents. The nations fitted by their geographic position to be our allies are not always

[49] *Op. cit.*, p. 18, my italics.
[50] *Ibid.*, p. 216, my italics.

those we might, on other grounds, wish to have for friends. This is notably true of Japan. But, says Mr. Spykman, "Alliances are made in terms of geography and balance of power, not in terms of sentiment, and if there is a certain friendly feeling toward an ally, it is usually the effect and not the cause of political cooperation." [51] Geography is of the essence of the case, sentiment is not. And so, to sum the whole thing up, "The search for power is not made for the achievement of moral values: moral values are used to facilitate the achievement of power." [52] And it is the struggle for power that is "the underlying reality," whether our ideology will admit it or not.

There is, again, much truth in this. The men who make the peace at the end of this war will need all the information they can get about strategic requirements for the maintenance of their power position. But what they can learn from political geography—or "geo-politics"—on matters of policy will make sense only when it is combined with much else that geo-politics can hardly tell them. The "demands" that determine the policy of a country are not those of "space" or of geography but of men who intend to use their spatial and strategic position for human ends. If they can see no better end for national policy than continued national aggrandizement, they will use their knowledge of political geography to direct the seizure, by intimidation or war, of the strategic bases which insure military domination. If, unlike Hitler and Carlyle's celebrated bootblack but like Mr. Spykman, they are content to control only a section of the world, though one considerably larger than our present national boundaries, they will seek a balance of power in which that status will be recognized by other interested parties, while those who might object to it can be speedily put down by force. That is what political geography tells you to do, if that is the

51 *Ibid.*, p. 256.
52 *Ibid.*, p. 18.

kind of world you want to live in. But the continents would not need to change their shape, nor the leopard his spots, to make sense of a different kind of political set-up, one in which a shared common interest in security against the recurrence of just such "geo-political" enterprises as that which Hitler has now undertaken, would lead nations to pool their forces against a common aggressor, and to keep the peace. That has never happened yet, but it could happen and would be worth great risk and effort to secure. The difficulties that stand in its way are not geographical, nor technological, they are in considerable part moral. So long as politicians agree with Mr. Spykman that morals are useful only, or primarily to facilitate the struggle for power, it quite certainly will not happen. For in that case there will be no virtue in a promise nor security in a common understanding except in so far as the keeping of it is advantageous, on the level of power politic "realistically" conceived, and one man or nation would be a fool to trust another on any such basis. What Mr. Spykman calls "the last instance" would then be the only possible instance, and the only security against war would be for each nation to try to achieve a position of such dominance that the threat of violence could thereafter take the place of the exercise of it. It was the attempt of one nation, with its allies to reach that position that brought on the present war, and the continuance of such a policy that will as surely bring on others. What Mr. Spykman's appeal to the "last instance" actually does, therefore, is to normalize the present chaotic situation as the "underlying reality" to which all efforts at future improvement must conform. This has the look of being very hard headed. But it is also very short sighted. *Of course* nations will fight if worse comes to worst, just as men will in many cases lie and steal and murder for bread if they are reduced by starvation to so low a level. Every decent trait in human nature requires some degree of organized adjustment in the individual and between the individual and his

environment for its effective exercise. As Hitler characteristically observed, "The greatest of spirits can be liquidated if
its bearer is beaten to death with a rubber truncheon." That,
too, is a truth about human nature "in the last instance." But
it is precisely the business of rationally directed human action
to see to it that the conditions of this "last instance" do not
occur, that the breakdown on the level of human behavior
which makes them possible is forestalled. To claim that this
can securely be accomplished, where the relations of national
states are in question, is to go beyond the present facts to a
possible and desired future outcome. But to deny that it can
be done and to set up as the "underlying reality" of political
action a projection of our present failures into the indefinite
future is also to go beyond the present facts, and less intelligently. The cynicism of its conclusion is the reflection
of its initial choice of "realities." It rationalizes the morally
uninhibited struggle for power by depicting the international
situation as one in which "in the last instance" nothing else is
effective and acclaims as a realist the man who acts on the
assumption that nothing else matters. This is not any longer
a refusal to make judgments on ideological issues, but a way
of so making them that only one side—and the worse—on
social issues can present a case. It is the appropriate fruit of
that trained incapacity to see moral issues which we have
been examining.

(5) There is but one further step to be taken in this unhappy history of a state of mind. From "realistic" acquies-
cence in a state of affairs to which moral scruples, having no
standing in the "realities" of the world, are merely inappropriate, we pass to the bandwagon stage of joining forces
with the winning side. "There is no fighting the wave of the
future." Now the winning side—however much we may de-
plore its methods—is the side of the future, hence of "progress" and advance. Naturally, "dynamic" and "vital" forces
must break with the past and its morality—which was after all

no better than it should have been—how else can the new be created? The particular episode in our own political history with which *The Wave of the Future* was associated is already well in the past. But the state of mind it felicitously expressed is still with us. We can see it, in learned works as well as in the ten cent weeklies, in the identification of the "natural"—the way things are whether we like it or not— with the "normal"—the only way things could reasonably be expected to be—and then with what is reasonably to be accepted—which a healthy mind will acquiesce and collaborate in with no "idealistic" nonsense. What it amounts to is the use of what *is*—from which all suggestion of what ought to be has been scrupulously eliminated—as the standard for what ought to be. It is the normative use of "facts" previously emptied of all normative significance. And that, in the context of the use of ideals for the determination of social policy, is the ultimate disloyalty to human reason. Is it not "natural" for "dynamic" powers to snatch and grab from their weaker brethren? We do not *like* it of course and are not to be quoted as approving. But after all, we did not make the world. And surely "Vitally strong states, possessing only limited space, *owe it to themselves* to enlarge their space by colonization, amalgamation or conquest." [53] It is the way of nature, after all, which is also the way of growth. Naturally then, the "vitally strongest state," which has shown its disposition and capacity to grab the most, can plead "its *right* to natural and necessary growth." [54] To acknowledge the right of the strong against the weak, of the bully to his spoils as long as he can hold on to them since his success in bullying is, in the circumstances, the evidence of his dynamism and presumptive hold upon the future, is the final stage in this curious pilgrim's progress of the emancipated mind.

[53] Quoted from H. Kjellen, Swedish professor of geo-politics in R. Strauss-Hupe, *Geopolitics*, p. 43, my italics.

[54] *Ibid.*, my italics.

The attitude it expresses is untenable not because it offends the canons of an outworn moral code but because it violates the principles of elementary good sense. What can "right" possibly mean in a situation antecedently emptied of all moral content? It is "natural" for states that manifest their creative dynamism in the systematic destruction of the lives or liberties of their neighbors so to behave—i.e., it is the case that they do so behave in the given circumstances. It is no less natural for their intended victims to resist if they can and in the process sometimes to alter premature estimates as to precisely what the "inevitable" is to be and who, therefore, are its accredited agents. To talk of "rights" on this level is to talk misleading nonsense. "Vitality," again, is an honorific term only when we know that it is the vitality of a force that makes for good, rather than the malignant growth of a cancer, which also has a "dynamism" of its own. There is a significant difference between that break with old standards that is the necessary prelude to humanly valuable creation and the random destructiveness of the "blond beast" on the prowl, but it is not to be made out except on the basis of a standard of values, of what ought to be, that can justify itself in terms of the best we know. The future will be what it will, though that is hardly an enlightening discovery. But there is no escaping the responsibility of rational judgment on the "creative" possibilities of the present and our own obligations in respect to them, save by descending to a level on which the categories of discriminating valuation no longer have a meaning. The confusion of the two levels in an apology for moral surrender masquerading as a factual acknowledgment of things as they are is an ingenious way of having the worst of both levels. There is not much else to be said for it.

An amusing instance of this curious confusion of categories is provided by a work of Spengler's which did not lack admirers in this country. His *Hour of Decision* is offered as no "wish-picture" of the future, but a clear delineation of the facts as they are and will be. The future is forbidding indeed, but Spengler can take it, and the reader who is prepared to follow him can expect no comfort for his "illusions." He may, however, if he can be one of those "big and strong beasts of prey" whom the author admires, find much to flatter his vanity. Consider, for example, the notion of equality. It is obvious to the *man of facts* that "society rests on the inequality of men. That is a natural fact. There are strong and weak natures, natures born to lead or not to lead, creative and untalented, honorable, lazy, ambitious and placid natures. Each has its place in the general order of things. The more significant the Culture, the more it resembles the structure of a noble animal or vegetable body and the greater are the differences between its constituent elements." [55] What more natural than that those who are by nature marked as superior should have a preponderant share of this world's goods? *"High culture is essentially bound up with luxury and wealth,"* [56] and "a refined craving for luxurious conditions" is a mark of true breeding.

Not luxury for everyone, however, by any means. The proletariat is not by nature and history designed for luxury and has no business at all to ask for it. Its leaders, however, with "morbid vanity" and a "vulgar greed for power"—quite different, it would appear from the predatory instinct of the noble beast of prey—have led the workers to rebel against this natural ordering of things. This is regrettable. For the desire of the poor for a better way of life is not as genteel as is a "refined craving for luxurious conditions." It is something quite disgraceful from the standpoint, of course, of the facts of history. It is materialism. "As soon as one mixes up the concepts of poverty, hunger, distress, work and wages (with the moral undertone of rich and poor, right and wrong

[55] *Op. cit.,* p. 92.
[56] *Ibid.,* p. 102. Italics in text.

and is led thereby to join in the social and economic demands of the proletarian sort—that is, money demands—one is a materialist." [57]

The pity of it is that this materialism is sometimes successful and "we are shown that everything that the few big and strong beasts of prey, the statesmen and conquerors, have created throughout the centuries can be gnawed away in a short space of time by the mass of small animals, the human vermin. The old and honorable forms of the State lie in ruins." [58] This was written before Hitler's regime had got under way. At the end of his volume Spengler was asking: "Who will lead the legions of the next Caesar?" He lived to get some intimation of the answer, though hardly its full significance.

Is it necessary to comment further on all this? Since men who should know better have been imposed on by it, perhaps it is. The fact-minded Spengler has simply identified the order of his social and economic preference with the order of nature and history. Prowess manifest within the limits set by this order is proof of natural superiority, and to the victor belong the spoils. But success in modifying the regime or setting up another in its place is in no wise a proof of merit; quite the contrary. The strong are still strong, though defeated by the weak, who qualify in consequence not as members in good standing of the predatory class, but rather as human vermin. Yet vermin too are predatory and it is the insects, we are told by the scientists, who shall inherit the earth. There is no fighting the wave of the future. It is all very confusing and not a little confused, a fraudulent identification of *de facto* power with excellence which refuses to accept the consequence of its commitment when its side is losing. Spoiled children and willful, irresponsible men often think and speak in this fashion. It is only in the new enlighten-

[57] *Ibid.*, pp. 130-131.
[58] *Ibid.*, p. 145.

ment that it has been made to serve as a model for a truly historical understanding of things as they "ultimately" are.

The moral of this unmoral tale is plain enough. There is, in the context of the reasonable determination of social policy, no valid substitute for enlightened moral judgment on the attainable good to which men, in virtue of their common needs and interests, are committed, and in the pursuit of which they share responsibly in reciprocal rights and duties. An ideal that can meet the demands of this activity is a valid, rationally grounded, ideal, worthy of the allegiance of men of good will. One that falls short of it is not. The refusal to make this distinction between right and wrong, valid and invalid, when issues of social policy are at stake, is not a mark of intellectual emancipation, based on new discoveries about the working of the human mind in its social environment. It is a failure to face social issues rationally, with due regard for factors essential to their just evaluation. We have seen enough of the nature and consequences of that failure. It is time to consider more fully the conditions and possibility of success.

CHAPTER III

THE EFFICACY OF REASON

We are now in a position to deal affirmatively with the issue whose mishandling, as was seen in the preceding chapter, has led to so much confusion. In what sense are social ideals true? How do they or ought they to correspond to facts, "realities," "the actual direction of events" and the "imperatives" of history? And what bearing has such correspondence or the lack of it on their validity as ideals and on the claims their protagonists make for our support? In outline, the answer has already been given. A valid ideal is a genuine and attainable good proposed as a goal for action and capable of uniting and directing the activity of the group to which it is addressed in the just and effective pursuit of the good it represents. That is what it ought to be, if its acceptance is to be reasonably justified, and that is what, when it proves reasonably justifiable, it is. Questions of factual truth are inseparably bound up with the assessment of the validity of ideals, and the determination of truth must here be made, as elsewhere, without appeals to any special insight, or authority or metaphysical illumination that transcends the pedestrian methods of fact-finding appropriate to the discovery of what is happening, has happened and is likely to happen in the world in which our bodies and their perceptually observable environment are palpably involved. But since questions of what has happened, is happening or will probably happen are here considered in their bearing on what is desirable as a goal for action, and since what is desirable, on the human level, is a question not only of what is actual and possible but also of what is good, the factual question is not the only one at issue. Information about matters of fact thus determined is necessary but not sufficient to the adequate validation of ideal claims. If this is what those have meant who tell us that an ideology cannot, from its very nature, claim "scientific" truth, but that it must none the less correspond to the conditions of actuality, then so far their pronouncement has been correct, though most unhappily stated. The manner of this correspondence, however, is what has been most radically misconceived. A valid ideal is itself neither a report nor the expression of an attitude or wish, but an estimate, based on reports, of the good worth pursuing under actual conditions in which a variety of wishes and attitudes in themselves incoherent and full of potential conflicts can attain a reasonable satisfaction. To call it irrational or mythical because it represents a good not now actual or capable of "verification" as a report of an existing state of affairs, is to apply an impertinent and wholly misleading criterion. In the context of social action, which is that of its relevant use, an ideal would be irrational, because inadequate to its essential intent, if it did *not* represent a good not now actual. For anyone who could suppose that the continuance of the existing state of affairs represented the best goal attainable for cooperative human action would be almost incredibly unwise. To call such ideals "myths" is misleading. "Myths" are, in common usage, ideas that have been found to lack a kind of validity which those who seriously accepted them supposed them to have, while a valid social ideal need not lack anything whatever that is required for a reasonable acceptance of its claims. The suggestion, bound up with the use of the terms "myth," and "stereotype," that those who take social ideals seriously as standards for conduct are fooling themselves and are as deluded as those who thought to see Jupiter emerge from the heavens or Venus from the waves, is thoroughly unwarranted. The cynicism it engenders is less the fruit of uncommon penetration than of the uncritical use of an uncommonly careless terminology.

We can also reject as mistaken the view that the determination of what is good, as an ideal for cooperative social action, is a merely arbitrary affair. This view proceeds on the assumption that no other rational discipline is attainable than that which restricts its activity to the collection and reporting of facts and that this would, in the circumstances, be inadequate to justify the choice of an ideal. It gains its plausibility in part from the quite arbitrary classification on which it is based, everything not scientifically verifiable being relegated to the limbo of sentimental fantasy and the like. But it survives, also, through the ignorance, which a triumphant scientific specialism has fostered, of that rational discipline in which the facts of the sciences are organized for purposes of constructive and comprehensive wisdom in the direction of policy. We must try, therefore, to make clear the nature of this discipline and the way that reason can work, and does work, in the context of social action.

Social Science and Social Ideals. The proximate area of such activity, now, alas, a battleground for contending sects rather than a well developed field of inquiry, is that in which social scientists and their followers dispute about the social meaning and use of their findings. Should investigators in the fields of politics, economics and psychology maintain the "impartial objectivity" elsewhere associated with scholarly research, or is it rather their business to direct their activity to the promotion of causes whose merits they, more than other men, are in a position accurately to assess? The academic tradition still reveres what Mr. Lancelot Hogben calls the "idol of purity" in research, but an increasing number of practical minded researchers, Mr. Hogben among them, preach the duty of carrying through the implications of scientific findings to controversial and tendencious applications. And they practice what they preach. Mr. Robert Lynd, in a provocatively entitled volume *Knowledge for What?* has stated the case for the "tendencious" sect very ably, and I shall make use of his analysis in what follows.

It might be supposed that since the issue, basically, is that of the propriety of the social scientist sponsoring the use of his findings as guides for social policy, some careful attention would normally be given to the question of the bearing of these findings on issues of social action, and the kind of contribution a scientist can best make to their adjudication. It is just here, however, that the confusion has been greatest, with the result—not unusual in such cases—that each side in the controversy maintains with fervor a half truth which it, and its antagonists, are unable to keep distinct from a whole error. Each, therefore, in defending his own morsel of insight against his opponent's error, commits an error of his own which that opponent is justified in exposing, and the exposure of which he takes as the sufficient justification for the complementary error he has mistakenly espoused. This sort of thing can go on indefinitely, and does.

The defenders of "objective impartiality" in the social sciences stand initially on firm ground. The first, most basic, and most indispensable contribution that the social sciences can make to the adjudication of social issues is to supply reliable information on relevant matters of fact. This will be information about what happens, or would probably happen, under determinable conditions, and nothing is more painfully clear than that many well intentioned social policies have failed for lack of just such information. Under these conditions what matters is that the information should be accurate, and that its relevance to the probable success or failure of a proposed course of action should be clearly made out. The information may well be of a disappointingly un-ideal character. It may be such as to warrant the rejection of ideals which appeal to the best in human nature and which we should all like to subscribe to if we could. But if it is information that accurately portrays the situation within which our ideal activities must be carried on, it is the responsibility of reasonable men to take account of it and refuse to be deceived by false hopes.

Now, what the defenders of objectivity rightly affirm is that in the gathering and reporting of such factual information the researcher's first duty is to see things as they are or can be, not as he would like them to be, and that he must, in the pursuit of truth, rigidly repress his own desires and preferences and social enthusiasms. If he feels called upon to justify conclusions antecedently determined by the interests of the class or race or religious sect to which he belongs, and to accommodate his findings to such interests, he is selling his scientific birthright for a mess of pottage. Nothing that the scientist can contribute as seer, or sectarian propagandist, or lay preacher, can compare in value with what he contributes as purveyor of reliable—though sometimes discouraging—information about the nature of the world. It is, therefore, of the utmost importance that, as a researcher, he respect the canons of "purity," or of logical and factual accuracy which, here as elsewhere, are our best available means for distinguishing what in fact occurs from mistaken, though frequently attractive, beliefs and opinions about it. "The facts" apart from an evaluation of their social significance may be of little use; but the social significance of "facts" which are not facts at all is hardly an improvement on them. What is of supreme value is an adequate interpretation of facts which are genuinely what they purport to be. But for that we must first of all have the facts, and a zeal for social significance which gets in the way of their accurate determination is no help at all either to science or to society.

It might seem that this would go without saying—that no one worth considering would seriously question it. And there are indeed few, in this country at least, who would care to challenge it explicitly. There are plenty, however, who are

prepared to deny its implications when they prove inconvenient. Nor is their procedure wanting in a kind of specious
plausibility. For *mere* facts are quite surely not sufficient to
provide a just basis for the criticism of a social ideal, and the
disciples of "the facts, and nothing but the facts" have often
supposed that they were sufficient. Hence, the reaffirmation
of "spiritual" values, against the ostensible denial of "meanings" that "transcend" the facts can easily be made the basis
for a resurgent idealism that will not stop until it has made
its own deeper desires the measure of what is "ultimately" or
"really" the case. Such enthusiasts need not call themselves
idealists—they may be aggressively materialistic in their philosophy and still proclaim a doctrine of "the unity of theory
and practice" which means in practice that no theory is to be
accepted as true which is not subservient to the doctrines and
policies they consider essential to the success of their cause.
Or they may be racists who find in the deeper promptings
of their "blood" a truth for which the abstractions of the
sciences are but a feeble substitute. Against these forms of
obscurantism, and others like them, it therefore remains pertinent to affirm that where a claim to factual knowledge is in
question there is nothing so "ultimate" or worthy of credence
as the evidence which bears on the factual truth or accuracy
of statements made, and that the proper standard for the
estimation of this evidence is not practical but theoretical.
For this is a question of what is in fact the case, whether
we like it or not, and however much or little the knowledge
of it may contribute to the peace of the soul, the progress of
the class struggle, or the meaning of life. And this, as we
have seen, is not without bearing on the determination of
social policy. For it is a primary obligation of a good society
to keep open the channels of free inquiry and responsible research, without which the relevant facts cannot be found out
and made available for the enlightened direction of action.
So much has been already established, and its pertinence to

the issue of "objectivity" in the social sciences is obvious. A science that refuses to be "practical"—in the sense that it refuses subservience, direct or indirect, to any other interest than the discovery and publication of the truth, within the area of its factual investigation—is one of the most practical —i.e., useful and valuable—factors in a civilized society. It should be valued and respected as such.

The question of the bearing of the findings of scientific research on social policy none the less remains. The interpretation must not be allowed to prejudice the facts, but the facts are of little use without the interpretation. What the more judicious advocates of a tendencious social science mean to say, I think, is that the scientist has not completed his work until he has shown what action the facts warrant and lent his active support to such action. "If one is not simply observing the inner orderliness of nature, the essence of science is to analyze, to draw inferences, *and then to implement action*." [1] Action to what end? Is the scientist also to tell us that? Mr. Lynd thinks that he is. It is the sort of task once left to ethics, which was supposed to criticize ends, where the sciences gave information only concerning means. This distinction, Lynd believes, is no longer defensible. "The old, aloof ethics has evaporated, and ethics is today but a component in the cravings of persons going about the daily round of living with each other. And the science of human behavior in culture as the science charged with appraising man's optional futures in the light of himself and of present favoring and limiting conditions, can no more escape dealing with man's deep values and the potential futures they suggest than it can avoid dealing with the expressions, overlayings, and distortions of man's cravings which appear in the institutions of a particular culture." [2]

There is little point in arguing whether it is "the scientist"

[1] Robert Lynd, *Knowledge for What?* p. 166. Italics in text.
[2] *Ibid.*, p. 191.

or "the philosopher" who is licensed to perform a particular job. Anyone who can do it well ought by all means to do it, whatever his academic designation. But what are the requirements for doing this job well? That is an important question, and I do not think that even Mr. Lynd, who does much better at it than most of his colleagues, has given a satisfactory answer. How are we to "deal with" man's deepest cravings when our problem is to determine which social policies are desirable and which are not? We can, of course, catalogue them, and report on the way in which they manifest themselves in a variety of social conditions, but what we want to know is how they ought to be manifest in a social organization judged to be worth attaining. That such an organization ought to be such as to satisfy all our "deepest" cravings is a sound moral judgment—but it *is* a moral judgment and not a report of things as they are nor a prediction as to what in fact they will become. It involves an estimate of what they could become, under favorable conditions, but many other eventualities are just as possible, and some of them much more probable, unless a concern for what is felt to be right and good acts as a considerable motivating force in human behavior. Nor is the manner of this organization an affair merely of adjusting "cravings" to each other, so that all will continue to function without overt conflict. It is a matter of adjusting them all to the demands of responsible persons who act at times for ends they judge to be right and reasonable. If it is less than this, it is, as we have seen, a misrepresentation of the requirements for reasonable social action.

The trouble is that scientists, in their professional capacity, have been very chary of using terms like "justice" in an evaluative sense, or of making judgments about what ought to be. Hence, when they feel called upon to pass judgment on the ends of reasonable action they are tempted to govern their estimate of this total situation by those factors which they have found pertinent and reliable in a more limited field of inquiry. "Cravings" are factual enough—everybody can identify them. What these cravings "demand" can perhaps be listed, and might even be measured, if we were just a little further advanced in these matters. But the question that has to be settled is not what these cravings or drives demand but what practical wisdom demands when drives are harmonized and disciplined with reference to a represented good which justifies and lends meaning to their inarticulate urgency. Again, it may be possible to estimate what our present technological equipment "demands" for its maximum efficient use, and there are bright young men who write as though the "demands" of technology stood as unconditional imperatives to which the rest of human life must accommodate itself on such terms as it can make. There are also "imperatives" of history, of geography, and even of thermo-dynamics [3] which are invoked to tell us scientifically what men and nations require and what, in consequence, they ought to have and to be. In the context of reasonable social action, however, all these are hypothetical imperatives—they are addressed not to partially embodied abstractions which reflect the limits of professional specialization, but to men whose business it is to decide how, in the kind of world the sciences describe to them, they want to live, and to what end. There is, however, one categorical imperative for men of good will, and that is that they consider their fellows as ends—as responsible moral agents—not merely as means to the ends set by considerations of economics, or geo-politics, or the adjustment of "drives" on a level at which a rat will do as well as a man or, in some cases, even better.

To say that the sciences deal with "abstractions" and that their results are therefore to be viewed with suspicion is to say very little, as has been seen. *All* effective thinking is abstract and, where what it abstracts from is irrelevant to the problem

[3] Cf. L. Hogben, *The Retreat from Reason*, p. 70ff. The page references are to the British edition.

considered, the better for it. But where something is left out
that is, in a further context, relevant and even decisive, the
abstraction is illegitimate and misleading in that new context,
and an insistence upon its use because it has *elsewhere* proved
its scientific cogency is simply stupid. It is that kind of
stupidity with which we are faced when a judgment of the
ends for which men can wisely strive, a judgment that ought,
in its comprehensive understanding, to treat nothing as alien
that can be harmoniously included in a life worthy of man's
humanity, is "scientifically" reduced to a statement of the
thermo-dynamic or biological "requirements" of the human
organism. Mr. Lancelot Hogben has offered expert testimony
on the results of such an analysis of "scientific research into
the character of the fundamental requirements and the material resources available for gratifying them." [4] He finds that
the organism *requires* radium and does not require "chairs of
verbal logic," the importance of which, measured by Mr.
Hogben's standards, is indeed somewhat difficult to make out.
There is, of course, in this case and others, the supposed
"cultural value" of activities the bearing of which on "fundamental human requirements" as specified by the expert, is
obscure. But there is a short way of dealing with that. "When
knowledge is said to have cultural value, further inquiry is
usually closed by the statement that it is worth having for
its own sake. This is another way of saying that we value
it as individuals without knowing any good reason to com-
mend it to anyone else." [5] The bumptious philistinism of this
sort of writing illustrates what happens when abstractions are
misapplied and "experts," in the name of the "scientific outlook," take pride in not understanding aspects of human
culture on which they none the less pass judgment with great
assurance. If Mr. Hogben had taken serious account of
Platonic dialogues he would have discovered that the claim

[4] *Ibid.*, p. 49.
[5] *Ibid.*, p. 55.

that something is of value for its own sake, whatever else it is, is not a way of closing inquiry and discussion, but of opening it to ranges of experience the meaning of which, in twenty-five hundred years of subsequent discussion, has by no means been exhausted. But Mr. Hogben has decided that Plato was a "mystic" and no scientist, and he feels no obligation to take account of this great source of human wisdom before setting down the "requirements" of human life with an assurance which would have amazed—and perhaps amused —the skeptical Socrates. It took a reading of Korzybski and Ogden and Richards to assure Mr. Stuart Chase that his failure to understand the great philosophers was their fault and not his,[6] but Mr. Hogben, apparently, needed no such reassurance. He knew thermo-dynamics, bio-chemistry, mathematics and related special subjects. If more is required for a comprehensive grasp of the ends of human living, it has not been apparent to the scientific mind of Mr. Hogben.

In the context of the determination of social policy, which is the determination of the good toward whose attainment groups of men can reasonably direct their cooperative effort, the findings of the several sciences are abstractions in need of supplementation and correction. They state the "needs" of human nature, and its capacities, and the "requirements" of the social situation in terms of some only of the factors of which a wise man will reasonably take account in reaching a decision. An analytic inquiry into the geo-political factors in national policy, considered in abstraction from further questions of the relation of strategy to the kind of world we want to live in and the level of cooperation we want to maintain in it, is a legitimate and possibly fruitful inquiry. But a statesman or a nation in whose policy geo-political considerations were allowed to dominate all other interests would be an offender against the possibility of international amity and enduring peace. It is in the name of that

[6] *Op. cit.*, p. 4.

possibility, accepted as an ideal worth working for, that we condemn such nations today, and rightly condemn them. To understand the nature and grounds for that condemnation, however, one must know something of the good to which human nature, at its best, aspires, and that is not a theme for, or a subdivision within, the science of geo-politics. It is a question of what men want when they understand their more limited interests from the standpoint of an inclusive good in which what is confused and partial in them is enlightened and made complete. The discernment of such a good, not as an eternal pattern of super-mundane grandeur, but as a right ordering of actual human interests to the end of their harmonious satisfaction on the level of cooperative human action, is a task of great difficulty. The best intelligence we have may fail to accomplish it, though there is still no good reason to conclude that it will. But it will need the best, most comprehensive, and most sympathetic understanding of all the factors involved in a good life that we can bring to it. And here Socratic dialectic is not only a better, but an incomparably better, discipline than that professional ignorance of spiritual goods which is the current contribution of the specialized "expert" to the subject.

When, therefore, we express considerable doubt concerning the crusading social scientist as an arbiter of social policy, the reason is clear. The social scientist is also a man, and he may be a wise and conscientious one. If he is wise, his judgment on issues of social policy will be most valuable, and if he is conscientious he will want to bear his full share in supporting good causes. Let him by all means be as practical in both these ways as he can. But if he insists on guiding his practical decisions by the abstractions which have proved their use in his theoretical inquiry, and if he assumes in his support of practical causes the right to exclude from human concern everything that would be out of place in his scientific calculations, he will, at best, be wasting his time and ours. "The union of theory and practice" is a fine thing, if it means that plans for action are to have the benefit of reliable information, obtained by the soundest of theoretical methods, and that the results of theory are in this way to be put to practical use. But the confusion of theory and practice is a very bad thing and, at present, a very pervasive one. Those who suborn the pursuit of truth for "practical" purposes, and those who distort sound practical judgment by restricting its subject-matter to the abstractions with which their scientific inquiry has been professionally concerned, are more nearly related than either party would care to admit. They both have failed to distinguish the respective contexts of theoretical inquiry and practical judgment, and to observe in each the rational discipline proper to its effective exercise.

Should the social scientist deal with "values"? By all means. If he is "dealing with" them descriptively, in terms of the occurrence of valuations or their causes and effects, he can doubtless tell us a great deal that is both interesting on its own account and relevant to our further problems. The fact that he disapproves of some of these valuations, or wishes that they were more easily controlled by considerations of which he does approve should in no way influence the accuracy of his reporting. If it did, the report would be less genuinely "practical" than it ought to be—less reliable as information about what happens. If he is dealing with them evaluatively, from the standpoint of their worth as social ideals, he may again have something valuable to tell us. But it must be realized that he is here speaking from a different standpoint and that if he proposes to assume the authority of that standpoint, and in consequence to tell men categorically what their lives require and what they ought to value, he must accept its responsibilities. And here the requirements of reason are comprehensive wisdom and sound judgment in the determination of a good worth living for, not simplicity and accuracy in the description of selected aspects of behavior. If he is not called to this task or competent to perform it, he is under no obligation to undertake it. His scientific work is a sufficient and indispensable contribution to the good of the society in which he functions. But if he does undertake it he ought to do so responsibly and with an adequate knowledge of what he is about. Lacking this he gives us social cynicism in the guise of "objectivity" and insensitiveness to cultural values as "scientific humanism." We have had more than enough of both.

Ideological Manipulation and the Appeal to Reason. One of the considerations that figured most largely in the debunking crusade against reason was the discovery that social ideals can be, and frequently are, used as instruments for manipulating the people who accept them for ends quite other than those to which they are ostensibly directed. Men fight for "democracy," when they would not fight for the profits of businessmen, but it is the businessmen who profit, we are told, not "democracy," and those who understand these things can add to that profit at but little cost to themselves by playing suitably on the loyalties and idealism of their countrymen. So runs the story, and we have seen the lengths to which it can be carried. We are now in a position, I think, to discriminate reliably between an ideology thus employed and a valid ideal to which men reasonably appeal to enlist cooperative action. It was the failure to make this discrimination which led to the destructive cynicism of the "detectors" of propaganda and their like.

In the first place there are obviously points of agreement. A valid social ideal and an ideology employed as a false front for action which could not, on its own merits, win support, are alike in being designed to influence the behavior of others. The wisest of statesmen, like the most disingenuous of rabble-rousers, wants to get something out of the people to whom he appeals. He wants to use them for a purpose, and unless he succeeds in this, the ideals he invokes as a justification for

action have failed in their purpose. Whatever the goodness
of an ideal consists in, it does not consist in its ineffectiveness
as a means of securing resolute and united action. The social
use of ideas thus falls within the field of "propaganda" as the
Institute for Propaganda Analysis defined it.

Moreover, effective social idealism appeals to men's emotions and, other things being equal, the more potent the
appeal the better. If we could only be rational about things
we did not care about, or recognize truth in instances where
its recognition had not sufficient connection with issues of
urgent concern to stir our emotions, it would be of little use
indeed to appeal to reason. The appeal to reason on issues of
social policy is an appeal to men to act under the guidance
of valid principles and ideals and these rightly make a powerful claim on our emotions. Those who warn us that propa-
gandists appeal to our emotions and invite us to assume an
attitude different from that in which events are merely observed, classified or used as evidence of further happenings
can say the same of any appeal to reason in the context of
social action. The differences, however, are of considerable
significance. For while both the statesman and the rabble-
rouser appeal to our emotions, the one does it in the name
of an ideal that will stand inspection while the other does
not. We are asked to "give our all" for "America" or "Freedom" or "Democracy." The words are shop-worn and may
mean much, or nothing at all. What do they stand for in the
use the speaker makes of them? Is the "America" for which
he asks our support worth supporting? Is the action he proposes one that will, within the limits of reasonable proba-
bility, contribute to its support in a desirable way? Are the
"American" ideals he invokes principles by which he also
is prepared to stand in carrying out the proposed plan of
action, so that we can trust him to behave responsibly as our
agent in the furtherance of a common cause in which we are
jointly concerned? If these questions are answerable in the

affirmative then we are not being fooled when we respond to such an appeal with emotional fervor. We should rather be fools if we failed to respond and were led through indifference or laziness or cynicism to neglect the action on which our security and future happiness may profoundly depend. To follow such ideals *blindly* would be stupid enough, for men have often been led by those who professed them into futile and costly errors. But not to follow them at all, on the ground that we might be being deceived, and thus to fail to discriminate, when the means of discrimination are available, between deceptive manipulation and rationally justifiable persuasion, is only a more sophisticated kind of stupidity or incapacity to distinguish the genuine from the illusory in the situations in which that distinction is essential to intelligent action.

There is a further factor in this situation which needs special attention at present. The terminology of "ideology" and the "manipulation of the masses" has flattered some of the more unlovely tendencies in human nature, and in the natures of scientists, teachers, and publicists in particular. For it has encouraged those whose responsibility it is to expound the ideas necessary for effective social action to regard themselves as experts "controlling" the reactions of the uninstructed and still idealistic populace rather than as co-workers with their fellow-countrymen in the pursuance of ends to which all are alike committed. A drop of acid on a frog's leg will cause the leg to twitch. A judicious drop of idealism in a popular weekly will cause the reading public to twitch and thus further the cause that the "expert" in the control of public opinion has in mind. If the device is merely manipulative, its purpose is served when the anticipated response has been elicited, and that is the end of it. But the subjects manipulated are in this case human beings with minds of their own, and the device by which they are persuaded is an appeal to principles which the manipulator professes to respect as well. If he does not respect them, or the judgment of the people whose "reactions" he is controlling, but is using both simply as means to an end of his own or that of the "élite" he serves, his action is both unintelligent and unmoral. It is unintelligent because men have longer memories than frogs. They are asked not merely to twitch but to believe and there are limits, especially where the means of free inquiry are still open to them, to what and whom they will believe. And it is unmoral because it violates the categorical imperative of all decent cooperative action—it uses men and their ideals not as means—that is inevitable and proper—but as means *merely*, to an end in which they cannot share on the level of responsible humanity. The clear-eyed young experts who like to run things and are not squeamish about the conformity between their words and their performance, so long as they get things done, have perhaps not heard of this principle of conduct, or, what is more likely, would not understand it if they did. It has, none the less, a pertinence to a democratic—as distinct from a managerial—society, that should not be overlooked.

The "liberalism" of John Locke has, in recent years, had some hard things said about it. Yet no one ever saw this point more clearly or stated it more cogently than he. Defending popular government against the charge that it may lead to disturbance or revolution when the people become suspicious of their rulers, he makes these pertinent queries: "Are the people to be blamed if they have the sense of rational creatures, and can think of things no otherwise than as they find and feel them? And is it not rather their fault who put things in such a posture that they would not have them thought as they are?" It would be well for the molders of public opinion to remember that now, not less than in the seventeenth century, the men with whom politicians deal are rational creatures, and that those who undermine the foundations of political honesty—who "put things in such a posture that they would not have them thought as they are"—have only themselves to blame for the breakdown in public confidence that results.

Yet it is not surprising that we have forgotten the truth of Locke's teaching. It rests on a distinction that can only be made when social action is considered from the standpoint of practical reason—when, that is, the ideals on which men are asked to act are not tools by which the shrewd get what they want from the gullible but principles recognized as valid by those who profess them. Part, at least, of the value traditionally attached in this country to the ideal of "a government of laws, not of men" derives from this rationalistic and quite old-fashioned notion that rules and principles, binding on all alike and administered impartially in the name of common justice, ought to govern the conduct of public officials, who are also public servants. It is heartening to observe that this is a generality that has not lost its glitter, even for some of our more skeptical contemporaries. Thus Mr. Thurman Arnold tells us, "I have no doubt as to the practical desirability of a society where principles and ideals are more important than individuals. It is an observable fact that such a society is more secure spiritually and hence more tolerant." [7] It is also the sort of society in which it is supremely important that the ideals and principles professed be also practiced by those who make use of them.

A practical instance will help to make the point here. In trying to build a common front against the Axis powers, our leaders have rightly made much use of the notion of "freedom," not only for ourselves but for all nations willing to unite with us in a common cause. The good they promise is the greatest of all political goods, it is gravely threatened at present, and there seems to be a real chance that we can, through victory in this war, be in a better position than ever before to make it secure. It is therefore a valid ideal, provided

[7] Thurman Arnold, *The Folklore of Capitalism*, p. 393.

that we mean what we say and are prepared to stand by it. But *if* it is a valid ideal, it is not merely a slogan for enlisting support at present but a commitment to a kind of action in the future. It not only elicits a response now, but it makes a promise and arouses an expectation which will later call for fulfilment. That is the sort of thing that moralists sometimes mean when they speak of an "obligation," the kind of engagement that binds men not in so far as they are the subordinates, or dupes of others, but in so far as they are free.

It would be well, then, for the manipulators of opinion, who are now expected to be expert in their knowledge of the appropriate psychological techniques for producing desired responses, to be at least equally mindful of the moral cogency of familiar rules for truth-telling, open dealing and, above all, a decent respect for the opinions of their fellowmen. "The masses" are often wrong, no doubt, about many things that the experts know a great deal about. But when it comes to the management of their own affairs, which are also, in part, the public affairs of the country of which they are citizens, "the masses" are and of right ought to be, individuals with minds of their own, to be made up in their own way and on their own responsibility. It is a great responsibility, and it lays certain moral limits on the manipulative zeal of those who work to unite them effectively in a common cause. It is, none the less, the kind of responsibility without which "freedom" is only a high-pressure word, and nothing that salesmanship in ideas that "curb" the masses can offer is good enough to take its place.

The difference, then, between an ideology that is a tool merely, in the struggle for power of groups, classes or nations on the make, and a social ideal to which free men give their allegiance, knowing what they are doing and to what they are committed, is primarily a moral difference—it concerns the level on which collaboration is achieved and the ends to which it is directed. Those of us who believe that this difference is profoundly important in the determination of social policy maintain that no end to which the efficiency achieved in the competition for power can be directed is worth having, if it means the sacrifice of the human dignity and integrity of the people—quite ordinary people for the most part—who are used as means to its attainment. There are other goods, of course, power and glory for the masters, whoever they may be, and bread, circuses and, perhaps, a kind of security for those who submit. When we say that these other goods are not enough, and that those who willingly submit to tyranny, even a comfortable tyranny, and those who exercise it at what appears to be a great profit to themselves, have lost something that is better than power and glory, better even than circuses and bread, we are making a judgment about ends, not means, the kind of judgment that Mr. Hogben views with scientific suspicion. The aim, however, is not to shut off discussion, but to place it on a level on which the issues of social policy can be apprehended in their widest human significance. And we hold that those who are willing to decide these issues on any narrower basis are, in the long run, simply selling their birthright, and ours, for shoddy goods by no means worth the price.

The Relativity of Principles and the "Taint of Ideology." "But whence," we shall be asked, "are these lofty principles and impartial ideals supposed to be derived?" Men act, even at the best, from a partial and limited standpoint within the natural and social world, and their preferences will inevitably reflect the bias of that standpoint. The nations that fight for the freedom of mankind visualize freedom in the local terms with which they are familiar and have curious difficulty in focussing their moral insight on applications of the principle which would impair their own more mundane interests. "History relativizes all ideals," as Reinhold Niebuhr has remarked, and human beings and their ideas are creatures of time, circumstance and history.

This is true, and a clear understanding of it is indispensable to a just estimate of the rational cogency of social ideals. To quote Niebuhr again: "Man's ideas are conditioned not only by the means of production upon which he depends and the economic interests which he seeks to defend; they are also conditioned by racial history, geographic influences, family traditions, and every conceivable partial perspective of a mind embedded in a finite organism. Yet this creature of finitude touches the fringes of the infinite, and every awakened human mind reaches for the universally valid value and the unconditioned truth." [8]

So it is, and so, with any reasonably adequate grasp of the history of ideas, we should have expected it to be. Moreover, we use these very limited ideas as the means through which we reach for the values that are genuinely valid and the truths that are unconditionally true. And sometimes we reach our goal, though not quite in the manner that Mr. Niebuhr seems to suppose. If there is any mystery in this, and great mystery has been made of it for purposes of edification, there are two considerations about the functioning of human reason which can contribute substantially to its resolution. We have encountered them before, and can use them here, I believe, with some profit to the subject in hand.

The first is the observation that the conditions of the relativity of human ideals are also the conditions of their relevance to the needs and problems of the people who are to make use of them. Every claim to the recognition of a value is meaningfully addressed only "to whom it may concern," and it is the concerns of men who live at a point in time and a locality in space, with families, work to do, loyalties to acknowledge, and hopes that a reasonable ideal may redirect and clarify but cannot initially create, that form the stuff of purpose of which social action must be made. Nor is this a defect in their nature. If the Word is to become flesh and

8 Reinhold Niebuhr, *Christianity and Power Politics*, p. 155.

the Logos to achieve an historical incarnation it must acquire a local habitation and genealogy in the process. Nor is this a mystery which achieves its idealizing effect once only, or in a single place. "The gods of the Ethiopians are black," said a cynical philosopher, and those who saw, and understood, Marc Connelley's *The Green Pastures* will add that it is well that it should be so. The content of valid human ideals is the content of human experience, organized, clarified and focussed on a represented good that can direct action that would otherwise be frustrated and incomplete to a fruitful and coherent issue. Those who, like Mr. T. S. Eliot, can find a good worth seeking only in dark adumbrations of an unspeakable revelation are indeed fastidious. They are also, in the context of social action, remarkably unperceptive. It is only a four dimensional ideal, of the earth, though not altogether earthy, and the people who live in it, that is good enough to find a place in the affairs of men. If we are still saddled with a view about practical reason which maintains its purity by divorcing itself from the context of its effective use, this might seem surprising enough. But we have seen good reasons for rejecting that view, and are, therefore, not inclined to be alarmed or intimidated when its unhappy implications parade as witnesses of a sinful bias in thinking that fails to conform to its arbitrary specifications.

For, and this is our second consideration, "bias" in any sense in which it is humanly or rationally objectionable, is not an affair of the origin of ideas, but of the way in which they are used in the situations in which they function. A limited ideal—and all ideals within the range of social action are limited—may be used narrowly and stupidly, to blind those who accept it to possibilities of good which fall outside its scope. So far as this is the case it represents an interest which, relative to the good attainable in that situation, is partial and merely special. But if it is reasonably condemned it can only be in the light of a better ideal, one which also has its human origins and represents specific interests. If the latter interests define a more inclusive attainable good they are, *in that situation,* on the side of reason, which works through them to secure the best there attainable. To condemn an ideal as "biased" from the standpoint of a universal good which is not, in that situation, a real possibility, may be profound in some higher sense, but, in the context of social action, it is dangerously misleading and inept.

Mr. Niebuhr has seen this clearly and his insistence on it does much to compensate for the obscurities of his theology. Doubtless the spokesmen for freedom in this war have sinned as, indeed, from the standpoint of a wholly "unbiased" goodness, all men must. Nevertheless, the question that concerns us is whether the ideal they offer is a better goal for action than the alternative presented. On this point there can be no reasonable doubt, though when Niebuhr's book was written there was much doubt and contention among the theologians about it. For "it is sheer moral perversity to equate the inconsistencies of a democratic civilization with the brutalities which modern tyrannical states practice. If we cannot make a distinction here, there are no historical distinctions which have any value. *All the distinctions upon which the fate of civilization has turned in the history of mankind have been just such relative distinctions.*" [9] In so far, then, as it is the function of reason in social action to help us to make just such decisions wisely, it is a relative good, which is also a genuine one, that we must expect to support. But not a "merely" relative and therefore arbitrary one. For the situation in which we act is one in which distinctions of better and worse are made from the standpoint of responsible moral action. The "justice" achieved will not be eternal nor its application independent of habits of thought about fair dealing which are local (like everything else that is capable of growth) in their origin, and limited in their scope. If it is, for

[9] *Ibid.*, pp. 16-17, my italics.

all that, the means of achieving a measure of shared well-being not otherwise procurable, and if the effort to secure it favors, on the whole, the agencies and interests through which a further progress can later be made, it is right and reasonable and ought to be accepted by those responsible, in the given situation, for reaching a decision on its merits.

So it is with the ideals of traditional liberalism. The interest of a rising middle class can be at some time a genuinely liberalizing agency which even those who profit only indirectly will be well advised to support. The freedom it achieves will be colored by its preconceptions and predilections. It will see the welfare of the community more seriously menaced in a threat to business than in widespread suffering of the lower classes, and the limits of its "practical" concern will tend also, though by no means completely, to be the limits of its sense of justice. None the less it would be unjustly cynical to deny that an effective sense of social justice worked in it and that goods not only for the body but for the spirit of man were achieved through its agency that would not otherwise have been secured. To indict the liberalism of the eighteenth century it would be necessary not merely to expose the "ideological taint," which all men share, but to show that a different social ideal, in that situation capable of enlisting support and directing activity, could have served a better purpose.

Because such ideals are limited and shaped to meet existing conditions, they may, of course, become impediments to further progress when conditions change and new needs and possibilities are to be dealt with. They have no inherent sanctity about them; their virtue is in their capacity to organize human purposes to an attainable good. The failure of traditional individualism to meet twentieth century needs is not proof that our ancestors were fooling themselves but that we should be fooling ourselves if we failed to apply to our problems as independent and discriminating a judgment about relevant ideals as they applied to theirs. The essential condition for the rational use of ideals is the capacity to refashion and readjust them to the requirements of changed conditions and, it is to be hoped, a broadening concern for human welfare. Those that can be so refashioned, that are in this way on the side of growth and humanity, are on the side of reason, and the interests which support them in this activity are, in their functioning, rational interests. Those that oppose them, though they speak with the authority of a good beyond space and time are, in this situation, anti-rational and their claim is an arbitrary and illegitimate one. For reason lives in its work, not in the monuments of its past success, and its work is in the world in which men discover what is true and use their knowledge to clarify and strengthen their common interests through cooperative activity that can complete itself in a common good. From the standpoint of this activity and no other is any social ideal properly judged as rational or irrational, "tainted" or pure.

Reason and the Future. There has been much said in the preceding chapters about foreseeing the future and acting under the guidance of ideals which present an anticipated good which functions, in the minds of reasonable men, in the organization of present conduct. But it needs only a little acquaintance with the history of ideas to convince us that our capacity to foresee the future, especially at the complicated level of social planning, is limited indeed, and that things rarely turn out as those who planned for them had anticipated. The Constitution of the United States has proved to be one of the most enduring of political structures, but what its framers looked forward to when they planned it was, as we are often told, something very different from the country which today operates under the law they framed. Jefferson is honored as one of the founders of our democracy, but the country that honors him is by no means a Jeffersonian democracy. And these are instances in which the work of the planners has endured. The record of the many schemes that have failed or fallen short of their goal is, of course, far less encouraging.

The picture, so far as it goes, is accurate. It is even, in a sense, a somewhat comforting one. For it at least serves to release us from the spell of the "necessities" and "imperatives" which the professionally clairvoyant have tried to impose upon us as "the future" to which we must accommodate ourselves, whether we like it or not. The future that concerns us and our action is not a thin thread of tendency, precariously abstracted from the complexities of past and present happenings and strung out through an otherwise vacant series of coming events as the inevitable pattern of the world that is to be. That is the way the future looks to zealous and humorless specialists, intent on reducing the world in advance to the measure of present ideas concerning it. The future we shall have to live in will not, in that sense, be a "future" at all— it will, when it happens, be another present, as complex and multi-dimensional as the one we work in now, with *its* past limiting the scope of effective action within it, and *its* future ahead of it, seeming as puzzling and unpredictable, no doubt, as the one which concerns us today. Barriers that to us seemed impassable will be down, and men will wonder why their ancestors were ever so stupid as not to see over or through them. And clouds today no bigger than a man's hand will darken that horizon with storms which our present social barometers are far too rudimentary to predict. So it has happened many times before, and so, we have every reason to suppose, it will fall out again. A remark about the plans of mice and men would seem at this point to be in order, but I shall illustrate the unpredictability of human conduct by refusing to make it.

Yet, and the observation, though obvious, is important, it is not what we do not know about the future but what we very reasonably anticipate concerning it that enables us to make the foregoing judicious and somewhat skeptical observation. If we had not been able to learn from past experience and to use the dividend of that experience as a present basis for judgment with a future reference, we should not now be able to discount the over eager extrapolations through which a few soundings in the current of events are made to serve as the sufficient basis for a chart of the whole channel ahead. Nor is there anything tricky or over subtle in the further claim that if we can foresee that the future will be in some respects unforeseeable, it is the part of wisdom to use that foresight in making up our minds about the kind of social ideals we ought to accept, and the way in which we ought to use them. All that reason asks us, here as elsewhere, is to use such knowledge as we can get to the best advantage possible. What we cannot know about the future will not be known no matter how hard the prophets stare into their assorted crystals; but what can be known, and it is, on the skeptic's own showing, far from negligible, can be rationally used to carry us into the future with some understanding of what we are doing, and of the resources on which we can draw to meet its risks and surprises, whatever they may prove to be, with intelligence and resolution.

One maxim at least we can affirm with some confidence. *There is no short cut to the future.* Forces we can now discern will indeed shape the "world of tomorrow," for it is through what now is that what is to be is made actual. But they will operate in conjunction with others we have barely been able to make out and they will, in the context of social action, function not as iron laws of destiny but as conditions and possibilities, setting problems for that future present to solve but by no means dictating in advance the inescapable terms of that solution. There is little use in transporting ourselves with our existing entanglement in the past and lack of adequate knowledge of the present, to a future peace conference, to lay down in advance the terms on which the nations of the world as they then will be are to live together. Not only is the world going then to be different, but we ourselves are going to be different, also. Effective decisions are made not in a now projected future but in the present in which that future becomes actual, and while we hope to have a hand in making those decisions, it doth not yet appear what we shall be.

Does this mean that there is no use in making plans, or in trying to see ahead? By no means. But it does have some bearing on the nature of our plans, and on the way in which we can reasonably use them. What we can determine, in *our* present, is not "the future" in its concrete complexity, with the decisions that will have to adjust themselves to that complexity if they are to be intelligent. It is rather the past, by which that future, when it becomes a present, will be conditioned. Nobody doubts that what we are and do today is tied down at every turn by what has gone before and cannot now be changed. We would change it if we could, but the time for that has gone by. But our present will be a part of the past by which the possibility of future good is, in its turn, determined. We cannot directly give our future selves a predetermined present, but we can give them a good past, and nothing will be more important or more valuable in the day when their decisions must be made. We cannot make those decisions now, but we can now help to make the selves who will make those decisions and the conditions under which the decisions can be wisely and perhaps even generously arrived at.

To turn to a concrete instance. The Russia and America that will meet to adjust their interests at the close of this war are still in the making. To lay down in advance the conditions on which they will meet and the demands to which each must then conform would be futile, or, if we insisted on prejudicing the future by an insistence that such issues be settled in advance, would be altogether mistaken. But if the future is still in the making, our present action is one of the factors that will help to make it what it will be. If Russia and America come to a peace conference with good relations built up by fruitful collaboration in their recent past, they may then be able to reach agreements which in advance would seem quixotic. If they come to it embittered and divided by quarrels which our stupidity has helped engender, no plan for "world government" now worked out, even by the most starry-eyed of peace groups, will be of pertinence or use. The future will be what it will be, and no man is wise enough to lay down in advance the rules to which wise future action must conform. But reasonable men, without any superhuman endowments, can often make out the rules according to which *present* action can be carried on in guaranteeing to that future resources and capacities which our own foresight has helped to prepare. It is in that spirit and with that end in view —a future end, like any other, toward which we try to work with the best knowledge available—that reasonable social action can fruitfully proceed.

Among these capacities, none has better proved its right to our continued confidence than the capacity to learn by experience—which is the capacity to make up one's mind on the basis of the best evidence available and to change one's mind when new evidence shows the wisdom of such change. And nowhere is the pertinence of what has just been said about the relation of present planning to future decision more obvious than here. It is to be expected that many of our present ideas about social policy will have to be altered, and ought to be altered, in the light of events that have not yet transpired. We cannot protect ourselves in advance against the necessity of having to change our minds, in the light of new knowledge, though some philosophers seem to think that there ought to be some epistemological or metaphysical device which would afford such protection—by supplying us in advance with certainties exempt from the vicissitudes of further inquiry. If such certainties anywhere exist, they are too empty, or too exalted, to be of serious use in the determination of social policy. But we can now develop the discipline which enables those who follow it to change their minds reasonably and thus to welcome and profit by new experience, not merely to ignore or be upset by it. And while our knowledge of the future is precarious and limited, there is good reason, based on four centuries of success in scientific inquiry, to believe that those who are prepared to learn in this way will find out much that is to their advantage.

The metaphor of the wave of the future is, when you think it through, a peculiarly instructive one. For there are a variety of ways of dealing with waves, and each has its lesson for a perceptive mind. We are told that King Canute ordered his henchmen to sweep back the sea. It was a futile gesture, but there was more human dignity in it than in the foolish posture of those who prostrate themselves before the mindless forces of wind and water, in the mistaken belief that destructive violence is a unique manifestation of creative power. Nor should we fail to note the ingenuity of those who, having provided themselves with the latest model of ideological surfboard, propose to ride in just behind the crest of the wave, landing smoothly and somewhat ahead of their countrymen in the new order that they foresee. It is not the noblest form of navigation, but it has its rewards.

On a somewhat different level, the work in which the troubled Faust at last found his nearest earthly approach to the good he sought was that of fighting waves—reclaiming the land and wresting a livable environment from the sea. There could hardly be a better symbol of the efficacy of reason and of the way in which human effort at its best can sometimes triumph over chaos. Of those who engage in this work we can say, in the glowing words of Goethe's poem:

"They give the earth peace with herself at last,
To the proud waves they set their limits fast,
And put a mighty barrier round the sea."

There will be waves in the future, as there have been in the past, great enough to submerge whole nations and whole generations of men. Our hope must be that there will also be men who know how to build, against the chaos in both nature and society, a human habitation that will stand.

PART IV – THE PHILOSOPHIC USE OF REASON

CHAPTER I

THE DISCIPLINE OF PHILOSOPHY

There is, the metaphysicians tell us, no way of escaping "in the end" from ultimate reality, or the Universe, or the Absolute or the underlying and super-eminent Being, by whatever designation named, that is held to express the *final* ground of validation and reality for all that in any way is real or valid. Throughout this volume we have been trying to understand the uses and specific goodness of human reason in limited contexts and for limited purposes. We found the sciences prepared to supply reliable information about the natural world but not qualified to deal with a reality of any higher or more transcendent status. The moral order required to meet the needs of practical reason was seen to be a limited and conditioned one. And we were more interested in getting an untenable absoluteness out of social ideals than in considering them as manifestations of the Absolute. Ostensible "underlying realities" did indeed present themselves at various points in the analysis, but they proved hindrances rather than helps to its progress and their claims were at those points set aside as not capable of legitimation within the contexts with which we were there concerned. If, however, we are to carry through the justification of reason to its rational completion this process cannot go on indefinitely. We must at last accept the responsibility of measuring the claims and capacities of reason against the dimensions of reality itself, when and in so far as reality can be located and identified for examination. Even the transcendental Margaret Fuller, after some heart-searching, accepted the Universe and so, in our fashion, must we, and square our accounts with it.

The responsibility is a formidable one, and may seem at first to carry us far beyond the pedestrian investigation so far undertaken. There are, however, some lessons these inquiries have taught us, that even here will serve us well. One of the chief of these is that if we are to discuss a subject with profit, we need first to know what we are talking about. It would be a grave mistake to impose upon the terms employed in the exploration of "reality" a sense alien to that of their intelligible use in that activity. To avoid this error, of which the critics of speculative philosophy have too often been guilty, we shall begin our inquiry with an examination of the nature of this exploration of "Being" or "reality" and of the ideas used in carrying it on.

The Context of Philosophical Inquiry. In spite of the grandiose character of the final object of this investigation, we need not go far from the level of ordinary experience and quite commonplace thinking to discover ideas about "reality" at work. And it is here, at the point of their intersection with familiar issues and practical affairs, that we can best assess their function in the life of reason. Whenever we are told that something or other is true "ultimately," "finally" or "in the end," or are urged to turn from "abstractions" and mere daydreams to the concrete facts or the real world and to face "reality," we are up against a way of thinking that makes claims to philosophical finality, however little it may know, philosophically, what it is doing. The *content* of this "reality" may be anything you please—the "hard facts" of practical experience which only a "dreamer" would ignore, or an inclusive actuality in which dreams, too, have their meaning, and in comparison with which the "hard facts" are scornfully set down as "mere abstractions." Whatever the preferential "reality" proves to be, it can be known as philosophical by its function, its pretensions, and the grounds on which those pretensions are justified. Its function is to provide "a ground of legitimacy" for all that claims to be basically worthy of human credence and concern and thus "a guide in the normalization of knowledge," [1] by reference to what *really*, *ultimately* or *in the end* is the case. To try, misguidedly of course, to "escape from reality" is to refuse to accept as of primary importance for belief and conduct the *facts*—actual, concrete and hard—identified by the critic as of preeminent genuineness and importance. If these are held to be the dominant political and economic "imperatives" of the society in which one happens to be living, then to attempt an escape from reality will be to acknowledge as of primary importance other goods and imperatives than the idols of the market place venerated in that society. Such an "escape" may, from a different philosophical standpoint, be regarded as an evidence of uncommon cultural discrimination. But if men thus reject the "realities" of their time or group, it is in the name of some other and truer reality that they reject them, and this, in its turn, is set up as the standard to which all that is finally credible and humanly significant must conform, on penalty, if it fails to meet the test, of being set down as "unreal" and insubstantial. So Mr. T. S. Eliot, surveying contemporary society from the standpoint of a spiritual ideal which he believes to express the eternal reality of things, could without paradox write of pre-war London as an "unreal" city, and anyone who has entered into the spirit of *The Waste Land* will know what he means. And if the crowds that flow over London Bridge remain for the most part profoundly unmoved by Mr. Eliot's ontological abuse of their city, it is because, so far as they are concerned, the "realities" whose claims they understand and will respect have been determined in a different way, and

[1] These phrases are quoted from Thorstein Veblen, *The Place of Science in Modern Civilization*, p. 133. The account given in these essays of the functioning of philosophical preconceptions in economic theory is extremely penetrating and valuable.

there is no place among them for Mr. Eliot and his metaphysical malaise.

Lest it be thought that it is only on the borderline of fantasy that such considerations determine the course of our thinking, our next instance shall be from the more arid field of economics. Assessing the preconceptions of economic science in a masterly survey of the history of this discipline, Thorstein Veblen came to the conclusion that the final terms of economic theorizing are always of a metaphysical character. They prescribe the conditions to which the observable course of events must conform if it is to be accepted as natural, real, normal or, in the modern manner, rigorously and impersonally factual, and thus fit for acceptance in the scheme of knowledge. The direction of inquiry is thus in considerable part determined by "the received notions as to what constitutes the ultimate, self-legitimating term—the substantial reality—to which knowledge in any given case must penetrate. This ultimate term or ground of knowledge is always of a metaphysical character. It is something in the way of a preconception, accepted uncritically but applied in criticism and demonstration of all else with which the science is concerned." [2] Nor did Veblen think it possible to escape some preconceptions of a metaphysical nature. His claim was that the old preconceptions have ceased to be in harmony with habits of thought and action to which modern mechanical industry increasingly commits us. "To men thoroughly imbued with this matter-of-fact habit of mind, the laws and theorems of economics, and of the other sciences that treat of the normal course of things, have a character of 'unreality' and futility that bars out any serious interest in their discussion." [3] This does not mean that the old theorems have been disproved or that the new are less "metaphysical," in the sense

[2] *Ibid.*, p. 149.
[3] *Ibid.*, p. 80.

in which Veblen uses that term. It is simply that "matter-of-fact" has come, through a change in our habits of work and life, to function as the "ultimate, self-legitimating term" in place of "nature" and its normal and beneficent course. "Under the stress of modern technological exigencies, men's everyday habits of thought are falling into the lines that in the sciences constitute the evolutionary method; and knowledge which proceeds on a higher, more archaic plane is becoming alien and meaningless to them. The social and political sciences must follow the drift, for they are already caught in it."[4]

The way in which ideas about what is ultimately "real" actually *function*, here, even in the course of thought which is ostensibly, and sometimes aggressively, non-metaphysical, is to prescribe the area in which serious thinking is to work and, what is more important, the point at which it can with propriety stop, having reached the ultimate actualities for which no further justification is required and which will serve as the standard in terms of which all else that claims serious credence can be judged. The world thus defined may be no wider than the south side of Chicago, if it has an apartment and a place to work, and a chain store and a bank and a drug store and a motion picture theater and the *Tribune* inside it, or it may be broad enough to take account of all time and all existence. If it sets the boundaries of all that is accepted as worthy of a man's really serious concern and belief, and if whatever falls outside it, or is not reducible to its scale, is treated in fact as "unreal" in the sense defined, then it is, for those who honor it, the reality to which they are committed, and within the limits of which they effectively live.

This may be put in a more orthodox and edifying way, but to much the same effect, if we interrogate professional philosophers on the subject. "Philosophy," Whitehead tells us, "is an attempt to clarify those fundamental beliefs which

[4] *Ibid.*, p. 81.

finally determine the emphasis of attention that lies at the base of character." [5] He is speaking here of a reflective, or self critical philosophy, one which is not content merely to have and use a notion of reality, but seeks also to justify it from the standpoint of the widest knowledge available. We shall have more to say about this sort of philosophical activity presently. The point here is that the subject-matter on which it expends its clarifying effort is that of the fundamental beliefs which determine what we are to attend to, what we are prepared to take seriously, what, in short, we take to be the "realities" to which our thought and action should "finally" conform. The subject-matter of philosophy is the things that men take seriously, not for limited purposes, but in the basic commitments which determine, on the whole, what they make of their lives and of the world they live in. It was in this sense, of course, that William James was speaking when he made the much quoted observation, itself a quotation from Chesterton, that it is more important for a landlady to know a prospective lodger's philosophy than his bank balance, since his philosophy, in the long run, will have the larger influence on their mutual relations.[6] The term "philosophy" is not here used in a eulogistic sense. The lodger's philosophy may prove to be one he would have been better off without and its influence anything but praiseworthy. And it will frequently not be one that either lodger or landlady could formulate in the abstract terms usually associated with philosophical inquiry. But good or bad, inarticulate or verbose, it will make a difference and it is the kind of difference it makes and ought to make that is the subject for further philosophical investigation.

The aim of a reflective and responsible philosophy is to find the things worth taking seriously, the things to which the status designated by the terms "real" and "ultimately" can wisely be given, if not in virtue of their cosmic status—though

[5] A. N. Whitehead, *Adventures of Ideas*, p. 125.
[6] Wm. James, *Pragmatism*, p. 1ff.

this is usually a factor in the decision—at least in terms of their importance for human life and action. In making this his goal the philosopher may, as usual, quote Plato, speaking this time through the Athenian stranger in *The Laws*—"I say that about serious things a man should be serious, and about a matter that is not serious he should not be serious"—though he may also, as is not unusual, be in partial disagreement with Plato as to what the things worth taking seriously "finally" are. He will wish also to distinguish the serious from the solemn, and in this connection to remind his reader that the great Democritus was, by repute, a laughing philosopher, and that this is by no means out of harmony with Plato's dictum. For a just estimate of things not worth taking seriously in the kind of world we live in, provides many themes for mirth to a discerning mind.

The Methods of Philosophical Inquiry. So far we have located the context in which philosophical ideas function and the sort of decision to which they are pertinent. This brings philosophy down from heaven to earth, in a manner of speaking, but it leaves us with an almost embarrassing abundance of ultimates for further investigation. Many of these claims to finality and "underlying reality" are flatly incompatible with each other. Some, by current standards, have been a boon and an ornament to humanity. It is of such that Whitehead writes when he says that "It is our business . . . to recreate and renact a vision of the world, including those elements of reverence and order without which society lapses into riot, and penetrated through and through with unflinching rationality. Such a vision is the knowledge which Plato identified with virtue. Epochs for which, within the limits of their development, this vision has been widespread are the epochs unfading in the memory of mankind." [7] But it is no less the case that other philosophies, as sweeping in their pretensions, have been used as bulwarks for sheer, narrow-minded stupidity, and that still others, never reaching the level of reflective expression at all,

[7] A. N. Whitehead, *op. cit.*, p. 126.

have confused whole generations of well-intentioned seekers after truth. Common usage is here more revealing than professional eulogy. A "philosopher" may be a wise man who merits credence and respect, but he may also be an opinionated idiot who astounds the populace by the tenacity of his adherence to implausible preconceptions in the face of overwhelming evidence of their invalidity, or a garrulous ruminator on familiar themes to which he adds little but loose talk of a vaguely comforting character. If we are to proceed responsibly in this vast, important and equivocal field we shall need some method of discriminating the sort of philosophy that can reasonably justify its claims from the illegitimate pretender that cannot. It is not by its pretensions but by its performance that a sound philosophy is to be judged.

How can we be reasonable about the ultimate principles, categories and commitments in terms of which all further reasoning is to proceed? To answer this fundamental question, we shall have to make a distinction between two stages in the use of reason in philosophy which are frequently confused. The more obvious and familiar is that which proceeds, on the basis of a prior decision as to what is ultimately or "really" real, to legislate for the reality or unreality of the several phases of our experience, and of the world which they appear to disclose. If, for instance, all that really exists is spiritual in its nature, then the material world we observe perceptually cannot "in the end," be what it seems, or what the sciences, in any straightforward interpretation, seem to declare it to be. The task of reconciling the appearances with the underlying reality and showing how, on the terms it sets, they can be made to bear witness to the final satisfaction of our spiritual aspirations, provides a fascinating opportunity for the exercise of both constructive imagination and dialectical skill. The systems of speculation which have thus been developed are impressive demonstrations of the powers of human thought in this most difficult field.

A system of philosophy which offered no more than this, however, would not differ in principle, however much it differed in its degree of elaboration, from the varieties of uncritical philosophizing we considered in the preceding section. Reasoning on the basis of "ultimates" antecedently and non-rationally determined may lead us a long way, but it cannot escape, and cannot answer, the final questions: why *this* "ultimate" rather than some other should have been selected, and what reason there is to credit the system developed in its terms not merely as a speculative exercise but as the truth, indeed the "final" truth, about the world in which we live? To try to answer them by reiterating that whatever in the world fails to agree with the initial specifications for "reality" is therefore (if we accept these specifications) "unreal" and hence that whatever really exists must be what the system asserts all realities to be (since if it is not it does not *really* exist) prolongs the argument but does not meet the issue. It is no wonder that many intelligent specialists who have encountered this sort of argument in the writings of the professional philosophers have come to the conclusion that there is little in this field that can shed much light on their own philosophical problems. If we must in any case resort to arbitrary stipulations in these matters, it seems the part of good sense and frankness to do so explicitly and without the interminable arguments with which the metaphysicians seem to surround conclusions which "in the end" are no less arbitrary.

No first-rate philosopher ever does rest his case on so flimsy a foundation. His task is not merely to reason on the basis of assumed "ultimates" but to be reasonable about them, and thus to justify the standpoint from which his own survey of the world is made. This is the second (and more fundamental) stage in philosophical reasoning of which we spoke. Evidently, it cannot proceed in the same way as that which we have just discussed. To do so would be to beg the very questions which it is the aim of philosophy, on this level, to answer. Assuming the validity of the criteria for "reality" which speculative idealists apply, there is indeed no doubt that all that is (in this sense) real must be spiritual and that nothing non-spiritual can (in this sense) be real. This does not tell us why we ought reasonably to adopt the idealist's criteria but only what we should be dialectically committed to if we did. Yet while, as was said, no first-rate philosopher confuses the product of such unsubstantiated dialectical ingenuity with the philosophic wisdom which is his goal, there is plenty of second-rate philosophizing current among us, in both professional and non-professional circles, in which this confusion does occur. It is therefore important to be aware of it and clear of its unhappy consequences in our own thinking.

Now what would it mean to be reasonable *about* the "ultimates" to which our thinking commits us, as distinct from merely reasoning about the rest of our experience, however elaborately and portentously, on the basis they provide? To see the answer, we need only carry through the discussion of the preceding section. The "ultimates" with which our thinking begins are not in their own nature either rational or irrational. They reflect the urgency of quite specific human interests, each of which claims special importance or primacy in the organization of our activities and beliefs. But the urge to *justify* this claim, to show that the nature of the world, or of human experience, *entitles* the methods of the sciences or the assurances of religious faith to the final word in conflicts of belief or of policy, brings a new factor into the discussion. The proposed justification may in some cases be no more than skillfully disguised question-begging or special pleading. But it professes to be more than that. It claims to reach conclusions in which all aspects of experience, not merely that of its own preferential concern, receive a just and adequate interpretation, and its conclusions are supposed to be valid for all reasonable men, not merely for those of a particular sect or party. This claim entails responsibilities of clarity, comprehensiveness and adequacy which, when honestly met, will raise the inquiry in which they function to a new level—the level of philosophic understanding.

It is possible to be more or less accurate, more or less discerning, more or less just and adequate in one's acceptance and use of ideas about what is ultimate for human thought and action, as these ideas function in the organization of conduct and belief around our basic acceptances and commitments. To be as accurate, as discerning, and as adequate as possible in this use of them is, in this context, to be rational. This, in fact, is the philosophical use of reason for which we have been searching. Nor is this standard a merely arbitrary or question-begging one. Those who make no claim to *justify* their basic preconceptions but simply lay down the law in terms of them will continue to do so untroubled by scruples of philosophic reason. That which claims no rational warrant will not be undermined by the proof that it does not possess one. But those who do claim to speak from the standpoint of a doctrine which *rightly* and *reasonably* claims our respect and credence can fairly be asked to accept the responsibilities which this claim and this standpoint entail. The obscurantist may choose to be as unreasonable as he pleases in his "final" beliefs about the world. But if he claims that he is right in this attitude, because only superstition (or animal faith) can "finally" legislate on such matters, and if he presents this as a doctrine—supported by adequate evidence— which justifies his decision to reject the claims of reason, then the validity of his doctrine is by no means a matter of his own choosing. It is open to inspection in the light of the best we know. And, as we have seen in the earlier chapters of this volume, there is a good deal that we do know, in factual inquiry, in morals, and in social action, that will be relevant to any decision upon it. If he tells us that nothing better than "faith" is in any case open to us, and that his faith has thus as good a title as any other to legislate for matters of fact, we shall know that he is radically distorting an aspect of experience—that of factual inquiry—which is simply not what he claims it to be. He is using loose talk and looser thinking as an excuse for an intellectual commitment which, apart from such distortion, would not bear inspection. His claim is therefore "arbitrary," not in the trivial sense that it reflects a choice, but in the significant sense that it sins against a standard of accuracy and adequacy which he himself professes to respect and by reference to which his doctrine, therefore, can fairly and appropriately be judged.

The philosophic interest in attaining the sort of reasonable organization of experience in which all particular interests and claims are evaluated from the standpoint of a just, inclusive and discriminating wisdom, is not, by itself, a markedly strong or persistent one. It has often been attacked with impunity by fanatics, brushed aside by practical men in a hurry, and ridiculed by skeptics who see accurately enough how often it has been used as a cloak for dishonest and partisan pretensions, and see no more than that. Yet those who deny its claims do so at great cost to the human good they profess to honor. For while the philosophic interest *by itself* is of no great potency, it is of its essence not to work by or for itself, but to provide a standpoint from which other interests and activities, in themselves one-sided, partial and half-thought-out, can be ordered, understood and made complete. Apart from such completion they do not know what they are doing, or what their commitments mean. They shut out and deny much of what is best in their environment and themselves because they can only deal with fragments and patches of truth and are afraid or unprepared to follow through to a clear conclusion the ideals by which, in so far as it is anywhere clear and excellent, their work is guided. That the preaching of our time (both lay and clerical) is often angry, shrill and shallow, and its practice narrowly technical, shortsighted and without an organizing purpose or ideal, is, in the circumstances, hardly surprising. We lack the guiding discipline of philosophy, and the consequences of that lack are far reaching.

It is not my purpose to introduce at this point a systematic philosophy in whose terms our present perplexities can finally be resolved. We are not likely in this generation to achieve so comprehensive a doctrine and perhaps, on the whole, it is as well no longer to expect it. The world, as we have often been told, is very vast and complex; our ideas of it change radically and our perplexities shift to new pressure areas as we proceed. What is of preeminent importance to us at present is not philosophy as a final synthesis in which our minds could be at rest, but philosophy as a discipline under whose guidance our thinking can progress, attaining that measure of clarity, comprehensiveness and adequacy to the demands of rational living which is possible under existing conditions. The best possible will doubtless fall short of the hopes and ambitions of the great system-builders of the past, but it will none the less be vastly above the level of present performance. In this volume I have tried to apply this sort of philosophy to the clarification of issues of contemporary concern. In so doing, I have made use of methods long employed in philosophic inquiry. In this sense we have from the start been concerned with the philosophic use of reason, and with the distinction between conclusions which, by its standards, can rightly be set down as confused, one-sided or arbitrary and those which will stand inspection as warranted, and well-grounded and just. It will contribute, I think, to an understanding of what has been done, and of what is here to be understood as the philosophic use of reason, to distinguish explicitly the major criteria employed, and the methods used in their application. The best answer we can give to the question as to how we can be reasonable on philosophical issues, is to indicate explicitly how, in harmony with a great philosophical tradition, we have tried to be so. The reader will thus be able to judge the principles now presented in terms of the practice in which, from the start, they have been exemplified. We turn, then, to a survey of principles and methods.

(a) *Contextual Analysis.* It often surprises those who come in relative innocence to the study of the history of philosophy to find that many of its major achievements have been of a critical and restricting character. Philosophers like Hume and Kant and Bergson, for example, made their greatest contribution to the thought of their time by showing their contemporaries how *not* to philosophize, or how to avoid certain persistent errors and confusions to which we are naturally prone when we try to think philosophically without an adequate knowledge of what we are doing, or of the limits within which such thinking can properly be carried on. Nothing is more natural or more disastrous to clear thinking on ultimate issues than the uncritical generalization of ideas which have an intelligible use and meaning somewhere but are by no means adapted to serve as guides to what is always and everywhere true and valid. To use such ideas "philosophically" often means, for the uncritical, to spread them in all directions, though somewhat thinly, over the area of meaningful experience. If we hear of a theory of evolution that is valid in biology, we must have evolution everywhere, from anthropology to theology, until perhaps even a multiplication table that refuses to evolve will be set down in some quarters as a "static" and vacuous sort of contrivance which the new "Darwinism" in philosophy cannot tolerate. Perspectives in Einsteinian physics carry over to "perspectives" in education and morals, and the step from "Space-Time" to Deity was theologically an obvious and almost inevitable one. It is in this way that the legitimate findings of the sciences become, through a popularization which robs them of their specific contextual meaning, the idols of the market place for a reading public bent on keeping up with the times, and for those whose business it is to find sermons in stones, the vehicles of a new, if transitory, revelation. This is philosophy of a sort, but it is bad philosophy; for it assigns no new reliable sense to terms which it has stripped of their specific meaning and conduces rather to endlessly equivocal dispute with other pretenders to a similarly ubiquitous application than to knowledge of the world or of ourselves.

The remedy for this sort of confusion is simply to take particular pains to know what we are talking about, where statements made are supposed to apply, and how their truth-claim is to be tested. The greater part of so-called "critical philosophy" is an affair of taking pains in just this fashion and its result, when it is accurately and adequately done, is to make ideas clear, specific, and rationally usable in the context of philosophical inquiry. The task is one for philosophy since the problem with which it deals arises when we attempt to use ideas philosophically, or to estimate their significance and appropriate application from the standpoint of the rational organization of our experience as a whole. One currently fashionable version of this activity goes by the name of contextual analysis, and the name is a good one. What those who practice this type of analysis chiefly insist upon is that, for philosophical purposes, meaning can reliably be assigned to terms employed, and to ideas for which they purport to stand, only by reference to some determinate use that is to be made of them in some discoverable context of inquiry or activity. Terms and ideas, abstracted from such specific contexts, may, of course, be assigned a new use and meaning, other than that which they elsewhere possessed. But apart from such specification of meaning those who employ the terms will confuse themselves and their readers interminably with loose talk without determinate content or foreseeable end. Stated in this way, the claim seems obvious and empty enough. It has been found, however, to be uncommonly useful for critical philosophy, since many of the obstacles which impede the path of accurate thinking in this field can be eliminated by such analysis. We have already made extensive use of it in exploring the nature and uses of reason, and its utility for philosophical purposes should by this time be plain.

This sort of analysis is often regarded as a merely negative or critical instrument, a way perhaps of eliminating bad philosophy, but not a basis for establishing anything "constructive" in its place. There is some truth in this observation but on the whole it is misleading. It is indeed a purpose of contextual analysis to eliminate confusions, but if it is successful, what we shall see when the smoke of battle has cleared away is not merely the prostrate form of the enemy, but a whole world of earth and sky and men going about their affairs in clearer and more understandable ways. It is this world, not the misconceptions of past philosophers, with which we are primarily concerned. To see it as it is, in its variety and specific differences, as well as in such unity and order as can reliably be discerned in it, is the first requisite of a responsible philosophy. The business of contextual analysis as applied, for instance, to the understanding of "reason" and its uses, is to help us to see things as they are, by applying to their interpretation the ideas which genuinely articulate their structure or disclose their purpose and intent. As such, while not in itself a complete philosophy, it provides the foundation on which to build a "constructive" philosophy that will stand.

(b) *The Inclusiveness of Reason.* It is the business of a rational philosophy, we have said, to understand the several aspects of experience for what they are and for what can be made of them from the standpoint of an inclusive human wisdom. This imposes on the rational pursuit of this activity a responsibility which other disciplines need not meet, save in so far as they, too, make claims to philosophical validity. It is sometimes said that it is the duty of a sound philosophy to inform us as to the nature of reality or of life "as a whole," while the special sciences confine themselves to a single aspect only of the world. Hence philosophy deals with the concrete, the actual world in its fullness or totality, while the scientist must content himself with abstractions. And since we all want to get to concrete reality "in the end," and base our view of life upon it, philosophy has the further task of criticizing and correcting the abstractions of science from the vantage ground of its own completer knowledge.

The success of even the greatest philosophers in grasping the nature of the Universe as a whole and providing us with reliable information concerning it is, at least, debatable. A cautious man might well prefer to get along with abstractions which, whatever their limitations from the standpoint of the Universe, are better known and more reliably usable for merely human purposes than reality as a whole, of which the metaphysicians have such tenuous yet conflicting things to say, has so far proved to be. If he thinks, however, that he can in this way avoid the responsibilities of philosophical thinking, he will be mistaken and perhaps, in the end, disastrously so. Whatever "reality as a whole" may be, and I agree that we know very little about it, the need remains for us, if we are to make the most of our experience, so to understand and interpret it that nothing that is humanly significant will be needlessly excluded, and nothing included in such fashion that it distorts or blinds us to the possibilities of significant experience elsewhere. There is an important difference between a way of looking at things philosophically that is "abstract," in the derogatory sense, because it leaves out or reduces to insignificance everything that falls outside the limits of a narrowly specialized interest, and one that is flexible, comprehensive and discriminating enough to include coherently ranges of experience which a more restricted view would arbitrarily have excluded. There should be no question here of correcting the "abstractions" of the sciences about their own business, or of introducing into them a "concreteness" irrelevant to their purpose. What needs philosophical correction is not science but a philosophy in which nothing is considered worth taking seriously save that which can be measured by the standards which science provides. In the preceding section we made the acquaintance of some philosophies of that sort, and found a good meaning in the claim that their "abstractions" required correction before they could be put to rational use in the context of social action.

There are many factors that enter into the determination of the way a man looks at the world and the area within which he can make sense of it. The freshness and breadth of his perceptions, the range of his interest and sympathy, have much to do with it, and these are not initially the fruits of a reflective philosophy. But his view as to what is genuine and important is a factor in it as well, and may be a decisive one. To make this view as coherent, adequate and inclusive as possible, not in reference to an Absolute Experience in which we can hardly hope to share in any comprehensible way, but in the developing human experience in which is our point of contact with the "realities" which for us have meaning, is the aim of a rational philosophy.

Of the philosophers whose contribution has been chiefly in this field Hegel and William James will serve as instances. The Hegelian philosophy deals professedly with the total or Absolute Reality to which all our finite ideas refer and of which they are, as they stand, but fragmentary and contradictory expressions. What Hegel really meant to say about this Absolute Reality—whether it is personal or impersonal, timeless or temporal, or somehow both at once—is a matter about which experts disagree. It seems likely that he was by no means clear in his own mind about it. But what he had to say about the tendency in human thought which insists on taking some selected type or aspect of experience as self-complete, the kind of contradictions it gets into when it tries to maintain this false self-sufficiency against the demands of a wider experience, and the way in which these contradictions can be eliminated from a more inclusively rational standpoint, has proved to be of enduring value. Whether or not "the Truth is the Whole" and "the Real is the Rational"—whatever precisely these Hegelian dicta are supposed to mean—it is at least the case that the truth that counts for philosophy must be compatible with and contributory to what, *on the whole*, the world is found to be, and that no insight, however immediately luminous or urgent, which can maintain itself only through the exclusion of what is elsewhere, and reliably, found to be true, is worthy of philosophical acceptance. Hegel gave the name of "dialectic" to the process by which philosophical half-truths are set in their proper perspective from the standpoint of a wider truth that both includes and corrects them, and mistakenly assumed it to be a process dominating nature and history as well. We are concerned with it only as a factor in the history of the development of ideas, and of philosophical ideas in particular, since there is no good reason to believe that the sciences, whose interest is a different one, should follow a similar method. In this context, however, it has a good meaning and a valuable use. We are wiser, philosophically, for what Hegel and his disciples have taught us.

William James was no admirer of Hegelians and had little that was good to say of Hegel. Yet the interest that directed his philosophy was in important respects the same as theirs. What he saw clearly and argued eloquently was that our experience is frequently distorted and impoverished by the use of interpretative ideas too narrow and abstract to do justice to its immediate richness and variety. When men are so misguided as to accept not what they see and feel and live through but rather what their preconceptions tell them must be so, they are, according to James, the victims of a "vicious intellectualism," a philosophically illegitimate use of ideas to narrow rather than to widen the total area of significant experience. Since James was inclined at times to identify "logic" with reasoning that led to conclusions of this unhappy sort and since he could see that the conclusions were unsatisfactory without being able to see what was wrong with the logic that was supposed to justify them, he was no friend to logic and his lively assaults upon it have provided material for much less genial and well-intentioned versions of irrationalism since his time. Actually, however, his attack was not on the intellect but on "intellectualism," and his own best efforts were devoted to fashioning ideas that would organize experience more adequately and enable those factors which count in life and conduct to have their just place in a reasonable philosophy as well. In this he was never wholly successful and he remains, therefore, the spokesman for aspects of experience that are still, in his philosophy, only half articulate. But though he sometimes was content to purchase inclusiveness at the price of clarity, it was a philosophical inclusiveness that he sought and it is for a human wisdom immensely rich in its perceptions, broad in its sympathies, and philosophical in its scope that we rightly honor him.

The method employed in this volume differs in some respects from those of both Hegel and James, but its intent is the same. In judging the claims of reason, in the several contexts in which we could discover it at work, we have sought to interpret those claims in such fashion as to render them compatible with relevant experience elsewhere. We have accepted the responsibility for squaring accounts with any fact or theory from whatever source derived, that might reasonably be supposed to set aside on higher grounds the conclusions reached within the areas of inquiry with which we started. Our conclusions profess to be valid in the context to which we found them applicable, not merely provisionally, or for limited purposes, but in the light of the best knowledge and widest experience relevant to their adjudication. They do not apply to everything, but they apply to the particular things to which they are pertinent in a way that will stand philosophical inspection. It might at first appear that the method of contextual analysis is hostile to this more inclusive concern of philosophical reason. But we have not found it so. On the contrary, it is precisely when the several activities of reason are understood in the context of their specific usefulness that they *can* maintain themselves against the objections that have been brought against them and that each can be seen to make a valid and indispensable contribution to a wisely discriminating understanding of the world and our place in it. It is a curious notion, though a pervasive one, that the inclusive work of philosophy is best carried on when we are making claims to exclusive validity and unqualified cogency for some special interest or other—claims which rival pretenders will at once be bound to deny and which lead over therefore to that battle of the "isms" to which so much of professional philosophy has in recent years been confined. In offering a philosophical justification of human reason, not as such a pretender, but as a factor in activities which could not proceed as well without it and which are essential to life on the level of human excellence, we have had little to say of this battle. But we have been concerned with philosophical issues, nevertheless, and the result, if it is valid at all, is so from the standpoint of the kind of wisdom which enables us to make the most of experience by seeing its several factors for what they are and what they can contribute to a comprehensive adjustment to the world.

(c) *The "Ultimate" and the Human Standpoint.* If contextual analysis, however, is not enough, inclusiveness may be altogether too much for our philosophical purposes, if it is not modified by a recognition of other interests and needs. The human being is, from the necessities of his life and the manner of his thinking, a selective animal, and while we shall wish to include in our view of life all that we reasonably can, we cannot reasonably include all things on the same level or in the same order. Dreams have their significance as well as the experiences of waking life; but that significance can be justly appreciated only if we accord a certain primacy to what we learn when we are awake and judge the dream world in terms of it. It may be that, from the standpoint of some vaster experience, our waking life would seem as unsubstantial and wayward as a dream world does to us. In moments of exaltation poets and philosophers sometimes talk in this manner. They may be right. Until this vaster experience is made available, however, in some fashion that enables us to see what, in its terms, is "dream" and what is actuality, and to know how this further actuality bears on what *for us* is reliably certifiable waking life, it can make little sense of our experience. *For us* the world will have to be judged by what we can see of it from where we are, and learn of it by the means reliably at our disposal. It is from the standpoint which our human interests dictate and in which our human powers are exercised that we shall in any case make contact with the world around us. There is no trustworthy method yet discovered, either in philosophy or out of it, for "transcending" the limitations and the responsibilities of our humanity. The ultimate realities *for us* will have to be those that can make good their claims in the whole course of experience and action: the standards of truth and practical importance, those which we can stand on and stand by in the further conduct of life on the highest attainable level of human excellence. When we judge, therefore, of the worth of a philosophy that claims our support, a final and essential question to ask is what it commits us to take as ultimate, as decisive for thought and action, and whether this commitment is one that can be honestly and effectively maintained in our further relations with the world around us.

It is sometimes suggested that to introduce considerations of this sort into philosophical discussion is to reduce it to the level of a merely subjective and finally arbitrary expression of our own interests and limitations. Surely, it will be urged, the real world outside of us is what it is, whatever we poor humans, in our highly restricted corner of the Universe, may find useful to think or say of it. And surely it is. The sciences tell us a good deal about its nature and, as we have seen, there is good reason to suppose that much of this is literally and quite precisely true. But what we are asking for when we try to determine what is "ultimately" or "finally" real in it is not facts of that sort or similarly verifiable. The metaphysician who tells us that everything is matter, or spirit, or experience, or love, does not mean that everything can be discovered to be so by the methods of inquiry which suffice to show that tables are material, and that some human beings love each other, or, if he does, he is a very simple-minded metaphysician. What he means to say is rather that while the world undoubtedly contains much that *seems* not to fit his description of all that exists, this discrepancy is only apparent, since everything *ultimately* or *finally* or *in the end* is what he takes it to be. And that in turn will be found to mean that everything can be so regarded from a standpoint which he regards as peculiarly important or significant for certain assignable purposes. It is when viewed with eyes of love that the world confirms the faith of the optimist, and when measured by operations held to be peculiarly objective, scientific and commendable that it reduces to what a materialist claims to find in it. I am not objecting to this procedure; it is normal to the activity in question. What can be reasonably asked, however, is that it be coherently completed. That is, the assignment of "ultimacy" should be justified, not merely by repeated and frequently vituperative affirmations of its peculiar cogency against the defenders of a rival ultimate, but by an indication of why, when, and for what pur-

poses this particular standpoint is held to be valid in the organization of experience, and of how it can reasonably be related to other aspects of the world that, while set down as
"unreal" from the standpoint selected, are none the less of considerable significance and use for other purposes and in other
aspects of our lives. Thus, we know that it is important to
be as rigorously objective as possible in an exact description
of the motion of material objects. Is it equally well-advised
to eliminate from an account of social behavior everything
that would be irrelevant to the prediction of the future position and velocity of moving bodies? Perhaps it is—it is one of
the things that ought to be decided if the social sciences are
to proceed intelligently. But it will not be intelligently settled
by stipulating in advance that only what is material is "real"
and that in consequence whatever fails to make known its
presence by the tests accredited for material objects is "mysterious," "occult" or merely "subjective." Of course that is
so *if* we accept the criteria proposed as final or decisive tests
for everything that is to be accepted as genuine in the description of conduct. But why should we accept those criteria? Because what they disclose is ultimate reality and all
else mere appearance? But this is what was to be proved, and
the results achieved by the persistent use of such methods
tell us more about the materialist than about the Universe
in the name of which he purports to speak.

In fact, of course, the materialist has some reasons for the
choice he makes, though they are often only half-thought-
out and badly stated. He thinks, with good reason, that men
know what they are talking about when they keep to the
measurables of, e.g., physics in a way in which they frequently
do not when they talk of purposes and spiritual unities and
the like. And he rightly holds that it is important to know
what one is talking about and to think honestly and accurately concerning it. He knows, moreover, that those who
talk much of spiritual unities and unanalyzable values have

often used such talk to justify claims that ought to have been analyzed and to turn their "spiritual unities" into false fronts for snobbery, class selfishness, and reaction. He believes that it is important to avoid that sort of dishonesty at almost any cost, and he therefore places a high value on a way of describing human conduct which does seem to eliminate it, and to ground our beliefs securely on "realities" that will stand the most searching rational inspection. Perhaps he is right in this —perhaps not. How can we tell until we have seen what the costs would be, what we should be surrendering if we refused as philosophers to take seriously anything that could not justify its "reality" by this standard? In Part III we dealt at some length with this question, so far as it is related to the role of ideals in social action, and found reasons for concluding that the factors to be taken seriously in a social situation cannot properly be limited to those which the materialist's analysis accepts. This, I suggest, is the kind of way in which philosophical questions of this sort can be answered, soberly and piecemeal, by reference to the considerations which can reasonably justify a decision as to the *realities* worth taking account of in the world with which we have to deal. The notion that we have taken the argument to a deeper, more objective and less arbitrary level when we substitute for that kind of investigation a series of dicta as to what is ultimately real which beg at the outset the very questions they purport to settle is a mark not of philosophical profundity, but of philosophical confusion.

The reference of claims to "ultimacy" back to the standpoint of the commitments for thought and action they involve does not, therefore, come as an alien intrusion on a philosophical task that is or could be complete without it. On the contrary, it is only when the initially unqualified claim to *finality* for one interest, method of investigation or type of experience or another is clarified, made specific and related explicitly to the other claims and interests in terms of which we understand and act upon the world, that we can know what it means and how to judge the validity of its pretensions. Nor are such considerations merely arbitrary; it is precisely in their terms that we have to distinguish, in this type of inquiry, between what is arbitrary and what is not. Nothing is easier, given an initial tenacity of belief and some verbal and logical ingenuity in the manipulation of categories, than to set up any object of any interest as a reality on its own account and to show that, judged by its specifications, nothing can be "finally real" save as it contributes to the reality thus identified. If the interest that impels this identification is an urgent one and widely shared, the presentation of its un-qualified claim to primacy for thought and action as if it were inside information about the "deepest" reality at the heart of things will find considerable favor in cultured circles and such dissenters as there are can readily be put down with the crushing observation that they are shallow folk who have not penetrated to the truly *inner* nature of the ultimate reality in whose support of the interests closest to our hearts we surely cannot but believe. If we are reasonably to examine the exclusive claims of such a philosophical pretender there would seem to be but two alternatives. We may set up a rival reality of our own, and from that vantage ground estab-lish, without great difficulty, that those who disagree with us are merely wishful thinkers who substitute their "dreams" and "fantasies" for the realities which we, by honest, hard-headed and truthful thinking, have established. Who is right? Neither, really, is quite as arbitrary as he sounds. But the considerations which make sense of his position and would perhaps lead him, if they were fully understood, to develop and modify it by reference to other interests which also de-mand consideration in the rational organization of experience, simply do not come to adequate expression on the level at which he is arguing. *How* important are the values which, whether or not they lie at the heart of reality, are indubitably dear to the heart of the metaphysician? Where and for what purposes are they important? What claims to truth are involved in their acceptance and how far can these claims be checked by what we know elsewhere to be true? Would it be necessary if we were to accept them, to adopt along with them an attitude of hostility or disdain toward other claims, e.g., in morals, to which we are humanly committed? Would the commitment to which the metaphysician invites us supplement and sustain the work of reason as it operates in the context of social action, or would they impede that work? It is in terms of this sort of consideration that we can distinguish an arbitrary philosophy, one which can find no support outside its own initial demand for unqualified acceptance, from one that makes connection with the constructive forces in human nature and brings them to a rationally coherent expression.

But the objector still asks "does the outlook provided by such a philosophy correspond to 'reality'?" To what reality? To the reality at the heart of the Universe? Let us see what this reality is and we shall be in a position to answer. But how are we to know it when we see it? Is its recognition reserved for those who have first accepted the stipulations of a metaphysics which can produce no credentials beyond its own initial willfulness and the allegedly transcendent grandeur of the reality in whose name it speaks? If so we shall reject it, not as something too great for our comprehension and devotion, but as something too empty and meager. The only "reality" that is fit to serve as the measure of philosophical truth is that which we apprehend by the disciplined use of all our powers, when these are working together at the level of philosophical clarity, comprehensiveness and discrimination in the rational ordering of experience. We cannot expect more than this, for we have no special and self-authenticating organ for the disclosure of "ultimate reality," but we shall not be content with less.

This demand that a philosophy justify its commitments in terms of their capacity to meet the demands of life and conduct is in partial agreement with the claim of pragmatists and others that a valid philosophy must be practical, that it must satisfy the requirements not only of theory, but of life. The principles of philosophy, we have said, concern our basic or ultimate commitments, the things we are prepared to take a stand on and work with in the further organization of experience and direction of activity. Unless we can stand by them in action, and unless the activity in which they function is sustained and enlightened by their continued acceptance, they have failed in their purpose and are not in fact what they profess to be. This becomes clear as soon as one has sufficiently specified the claims of these philosophies themselves and the context in which their adequacy can reasonably be established.

There is a misunderstanding, however, that frequently accompanies statements of this sort and which it is particularly important to avoid. It is indeed the business of a sound philosophy to contribute to "life," but what it can properly contribute is not general edification or pleasantly oracular discourse on assorted topics, or support for special interests in need of ideological sanctions, but just a sound philosophy. A responsible philosopher is not a man who does intellectual odd jobs on the terms set by interests and activities other than his own, delivering a little homily here and a beautiful thought there, and turning off his little light as soon as it ceases to be called for by these other interests or might even become a source of embarrassment to them. It is not "life," lived just any sort of way to which a reasoned philosophical judgment is an instrument, but life at the level of human excellence which the principles of a sound philosophy themselves define. We shall have philosophical commitments in any case; there is no getting away from them. The discipline of philosophy is the means of making them intelligently, adequately and responsibly rather than in a confused, one-sided and arbitrary way. There is a difference here between a good and a bad philosophy which has nothing to do with usefulness for *other* purposes or convenience in the furtherance of *other* ends. Theory is rightly at the service of practice, but the only actions rightly judged "practical" are those which contribute to an attainable good, and no good is good enough for human life that does not contribute to the best of which that life, under those conditions, is capable. It is from the standpoint of a sound philosophy that we determine what that best is, and what the factors are that rightly contribute to its attainment. The philosophy that stops short of a decision, which it is prepared to maintain under the conditions of responsible action, on this primary issue, fails to perform its distinctive and appropriate function. It is hardly to be anticipated that it will succeed better in another.

The purpose of this chapter has been to clarify the conditions under which a decision about the philosophical ultimacy of the various elements in our experience can properly be arrived at. We have such a decision to make. For the adequacy of human reason when confronted with the ultimate problems of which philosophy is the custodian has been questioned, and it is a job for which we are responsible to answer that question if we can. We have now, I think, the means required for our answer.

CHAPTER II

REASON AND REALITY

The Ultimacy of Reason. The discerning reader may at this point observe that the claim that we are now ready to answer the question previously asked about the competence of reason to disclose "reality" is something of an understatement. In effect, we have already answered it, or at least have placed the problem in such a setting that only one answer can reasonably be given. The observation is a credit to his discernment. If he is also able to see that this setting is not an *ad hoc* construction, set up to justify a predetermined conclusion, but is the context in which questions of philosophical significance in fact arise, and can be settled, there will be little more that need be said to complete our case.

Is "reason" able to grasp the nature of reality and adequately to report it? What "reason" and what reality? If reason is identified with the procedures of the exact sciences and reality with what we enjoy in our most personally satisfying social relationships, then it will follow, as the night the day, that "reason" is a futile instrument indeed and all that we *really* care about lies beyond its scope. If we tell ourselves, like the melancholy Kierkegaard and his somewhat dismal followers, that "only the truth that edifies is truth for thee," we shall be able to say, with some show of profundity, that unedifying truths are, from the deep and urgent standpoint of the existential inwardness of a sick and seeking soul, not really true at all. Those who agree that "truth is inwardness" will find this dictum edifying and truthful, and will be able in consequence to ignore unedifying truths which, if acknowledged, might require the reconstruction of cherished, and edifying, beliefs. Their contempt for a "reason" which is, in their view, too shallow to grasp the reality to which their hearts are addressed and their affirmation of the "ultimate" irrationality of existence will, on this basis, be quite easy to understand. There are, in this procedure, two sorts of "irrationality," however. The first is the honorific status which attaches to those insights which "transcend" the capacities of a "reason" condemned in advance to deal with mere external and unedifying appearances. The second, less explicitly avowed but determining throughout the course of the discussion, is that willful self-centeredness which dignifies as philosophical wisdom its incapacity to learn from any other aspects of experience than those which minister to its unhappy soul-searching and seeks to excuse the arbitrariness of this unreasonable commitment by a general attack on "reason."

It is the "irrational" in this second sense that we are here concerned to examine. To "transcend" a "reason" identified with a method of inquiry rightly held to be insufficient for the adequate articulation of a particular subject-matter or type of experience may well be a philosophically just and discriminating procedure. What is not legitimate is the attempt to "transcend" the claims of philosophical clarity, adequacy, and responsible judgment in making the decisions in terms of which the "ultimacy" or "finality" of this favored reality and the preeminence claimed for it in the comprehensive organization of experience are justified. The irrational on this second level is not that which magnificently soars above the limits of mere reason but that which pretends to speak with philosophical authority, to *justify* its case in the light of the best we know, without accepting this responsibility. It is an incoherent and misguided procedure, and from it has come not the revelation of unutterable realities, but a lamentable breakdown in our means for achieving common understanding and shared good will. The heart may indeed have its more than rational reasons, but unless they are genuinely reasons as they claim to be, and reasonably defensible in a community of shared purpose and understanding, they will have little spiritual sustenance for a growing mind.

The method followed in this volume has been a different one. I am here preaching, as philosophical method, what has from the start been practiced and can now be judged by its fruits. The "reason" analyzed and philosophically defended was first identified outside the quarrels of both "rationalists" and "irrationalists," in specific contexts in which ideas are used, and in which the distinction between good thinking and bad, for the purposes of the activities in which ideas function, can reliably be made out. The "reality" in terms of which the validity of those uses of reason was judged was the "reality" which they themselves aimed at and were concerned about. We did not find the sciences probing the depths of reality as idealistic metaphysicians define it, but we did find them reaching true conclusions, on the basis of trustworthy evidence, about the course of events in the world around us. This truth was by no means always edifying, but it was not without its bearing on the concerns of edification. For those who edify also speak about the course of events, about what has happened and will probably happen, and they often want their statements to be accepted *as information*, without which their further teachings would have little bearing on the conduct of life. What we were justified in concluding was that, however far from "ultimate" the factually certified findings of the sciences may be for *other* purposes, *as information* about what has happened or is likely to happen they are reasonably held to be ultimate, and that any statements which conflict with them in this field which are not in the same way confirmable ought to be set down as probably mistaken.

This is a philosophical conclusion, and an important one. It is not just a statement about the way in which scientists, for their own inscrutable purposes, choose to talk, but about reasonably established truth, rightly held to be conclusive, on the subjects about which it speaks, as against any rivals or substitutes that purport to deal with these same subjects. This truth may not be directly usable for purposes of inspiration. It may even be highly inconvenient for some of the high-pressure inspirers of the time. It rightly claims authority in our thinking not as inspiring or convenient, but as true, in a quite matter-of-fact sense. If the edifiers try to conceal it, or its bearing on reasonably certifiable belief about the conditions and prospects of human life on this planet, they are behaving unreasonably, not just from the standpoint of "abstract science," which they scorn, but from the standpoint of a philosophy which claims for the factual conclusions of "abstract science" a primary place in all honest and accurate thinking. To say to oneself, philosophically, "only the truth that edifies is truth for thee," and to mean it, is to be willfully blind to available and well-established facts which ought to be taken account of in the direction of conduct. As a rule of philosophical procedure, it is manifestly indefensible.

So for the other uses of reason which we have considered. Each could be condemned as "irrational" from the standpoint of preconceptions inappropriate to the context of its significant application, but the notion that reason in these uses must conform to such preconceptions was itself seen to be philosophically unreasonable. A social ideal is indeed a myth if taken merely as a report of an existing state of affairs. Its "reality" lies in its efficacy in the organization of human purposes toward an anticipated good. The claims that, *in this context*, it makes on purposes of men who know what they are doing, are quite ultimate. If any philosophy, avowed as such or masquerading as scientific realism, condemns them as "dreams," "fantasies," or "fictions," meaning thereby to say that they have not the validity they there profess or do not deserve to be taken seriously, as of quite primary importance in the direction of conduct, that philosophy is mistaken. It has failed in philosophical accuracy, because it has failed to locate the context to which claims to the "reality" of ideals are pertinent, and to understand their significant use in this context. It has failed in adequacy because it arbitrarily excludes from the area of things worth taking seriously the concern for justice which must be a major constructive force in enlightened social action. And its "final" position is irresponsible and inadequate because the "realities" in which it puts its faith will not stand by themselves as a basis for intelligent and effective action. This is not something that we stipulate for purposes of metaphysical argument, but something we have found out by the use of philosophy to set the dispute about social ideals and their "reality" in the context in which their claim to "ultimacy" and their bearing on the things in life worth taking seriously can responsibly be determined.

Hence, as the discerning reader remarked, we do not come to the final question about "reason" and "ultimate reality" empty headed or empty handed. We know something about "realities" that are in their own kind ultimate and about their significance for human life. Moreover, we have acquired along the way enough philosophical sophistication to stand us in good stead here. We shall not be alarmed at the allegations that these limited "realities" of ours are not the ultimate reality, but only, by some higher standard, mere appearances. We are quite ready to agree that they are not any *other* reality than just what they are, and that there is doubtless far more in the world than they can compass. But, properly understood, they do not claim to be any other reality or to contain in themselves all that is meaningful in experience. Their finality consists not in their unconditioned all-inclusiveness but in their conditioned, and conditioning, cogency within the area of accurate thinking and effective action. The real world, we say again, may well contain much more than the methods of rational procedure we have examined are competent to disclose, but it cannot be less than what, by their means, we have found it to be. This truth will stand, and we take our stand upon it.

But is it enough? Are there not reaches of reality beyond it to which men invincibly aspire, whose exploration requires other methods and attitudes than those to which the use of reason has accustomed us? More specifically, ought we not to recognize that the *final* word on human destiny lies with religion, and that when it speaks even reason must be silent? These are formidable questions, and pertinent ones. I think, however, that we have the means to answer them. Nothing is enough, in the great enterprise of rational living, that stops short of the best of which the human mind and heart are capable. Are the affirmations of religion constituents in or constitutive of that best? They are, if they prove to be, that is, if they can make good their claim to that high place not by dogmatic affirmation or dialectically question-begging metaphysics, but by their contribution to what, on the whole, we can honestly commit ourselves to in the way of belief and action. That commitment need not be "rational" in the sense that either belief or action must exemplify a pattern of intelligibility derived from some other context and imposed here upon a subject-matter not fitted to receive it. There is no more reason that the validation of religious belief should conform to canons of scientific verifiability than that the substantiation of moral judgments should do so, save where it is with matters of fact, scientifically verifiable, that such belief is concerned. Let the religious believer speak in his own tongue and use the ideas which faith and practice have proved to be most suitable to the expression and communication of his unique experiences. There is nothing in the scientific exploration of the natural world that proves that nature, as thus disclosed, is all there is, and we have it on high authority that there are more things in heaven and earth than are dreamed of in our philosophies. We have, therefore, no standard of antecedent rationality which would justify us in rejecting the supernatural as incredible. Men in all times have found much in the world to inspire their awe and wonder, and it is by no means the function of reason to exclude the awe-inspiring and the wonderful from the sphere of human experience and concern.

We have, however, a standard of eventual rationality, or comprehensive reasonableness, that will prove no less pertinent here than elsewhere. The religious doctrines which have in the past proved vital and effective have developed in and been sustained by organizations which make very specific demands on their members in matters of both conduct and belief. This has been a great source of strength to them, and has given to the historic religions an authority and influence which mere philosophical reason could hardly hope to achieve. It has, however, raised serious problems for those who were concerned not only with the Absolute Being which, the theologians tell us, is the ultimate object of religious belief, but with the absolute or unqualified claims made by the leaders of religious organizations to pass final judgment on all matters of primary human concern, from factual truth, historical or scientific, to issues of secular social policy and procedure. The process by which, in the developments of modern Europe, one aspect of experience after another has claimed and finally made good its autonomy in science, politics and morals as against the previously maintained authority of the church, or churches, is well known. It is this progress of secular autonomy, rather than any special doctrinal difference or difficulty that today constitutes the major problem for an adequate philosophy of religion. The question it presents is this: can the commitments in the way of belief and conduct required to keep a religion alive and growing be maintained together and in working harmony with those of the activities in which we search for factual truth, pursue ideals of human freedom, and keep open the channels through which we can continue to learn about the world and ourselves?

There was a time when this question would have been answered by most philosophers in a cheerful affirmative. Without denying the conflicts which had often arisen between the representatives of secular and sacred interests, they would have maintained that the conflict was adventitious, due to mere misunderstanding and prejudice, and that between religion, rightly interpreted, and the claims of science and rational morality, correctly understood, no such conflict could occur. Today we are less optimistic. There is a serious question whether the progressive liberalization of traditional Christianity has not left at least some varieties of the faith with so attenuated a spiritual sustenance that they are no longer fit to live affirmatively and with vigor but only to die with maximum gentility. The reaction from this sort of religion has unquestionably favored more dogmatic and authoritarian doctrines, and these, in turn, have not hesitated to claim in principle, if not, as yet in educational and political practice, an exclusive and final authority in matters of belief and conduct that does conflict with the hard-won autonomies of modern secular culture, and even sets itself in explicit opposition to them. When assaults on "modernism" are made today, in the name of a deeper religious insight which, it is held, the modern world has lost and must regain, it is peculiarly important to identify the "modernism" in question. If it is that which denies all truth but that of science or all values but those of individual self-seeking, the criticism has some degree of justification. But if what is attacked is the "modernism" that affirms the secular autonomy of both factual inquiry and responsible moral judgment against the pretensions of religious organizations and religious teachers to final authority in such matters on all points at which the teachings and interests of such organizations are involved, the criticism is thoroughly mistaken. For this sort of "modernism" stands as the bulwark of that freedom of the mind which is one of the most essential of all the elements in our intellectual and moral heritage. It is important that well-intentioned spokesmen for religious values do not allow their understandable aversion to the negations of the former view to carry them in a position where they will no longer be willing to acknowledge the great affirmation on which the latter is based. It is that affirmation, inconvenient at times, but indispensable to the right ordering and interpretation of experience in the contexts in which we can best distinguish truth from falsehood and right from wrong, which sets the conditions to which any rationally justifiable religion must conform.

This, to be sure, is a somewhat different way of stating the issue than that which has been usual in this field. To show that religion—rightly interpreted—carries us to the very heart of reality—properly defined—is no difficult task, for those who know how to use an emotionally colored terminology for purposes of general edification. For our part, however, we have not been able to find any reality worth believing in that is less, or more, than the world we apprehend by the best use of all our powers and act in for their comprehensive expression and satisfaction. If the apprehension and valuation of this world as a supernatural order, with God as its author and final cause, can maintain itself together with the rest of what we know and value, as a constructive element in a total humanly understandable and attainable good, it will, in that process, receive its essential, and sufficient, philosophical justification. If, on the other hand, the belief that inspires it can be retained only in an atmosphere of suspicion and hostility toward the advance of secular knowledge in the fields in which such knowledge has proved its competence, if its authority must be buttressed by political alliances which claim a superhuman sanction but observably operate on a level considerably below that of the human best we elsewhere know and honor, if it is parasitic on interests and institutions which block the path of human freedom, then it is proved unreasonable not by what its opponents say about it, but by what, in its own operation, it shows itself to be. Such a religion is not too good for this world; it is, on the contrary, not good enough, and its appeal to faith as against mere reason is an appeal for special privileges which will not stand examination in the light of facts and ideals which we cannot justly or decently disavow. It is in that sense specifically that we contend that religion, like any other human activity, is subject to the principles of philosophic reason and rightly judged by the standard they provide. Nothing more than this can reasonably be required, but nothing less will suffice.

Can the religions as we know them meet this specification? They can if they can—that is, if there is in them the insight and good will and spiritual stamina to develop the doctrines to which they are committed to a point at which they enter into working harmony with the constructive forces in human nature and thought and thus to complete in common and communicable understanding the vision which their saints and prophets have seen. It will be a bad day for humanity when men cease to have visions, or to see the landscape around them lit at times with a radiance from worlds not quickened by the sun. But there are many sorts of vision; and those that fade in the light of common day will always be sentimental, inchoate and rudimentary in their human meaning compared with those that help us see, in that light, a world to live and work in, and to understand. The great ages of religion have been those in which such a synthesis was substantially achieved. The present is not one of them. Those religious leaders, and those philosophers of religion, who work to make it so are so far on the side of reason; and their success, in the measure that they achieve it, will be a further proof of the constructive efficacy of human reason when it reaches and can maintain itself on the level of philosophic adequacy and coherence. We welcome them as co-workers in our common enterprise.

This cooperative work will not be furthered, however, nor will the cause of rationally justifiable religion be advanced by those who claim unique authority for religious insight, not as an element in such a synthesis, but as a uniquely privileged aspect of experience outside it—qualified by the special sanctity of its doctrines and protagonists to pass final judgment not only on its own pretensions but on all other phases or aspects of experience with which its spokesmen see fit to concern themselves, and entitled to special and exclusive privileges for the propagation of its own doctrine and the condemnation of those who are unable to subscribe to its tenets. The faith that is worth having and believing will require no such sanctions, and a faith that can maintain itself only by means of them need not wait for our philosophical condemnation; it has, in process of its operation, pronounced its own.

This, then, is what we mean by the *philosophical* ultimacy of reason, or the ultimacy of reason in the context of the philosophical estimate of the rightness of decisions reached as to what is to be accepted as ultimate for thought and action. The world *may* be as "irrational" as the "irrationalists" say it is. But we shall have good grounds for supposing it to be so only if that hypothesis can maintain itself as more reasonable than any other, more fully consonant with the comprehensive wisdom which it is the task of philosophy to achieve. If the irrationalist asks us to accept his conclusion for no reason at all, and is prepared to rest his case on that basis, we shall at least understand each other. But if he advances as a reason for not giving any reason the allegation that reason is incompetent to deal with the high matters he reports on, we shall need to know how this judgment as to reason's competence is arrived at, and what reason there is to suppose it to be correct. If it, in its turn, is merely arbitrary, let it be frankly avowed as such and we shall know what to think of it. If it is not, then those who make it are bound to accept the responsibilities of justifying their assertions over the whole area of relevant experience in the most rational interpretation that can be given of it. For if anything is to be omitted, or excluded as irrelevant, it will be necessary to justify that omission not by fiat or special pleading, but by reference to what *on the whole* we have reason to believe and to prefer. The claim of reason in philosophy is not that the world is so constituted as to agree with some particular idea or set of ideas singled out in advance as peculiarly intelligible or rational. It is simply that whatever the world may be in itself, what we can reasonably believe about it is what, by the rational use of all our powers, we can find out, and that nothing is worthy of our acceptance that fails to justify itself in this manner. To this there is simply no reasonable alternative. There are, however, unreasonable alternatives which deck themselves out with reasons and to these it may be worth our while to devote some critical attention.

The Philosophical Alternatives to Reason. Against the finality of the verdict of reason in its philosophic use, concerning the legitimacy of all pretenders to ultimate reality, appeal has many times been made. There are understandable causes for this. They are discoverable in part as we have seen in the genuine grievance of reasonable men against a "reason," narrowly and arbitrarily defined, which has seemed to stand in the way of the just appreciation of aspects of experience of great human significance. They are also to be found in the willful urgency of interests which refuse to qualify their superrational claims by reference to what is known and valued elsewhere and demand instead a philosophy that can discover in an absolute and incomprehensible reality, beyond the reach of human judgment, an unqualified sanction for their own uncriticized preferences and preconceptions. It is not surprising that the Absolutes thus darkly discerned have often served an all-too-human function or that the demand for them continues. What is less easy to understand is what the authority is to which they appeal or what sense is to be made of their claims when they are addressed, not merely to the like-minded who are already persuaded, but to those who are not thus antecedently committed but are expected, none the less, to acknowledge the merits of their case.

The first step in the case for superrational Absolutes is, of course, an attempted proof of the frailties of human reason and of the sins of those who put their "final" trust in it. A vigorous version of this sort of argument has recently been offered by Mr. Peter Drucker, in a book which, on other issues of current social policy, has some valuable things to say.[1] The object of his attack is the "rationalist liberal," and the basis of the charge against this sort of liberal is that, by claiming that human reason is absolute, he paves the way for totalitarianism. For if liberals believe that they can, by mere human reason, *know* what is right and just, they will, he believes, seek to impose their judgment on others. And when they fail here, as they inevitably do, since they trust to the method of "rational conversion" to translate their principles into political action, they open the way for the dictator who will use their failure as the excuse for his own more drastic, and not less absolute, imperatives. In contrast to such "rationalist liberalism," Mr. Drucker places that "true liberalism" which, he tells us "grew out of a religious renunciation of rationalism,"[2] and which substitutes for "man made absolutes," a humble recognition that man is inherently imperfect and imperfectible and an acknowledgment that "there is absolute truth and absolute reason—though forever beyond man's grasp."[3]

[1] Peter Drucker, *The Future of Industrial Man, passim.*
[2] *Ibid.,* p. 193.
[3] *Ibid.,* p. 154.

Such a view, if justified, has social implications which Mr. Drucker does not explicitly develop, though the tone of his "conservative approach" to post-war problems suggests them. It purports to be a serious indictment of much that in this volume we have taken to be humanly excellent. But what, more precisely, does it mean? It is by no means easy to say, since the critical terms it employs are very loosely applied to a variety of referents which seem to agree chiefly in being common objects of the author's aversion. The case against "rationalist liberalism" is made out chiefly by a denunciation of Rousseau, who was not a rationalist, Marx who was not a liberal, and Hitler who is neither. We are therefore relieved, though a little surprised, to come upon Socrates in this curiously mixed company. Here, at least, is a defender of human reason, and of the freedom of the mind required for its responsible use, whom we can recognize as such. What has Mr. Drucker to say against him?

Chiefly this: that he believed "the good can be ascertained infallibly by man" [4] and this would naturally lead to a totalitarian position. "If Socrates really believed the oracle that he was the wisest man in all Greece—and he certainly acted on the assumption that he was the only wise man in Greece—he would have had the moral duty to set himself up as a tyrant." [5] Mr. Drucker does not add the rest of the familiar story, that what Socrates conceived his superior wisdom to consist in was his awareness of his own ignorance. This might well have had a deterrent effect on the sort of totalitarian urge to which the "rationalist" is supposed to be addicted. Actually, of course, the essential element in Socrates' claim was not that he was possessed of the "infallible" knowledge on ultimate issues which he so frequently disclaimed, nor that he was merely ignorant, but that he, like any other reasonable man, had the right and responsibility to distinguish ignorance from knowl-

[4] *Ibid.*, p. 214.
[5] *Ibid.*, p. 215.

edge, and to submit the claims of his contemporaries to the clearest, most thorough and most comprehensive judgment that could be brought to bear upon them. He was bitterly attacked for this in his own day, as he would be in ours, by those whose interests cannot stand that sort of scrutiny. But he was fortunate in being able to make his own *Apology*, and doubly so in having such a disciple as Plato to record it for posterity. It is pertinent to our present interest to recall that the gist of that apology is contained in the doctrine that "an unexamined life is not worth living." It is not surprising that those who object to that sort of rational scrutiny still find the Socrates of the *Apology* a dangerously "rationalist" antagonist. The defenders of the claims of reason, on the other hand, not in any "absolutist" pretensions but in its consistent and fearless use in the issues of conduct, could hardly ask for a worthier spokesman.

There is more to the matter than this, however. Mr. Drucker observes that the "rationalist liberal" is estopped from indulging his totalitarian propensities by his belief that his ends can be accomplished by rational conversion—that the good can be taught rationally and that those who understand it will accept it. This point, if he had seen its implications, would, of course, have undermined his whole case. For the "totalitarian," in any sense in which "totalitarianism" is morally or politically objectionable, is not simply a man who thinks he knows what ought to be done, but one who proposes to get it done by imposing his will on others, without respect for their right and responsibility to make up their own minds about it, and thus to decide freely and for themselves. With such "totalitarianism," the liberalism which is committed to a policy of "rational conversion" is, of course, in fundamental conflict. Its opposition, however, is not, like that of Mr. Drucker, based on the claim that human judgment and character are so "imperfect" that we cannot reasonably tell the difference between right and wrong. It rests rather on the claim—never better stated than by that other "rationalist liberal," John Locke—that man as a "rational creature" has a worth and dignity which are entitled to respect, and that free minds are persuaded by reasons, not intimidated by force. The "rationalist liberal" would maintain, I take it, that there is little point and less justice in holding man "responsible" for his choices (and Mr. Drucker lays great stress on such responsibility) unless he is capable of meeting that responsibility. Neither an awareness of his inherent imperfectibility nor a reference to an absolute truth and reason forever beyond his grasp is likely to be of as much use here as an intelligent use of such fragments of truth and reason as he *can* grasp to make the best of the situation in which he finds himself. If nobody knows what this superrational truth is how are we to distinguish it from the grossest errors, which sometimes also claim a more than rational sanction? And if other men tell us that they know what it is, thus in some curious way transcending the imperfections alleged to be inherent in the rest of mankind, and that we ought to believe what they tell us about it, how, save by the truth and reason which are *not* forever beyond our grasp, can we understand or rightly credit their claims? Man is indeed imperfect, but it is in virtue of the human capacities which he does possess that he can rightly claim the freedom which is essentially opposed to both totalitarian government and obscurantist philosophy.

This does not mean that the "liberal" need assume that reason operates in a disembodied form or independent of the conditions under which men live, though Mr. Drucker claims that it does. He tells us that the rationalist liberal assumes, like Socrates, "that it [his "rational absolutism"] is effective by its mere existence without any organization of power or any realization in institutions." [6] This is an odd view to attribute to the philosopher into whose mouth Plato thought it appropriate to put the doctrines of the *Republic*, and more

[6] *Ibid.*, p. 215.

curious still as applied to men like Bentham and Mill. It is quite certainly not the view of the modern reformers who insist on planning the future in such fashion that all men may have the health, economic security and education that will give them a chance to use their capacity for moral choice to the best advantage. The freedom that is worth while, as we saw in Part II, is not that which is independent of all natural conditions, but that which can be achieved *under* conditions which are in some measure within our power to bring about. But when the "rationalist liberal" talks about planning the conditions under which we are to act freely, Mr. Drucker accuses him of being a "psychological determinist"—whatever that is—and a denier of free will. There is, in fact, no pleasing him, it would seem. If the liberal relies on rational persuasion, he is denounced as ineffective. If he seeks to control the conditions under which rational persuasion can be an effective instrument of policy, he is supposed to have denied the freedom of the will. If he claims to know what he is doing and what he ought to do, he is branded a potential dictator, but he, like other men, is, none the less, held responsible for choosing rightly and apparently in accordance with an absolute truth and reason that are, unhappily, forever beyond his grasp. I think that at this point we can at least absolve Mr. Drucker of that "narrow" regard for consistency which is supposed to characterize the "rationalists" he attacks.

All this reaches its climax in a remarkable passage which will merit our closest scrutiny. "It is the essence of rationalist liberalism," Mr. Drucker tells us, "that it proclaims its absolutes to be rationally evident." This view is criticized as follows: "Absolute reason can, however, never be rational; it can never be proved or disproved by logic. Absolute reason is by its very nature above and before rational argument. Logical deduction can and must be based upon an absolute reason but can never prove it. If truly religious, an absolute principle is superrational—a true metaphysical principle which gives a valid basis of rational logic. If man-made and man-proclaimed, absolute reason must be irrational and in insoluble conflict with rational logic and rational means." [7]

I am not clear as to whether this is supposed to be super-rational reasoning or not. It seems to me to belong at least in the more general category of the unreasonable. What an "absolute reason" that is held to be "rationally evident" and is at the same time "above and beyond rational argument" and "logic," would be, I do not know. The appeal to self-evidence—if it is self-evidence that is open to rational inspection as, e.g., in the method of Descartes—is not something beyond rational analysis or logic, but is the most essential element *in* logic and indeed in all reasoning. "Deduction" to be sure cannot prove what is held to be *self*-evident—for it would be a contradiction in terms to hold that the self-evident derives its rational cogency from something else from which it is deduced. But reason is, on this view, not limited to deduction, but makes use of intuition as well. An absolute that was "man-made" would indeed be a dubious affair, but it is one of the peculiarities of the "rationalist" Drucker is attacking that he does not believe that the principles of right reason are his own invention but holds them, on the contrary, to have a cogency of their own which he, as a reasonable being, is bound to respect. As for principles, whether absolute or relative, which were not "man-proclaimed," I am at a loss to know how, apart from direct supernatural revelation, we should ever have heard of them. And what about an absolute "superrational" principle—a true metaphysical principle—which is said to give "a valid basis for rational logic"? How is its validity made out—by rational or superrational means? If the latter, what does "valid" mean in this use and what claim does it have to human credence? If the former, what does it mean to say that the principle in question is super-rational or forever beyond our grasp? Mr. Drucker does not

[7] *Ibid.*, p. 199.

answer these questions. Yet it is surely important that they should be answered, if we are not to be gravely misled on quite fundamental issues. For our own part we have no axe to grind for any "absolutes," rational or superrational, that are "above and before" rational argument—or rational examination. But we are greatly concerned about the capacity of human reason, working in a quite relative, provisional and mundane way, to distinguish true from false, right from wrong, and wisdom from folly, by reference to principles which it can grasp and see the meaning of. Those who reject this capacity or the validity of claims based upon its responsible use, as the best guide we have to right judgment and right action, take upon themselves a very grave responsibility. If there is a better way of deciding these vital matters, by all means let us hear of it. But what is it to be, and in whose name do its prophets speak? Do those who write vaguely of "religious humility" mean that we are to accept the verdict of some man or group of men as possessing superrational and superhuman authority in these matters? Are they themselves the oracles through which an Absolute—presumably not man-made or man-proclaimed—will speak? The injunction to consider our imperfections and be ready for superrational revelations which we cannot expect to understand but which we are none the less, in due humility, to accept, is not by itself a helpful one. It could be used by all sorts of agencies, for purposes that, on any merely rational level, are open to very grave suspicion. If it is not to be so used, those who proclaim it must tell us somewhat more plainly what they mean by it.

For this additional light we can turn with some hope to Mr. Reinhold Niebuhr. For Mr. Niebuhr is one of the authentic spiritual leaders of America today, and his judgment on the limits of human reason in dealing with ultimate issues is entitled to respect. Moreover, it is soundly grounded in an accurate, if somewhat disillusioned, estimate of the "ideological" element in all thinking, including theological thinking. It is the besetting sin of human nature, he holds, to make unconditioned claims for conditioned insights and values. And, from the nature of our human situation, all our insights and values, even the best, will in fact be thus conditioned. But if all human standards are thus relative, and if all are prone to claim an absoluteness that they do not merit, how are we rightly to judge limitations inherent even in the best of them and make the correction required for a just estimate of their cogency? Niebuhr answers: "It is only by an ultimate analysis from beyond all human standards that the particular guilt of the great and the good men of history is revealed." [8] This is as true, of course, of the men of "reason" as of any others, perhaps particularly true of them, since it is in the claim to absolute authority for merely human judgments that such pride is most clearly manifest. Where, then, shall we look for light? We shall find it only in the *true* and transcendent Absolute, beyond time and history, though operative in them. This reality, in transcending all human limitations, transcends our reason as well. Yet we can be satisfied with nothing short of it, and it is in its incomprehensible nature that we find the ultimate answer to our problems. "Man is thus in the position of being unable to comprehend himself in his full stature of freedom without a principle of comprehension that is beyond his comprehension," [9] and that is just because "Man is a creature who cannot find a true norm short of the nature of ultimate reality." [10]

There is much that is wise in this, but it seems, as it stands, curiously incomplete. Indeed, we do not want to stop short of ultimate reality, but neither do we want to stop short when we have merely named it. Will a principle that is beyond our comprehension tell us what this reality is, how we ought rightly to relate ourselves to it, or in what way we can cor-

[8] Reinhold Niebuhr, *The Nature and Destiny of Man*, Vol. I, p. 227.
[9] *Ibid.*, p. 125.
[10] *Ibid.*, p. 146.

rect our merely human judgments by reference to its transcendent truth? Mr. Niebuhr appears to know a good deal
about this incomprehensible reality, which proves, in fact,
to be of a recognizably Calvinistic complexion, and to require
of men something much more specific than the unqualified
affirmation of its incomprehensible transcendence. Perhaps he
is right in this but how are we to know? And how is he to
know? For while the transcendent reality may indeed pronounce judgment from a standpoint beyond all human standards, it is hard to see how Mr. Niebuhr can pretend to do so
without exhibiting the sin of pride in its most sinful form.
We seem to be involved in a dilemma. If the transcendent
and incomprehensible reality remains merely transcendent
and incomprehensible it serves no function in our thinking
save to condemn alike *all* our human beliefs and valuations,
as falling short of its unutterable greatness. If, on the other
hand, we pretend to say what is true about it—and it is only
in terms of what we know of it, not of what we do not know,
that this can be done—we must speak from a human standpoint and in that case the condemnation passed on *all* such
standpoints will have to be modified in favor of one among
them, that of Mr. Niebuhr, for example, which is held to be
more credible and reliable than others as a spokesman for
ultimate reality. And that claim cannot in its turn be justified by the observation that reality is incomprehensible and
it is sinful for us to try to judge it in human terms.

Actually the difficulty seems less than insurmountable. The
urge that sends us looking for more in the world than our
accepted categories can express is a genuinely reasonable one.
For there *is* more both in ourselves and in the world we experience than we have so far been able to articulate and make
use of. The unutterable is the perpetual theme of prophets
and artists and, indeed, of men of genius in every field, who
find the means of bringing to adequate expression what, until
they showed us how to say it, could not be said. Nor is there

room for doubt that more such discoveries are ahead, and that with the light they give us we shall yet see much that is now beyond our range of vision. In *that* sense the transcendent and the incomprehensible are perennial objects of human concern, and rightly so. To take what is now known as the sum of all that can be known, and thus to import into merely conditioned judgments an absoluteness that shuts off further inquiry is quite as sinful as Mr. Niebuhr takes it to be, and his insistence upon it is timely.

But what we rightly seek of the as yet unutterable is to utter it, and of the still incomprehensible to comprehend it— not completely, to be sure, since there will always be more to say and to comprehend than our human powers can grasp —but in such fashion as to bring it within the range of articulate experience and to give it the place it merits in relation to the rest of what we know and value. Apart from such comprehension—the best that it is within our human powers to give—how shall we distinguish the false prophet from the true, or the seer who speaks of Aryan supremacy from the one who comes in the name of the Lord our hearts and minds can honor?

I think Mr. Niebuhr does less than justice to the claims of religion in the following passage: " 'To know that there is a meaning but not to know the meaning,' declares the modern J. Middleton Murry, 'that is bliss.' That word is in the spirit of classical religion. It expresses a trust in life even when the immediate facts of life seem to outrage our conception of what life ought to be." [11] I should say, on the contrary, that it falls far short of the spirit of classical religion and leaves us instead the sentimentality of which Mr. Middleton Murry is so unique an exponent. To know there is a meaning and not to know the meaning is, for those whose end is the knowledge of God, to be endlessly dissatisfied, a state to which we may indeed be condemned in this life, but which

[11] *Christianity and Power Politics*, pp. 196-197.

is the mark of an imperfection later to be removed when we see no longer through a glass, darkly, but face to face. And the trust that found expression in St. Augustine, the *fides quarens intellectus*, is a stronger and better thing than its murky modern substitute. We must put up with a good deal of darkness in the kind of world we live in, and we have learned, at considerable human cost, not to be afraid of the dark, or to honor it as the medium of a special revelation. But we have been admonished, wisely, to walk, where we can, in the light, and to keep our own light burning. We propose to follow that admonition.

Nor is there any just reason for condemning this determination as a pride in reason which ought to be disavowed. If we identified our merely relative insights with complete and absolute truth we should be rightly open to this condemnation. But that is just what, so far as we use our reason, we do not do. On the contrary, it is precisely the right use of philosophical reason which enables us to keep from doing it—to find the proper ultimacy of reason *not* in pretensions to inside information on ultimate reality, but in its human function in enabling men to be as accurate and adequate as possible in their understanding of a world not made to their measure but demanding, for its philosophical comprehension, the best in disciplined intelligence that they can bring to it. It is not this philosophical use of reason that the Absolutist can properly condemn. Indeed, it is only through the discipline it provides that his own claims can escape the arbitrary absoluteness to which, as Niebuhr rightly insists, our human nature is so unhappily addicted. Is the prophet prepared not only to speak for the Absolute, but to accept the philosophical responsibilities of the human standpoint from which inevitably he speaks and to claim no more for it than can be made out reasonably in its relation to the rest of what we know? If so, then he has not "transcended" reason in its philosophical use, but is prepared to submit his claims to its adjudication. If not—if he does in fact claim for the human interest he represents an unconditional authority and incomprehensible validity—we shall know what to think of him, for Dr. Niebuhr has told us.

This issue is important. For there are apostles of the Absolute among us on whom Dr. Niebuhr's judgment ought to fall, and heavily. There is, for instance, Dr. P. Sorokin, who has recently announced the collapse of our sensate culture and the tragic degeneration of its values. Dr. Sorokin, viewing art, morals, law and philosophy from the vantage ground of a vast accumulation of statistical data and a peculiarly dogmatic and quite uncriticized value standard, takes a very harsh view of modern culture in its recent or "over-ripe" phase. Consider, for instance, the situation in the arts. In Greece, prior to the third century B.C. and in the Middle Ages, art was "the incarnation of absolute values in a relativistic, empirical world." "Nothing coarse, vulgar, debasing or pathological found a place in it." [12] How different is our modern art! "When we come to the art of the present day, the contrast . . . is well-nigh shocking. . . . In music and literature, painting and sculpture, the theater and drama, it chooses as its 'heroes' either the ordinary prosaic types of human beings or the negative and pathological. The same is true also of the events with which it deals. Housewives, farmers and laborers, business men and salesmen, stenographers, politicians, doctors, lawyers, and ministers, and especially detectives, criminals, gangsters, and 'double-crossers,' the cruel, the disloyal, hypocrites, prostitutes and mistresses, the sexually abnormal, the insane, clowns, street urchins, or adventurers—such are the 'heroes' of contemporary art in all of its principal fields. Even when—as an exception—a contemporary novel, biography, or historical work chooses a noble or heroic theme (such as George Washington, Byron or some saint) it proceeds, in accordance with the prevailing psychoanalytic method, thoroughly to 'debunk' its hero." [13] So it goes.

[12] P. Sorokin, *The Present Crises of Our Age*, p. 57.
[13] *Ibid.*, pp. 64-65.

"Even in such a specialized field as portraiture some 88 per cent of the foremost works of the masters of the twentieth century are devoted to the lower classes or the bourgeoisie, whereas in the medieval centuries only 9 per cent of all the portraits dealt with these classes, the rest representing royalty, aristocracy or the higher clergy." [14] Could more convincing statistical proof be given of the collapse of spiritual values in our culture?

There is much, much more of this, replete with judgments, statistically supported, of the inadequacy of our philosophy, the decline of science, and the collapse of morality. Such is the state of sensate culture in its decline. But a better day is coming, a day when man will once more be recognized as the image of the Absolute and when absolute values, "with their *'dura lex sed lex'* " will reign again, supplanting the "freedom" which, in Dr. Sorokin's opinion, has already failed us. As the prophet of the new reign of the Absolute, Sorokin ends on a note of hope if not of self-congratulation: *"Benedictus qui venit in nomine Domini."* [15]

But is it in the name of the Lord that he comes? For my own part I seemed to detect behind such passages as those just quoted, the strains not of the angelic choir, but of the chorus of Peers in *Iolanthe*—"Bow, ye lower middle classes, Bow, ye tradesmen, Bow, ye masses." The incarnation of absolute values seems here to be curiously arbitrary, not to say a snobbish affair. We do not need special access to ultimate reality or research assistance in the tabulation of the spiritual qualities of paintings through the ages, to tell us what is wrong with the picture it presents. A state of mind for which, "Washington, Byron or some saint" can be a properly "heroic" theme for genuinely spiritual art, while "housewives, farmers and laborers" are set with prostitutes, clowns and street urchins beyond the pale, is familiar enough

[14] *Ibid.*, pp. 66-67.
[15] *Ibid.*, p. 326.

on a merely human level. And it is on that level, until the Absolute is prepared to speak more unequivocally in its behalf, that it can properly be judged. I am sure that Dr. Sorokin, or his assistants, must have counted such a picture as Cézanne's "The Card Players" in their survey of our spiritual decline. It would be interesting to know whether, after it was counted, any of them stopped to look at it, and what, if anything, they saw.

This, of course, is only an instance, though in some ways a peculiarly instructive one. However it may be in Absolute Reality, in human experience there are many absolutes, each with its own exclusive claim to unconditional validity and its own short way of dealing with dissenters by denying reality or spirituality or meaning to everything that falls outside the scope of its initial insight. Those who tell us, therefore, as does Mr. Gilson,[16] that man is by nature a metaphysical animal, who demands "positive and dogmatic truth" about the ultimate ground of existence as a basis for ultimate assurances about morals and conduct, have a good deal of empirical evidence to support their case, more, perhaps, than they can altogether welcome when the variety of the ultimates actually current is borne in mind. What they say is true, but it is not the whole truth. For it is also true that man, under fortunate conditions, has found a way of measuring these claims against the equally human demand for an understanding broad and just enough to learn freely from all that a growing experience has to teach and to accept as finally true only what will stand the test of such experience in the most comprehensively rational interpretation that can be given it. In comparison to the total mass of human belief the amount of this kind of thinking is small, but so, as the parable tells us, is the yeast by which the whole loaf is leavened. The process of philosophic reason, when it is not restricted in its operation to metaphysical manipulation of the consequences of esoteric

[16] E. Gilson, *The Unity of Philosophical Experience*, p. 307.

intuitions whose unconditional validity only the faithful can discern, but works in and through the common stuff of public experience to clarify and complete the constructive insights contained in it, is not less human than the forces that at times oppose its work, and it is not less humanly valuable. Nor need it be opposed to the special insights whose spokesmen so frequently view it with alarm. Their insights may indeed be as unique and precious as they are claimed to be. There is no antecedent criterion of official rationality by which they can properly be condemned as "irrational" and unworthy of human credence. There is only the eventual criterion of their capacity to live and work with other claims and insights, no less initially persuasive, and in some instances more unequivocally authenticated in their known contribution to reliable knowledge and enlightened good will among men. The only irrational that a sound philosophy can properly condemn is that which refuses to justify its claims in this comprehensive and comprehensible way and demands instead that its dicta—whether these be dignified as self-evident truths, superrational intuitions or subrational urgencies of "blood" or "will to power"—be accepted unconditionally with a closed mind and a contrite heart, as the standard to which all further truth and value must conform. We have seen a good deal of that kind of irrationalism in the contemporary world—not all of it in Central Europe and Eastern Asia—and it has its philosophical apologists. It constitutes the only genuine alternative to the use of philosophical reason here defended that can seriously be presented.

The Final Option.

"Of the two dreams, night and day,
  What lover, what dreamer, would choose
  The one obscured by sleep?"
          Wallace Stevens, *Hymn from a Watermelon Pavilion*

At this point, then, we are confronted with a choice. The acceptance of reason, as we have come to understand it in its operation is a commitment, and it is only by use of the standard it supplies that the worth of the goods it promises can be made out. In a sense, therefore, the defense of reason here offered is circular. We have chosen reason rationally, and it is by means of a distinction, reasonably established, between what is reasonable and what is arbitrary, that the rightness of our final choice is established. But we need not now, I think, be much disturbed by that kind of circularity. For the circle is not that of a demonstration that begs illegitimately some assumption for which further substantiation ought to be provided; it is rather that of a process which completes itself by returning to its point of origin, preserving throughout the integrity of its rational structure. The Greeks had a great veneration for such processes and thought them peculiarly suited to the perfection of the heavenly bodies. But the "rationality" we have celebrated and tried to exemplify is not merely that of a geometrical pattern; it is rather and more properly that of a thought that gains in scope and meaning from progressive application without departing from the principles that defined its primary intent, or that of a life that is guided but not narrowed by ideals and centered in goods that do not lose their worth in being understood and shared. Reason, rightly understood, is like that, and if our defense of it has in some measure been rational, it has so far lived up to its professions. I should not wish to claim more for it.

As for the final choice, it is one that each man must make

for himself, when he has seen what is involved in it and what, for him, it means. The way it proposes for human thought and action is not an easy one; its wisest critics are those who have claimed that it asks too much of feeble human nature. Spinoza, who stands for all time as one of its greatest spokesmen, justified it on the ground that all excellent things are both rare and difficult—and there is much truth in what he said. But while difficult, as a sustained plan for life and action, the good of reason is by no means esoteric or unfamiliar. The undertaking to which it commits us is one we know and rightly value. It has proved its worth in the attainment of truth that will stand examination in the daylight, in ideals that work and have worked for human freedom, in comprehensive wisdom to which nothing is alien that contributes to the full realization of man's humanity. And it accepts these achievements, not as favored bits of final truth to be sheltered from rival claimants by urgent protestations of their unqualified validity, but as a working basis for further thought and action in the continuing enterprise of rational living. It is to that enterprise that our philosophy commits us. The task is great; it is for those of us who accept it to prove that we are worthy of its opportunities.

INDEX